FAMILY

FORGIVENESS

AND

RECONCILIATION

PEACE THROUGH BIBLICAL TRUTH

ROBERT KRAUS

High Bridge Books titles may be purchased in bulk for educational, business, fundraising, or sales promotional use. For information, please contact High Bridge Books at www.HighBridgeBooks.com/contact.

Family Forgiveness and Reconciliation primarily quotes *The Holy Bible*, English Standard Version® © 2001 by Crossway, a publishing ministry of Good News Publishers, for most Scripture references unless otherwise noted, and used by permission. All rights reserved.

In the English Standard Version, pronouns referring to God are not capitalized. To maintain consistency throughout *Family Forgiveness and Reconciliation*, pronouns referring to God are not capitalized.

FAMILY
FORGIVENESS
AND
RECONCILIATION

This book is dedicated to my best friend, faithful companion, and loving wife, Polly Kraus. Her sincere love for Jesus is evident in her forgiving spirit and readiness to reconcile—qualities that have strengthened our marriage and home for over fifty years.

Polly is the love of my life. I thank God for her daily and hold her in the highest esteem.

Visit the official book website:

familyforgiveness.org

Paperback | E-book | Audiobook

The Bible
is a portrait of love
painted on a canvas
of forgiveness.

-Robert Kraus

CONTENTS

PART ONE
A Foundation for Forgiveness and Reconciliation

1 What Is Forgiveness?..9

2 What Is Reconciliation? 35

3 Why Forgive..65

4 Why Reconcile 83

5 Love and Humility...97

PART TWO
Forgiveness and Reconciliation in Action

6 Wisdom in Action...115

7 Covenant Marriage...145

8 Mathematics and Forgiveness.................................163

9 When Forgiveness Seems Impossible.......................177

10 The Source of All Forgiveness................................203

INTERLUDE Peace for Our Families..........................231

11 The Transforming Power of Divine Forgiveness........241

12 Faith and Repentance 259

APPENDICES

ONE Voices We Cite...277

TWO Forgiveness Involving Finances 279

THREE Scripture Index...287

FOUR References and Supplementary Notes..............301

How to Use This Book

Family Forgiveness and Reconciliation is meant to be read thoughtfully and prayerfully at a pace that allows both truth and healing to take root. Meant to be read from beginning to end, each chapter of the book builds on the one before. Take your time; this is a journey not a race.

The reflection questions at the end of each chapter are designed for prayerful personal reflection. They invite thoughtful engagement with Scripture rather than quick answers or forced conclusions.

The appendices are provided as optional reference tools.

Appendix One offers brief biographical sketches of selected authors quoted throughout the book, noting when they lived and the lasting impact of their work. These short profiles allow readers to recognize the voices being referenced without interrupting the flow of the main chapters.

Appendix Two addresses questions that arise about forgiveness relating to financial obligations, and how to handle disputes involving individuals or institutions.

Appendixes Three and Four provide Scripture indexes, and references and supplementary notes.

For Group Study

Family Forgiveness and Reconciliation is designed to work well as a ten-week small group study:

- Week 1: Chapter 1
- Week 2: Chapter 2
- Week 3: Chapters 3 and 4
- Week 4: Chapter 5
- Week 5: Chapter 6
- Week 6: Chapter 7
- Week 7: Chapter 8
- Week 8: Chapter 9
- Week 9: Chapter 10 and the Interlude
- Week 10: Chapters 11 and 12

Groups that prefer a slower pace may choose to extend the study by covering one chapter each week.

Each chapter includes discussion questions designed to help readers reflect more deeply on the message. Groups are encouraged to read the assigned chapter before meeting and discuss all four questions, or select two or three if time is limited. Participants may choose to share personal experiences, offer general insights, or simply listen; there is no pressure to disclose private details. Every group should commit to confidentiality while also using wisdom and discretion in what is shared.

Introduction

When God's wisdom enters our hearts, forgiveness becomes possible, healing takes root, and reconciliation can begin in places once marked by hurt. Wisdom cannot be something we admire from afar; it must be lived out in the relationships where we spend most of our time.

One of the clearest examples of forgiveness and reconciliation in Scripture is the story of Joseph explored in Chapter 2. His journey shows how God can redeem deep wounds and transform painful wrongs into something good. Rather than seeking revenge, Joseph offered mercy, offering a model of wisdom that continues to guide families today.

Even with such powerful biblical examples for us, forgiveness remains one of the hardest things to practice. It reaches into the deepest parts of our lives, memories, pain, pride, and relationships. Scripture teaches that forgiveness is essential for our spiritual well-being and for the health of our families. When resentment takes root, it slowly poisons the heart; but when we release that burden, healing begins to flow.

The pages ahead take readers through God's wisdom for restoring what has been broken. Through Scripture, reflection, and prayer, we learn how forgiveness frees us and reconciliation renews us; and how both reveal the grace and mercy of our heavenly Father.

This book explores forgiveness and reconciliation through a guiding image: a portrait of love painted on a canvas of forgiveness. Like an artist preparing a canvas with care and intention, God purposes to make us one of his masterpieces—our lives shaped by grace, restored through mercy, and renewed by his love.

In Part One (Chapters 1–5), a foundation is laid for understanding forgiveness, how reconciliation works, and why both are essential in the Christian life. It also shows how love and humility prepare the heart, much like an artist prepares a studio—setting the light, selecting the tools, and envisioning the beauty that will one day appear.

Part Two (Chapters 6–12) explores how forgiveness and reconciliation unfold in daily life. Through stories, biblical wisdom, and practical guidance, the steps are explored that rebuild trust, restore peace, and bring healing where wounds have lingered. Reconciliation becomes visible, much like a painter adding color, depth, and detail stroke by stroke, choice by choice, revealing how God's grace transforms the places that need it most. Scripture itself uses color to describe God's restoring power: "Though your sins are like scarlet, they shall be as white as snow" (Isaiah 1:18). God is the Master Artist, and we are invited to trust his skillful hand as he shapes the story of forgiveness and reconciliation in our lives. This book aims to connect biblical truth with practical steps that help families find healing.

Forgiveness is urgent. When it is delayed, pain deepens and anger or bitterness can take root like weeds, slowly choking the life out of relationships. Yet forgiveness refreshes the heart like living water, freeing us to experience the peace God desires for our families.

Total forgiveness can feel costly because it asks us to let go of things we naturally cling to—our pride, our desire for justice, or the need to be right. Yet Scripture calls us to trust God more deeply as we forgive. When we place our natural inclinations in his hands, his grace strengthens us to heal, release, and walk in the freedom he provides.

This book focuses specifically on family forgiveness, as family relationships are among our most significant and often most challenging connections. Here you will find guidance for cultivating a life of forgiveness, and for families to heal, restore trust, and mend broken bonds. Forgiveness and reconciliation are priceless gifts, capable of soothing even the deepest wounds caused by betrayal, deceit, or misunderstanding.

This book also addresses some common misconceptions about forgiveness. Many assume that forgiveness means forgetting the offense or excusing the behavior. While the phrase "forgive and forget" sounds appealing, it is not realistic. True forgiveness does not deny what happened; it acknowledges the harm while choosing to release the offender from the debt of restitution and allowing the heart to let go of anger and resentment.

We learn here that forgiveness and reconciliation, though closely related, are not the same. Reconciliation is the renewal of a relationship after conflict, that is built on forgiveness, genuine repentance, and mutual trust. Forgiveness opens the door, and reconciliation walks through it. Understanding this distinction allows us to forgive freely, even when reconciliation might have to wait.

The purpose of this book is to focus on forgiving within families and forgiving others. In these pages we see that we are called to forgive, regardless of the offender's repentance or the severity of the offense.

PART ONE

A Foundation
for Forgiveness
and Reconciliation

*The Bible is a portrait of love
painted on a canvas of forgiveness.*

PART ONE
A Foundation for Forgiveness and Reconciliation

Before an artist begins a painting, the canvas is not chosen at random, but with careful attention to its grain and texture, and its ability to hold both light and shadow. It is placed on the easel where the illumination falls just right. Beside it, tubes of oil paint wait in careful array: rich crimsons, deep blues, brilliant golds, and tender whites. Each brush is selected for its purpose—some broad and bold, others fine enough to capture the smallest detail. Finally, the artist studies the subject to be painted. In this case, we are the subject; and the finished portrait reflects both the joy that forgiveness restores, and the renewed closeness reconciliation brings within our families and with others.

As already stated, Scripture also uses color to reveal God's restoring work. From the scarlet robe placed upon Jesus' shoulders to the water of the river of life, bright and clear as crystal, these vivid images remind us that the God who paints the universe with such beauty also restores our lives with grace and mercy. Truly, the Bible is a portrait of love painted on a canvas of forgiveness.

A similar preparation happens upon entering Part One. Here, forgiveness and reconciliation are defined, and both are shown as essential for a loving home. As the studio is prepared with canvas, paint, and brushes, so the heart is prepared with truth. Grace and mercy are not optional accents; they become warm, guiding tones that soften the heart and prepare it to become a portrait of love.

With the Part One foundation laid, painting will truly begin in Part Two—with the colors of forgiveness and reconciliation taking shape as the truths of Scripture are lived out.

CHAPTER 1
What Is Forgiveness?

Forgiveness is never easy, especially within a family where pain runs deep and lingers long. The burden grows heavier when the one who wounds us is our own flesh and blood. We wrestle with anger, resentment, and disappointment when the people we love most become the source of our deepest hurt. We feel the ache of an empty seat at the table, not because death has claimed someone, but because conflict or distance has created a silence that feels almost permanent.

We might picture a daughter absent from a family gathering after a painful disagreement, a son who has grown distant because we struggled to accept his choices, or a spouse slowly withdrawing behind years of unspoken wounds. These moments remind us how easily love can turn to distance when forgiveness is delayed and hearts grow guarded.

To understand forgiveness, particularly within our families, we need to pause and ask what God is truly calling us to do. Is forgiveness simply pretending the pain never happened, or is it something far deeper, reflecting the very heart of God? These questions are not distant or abstract; they reach into our everyday lives and invite us to experience the transforming power of grace and mercy in our closest relationships.

Grace and Mercy

Before exploring forgiveness, we need to understand the two words that give it life: grace and mercy. These work together at the center of God's heart and form the foundation for every act of forgiveness we offer.

Grace is the unearned and unconditional favor of God, offered to those who can do nothing to earn it. Grace reaches out long before worthiness is proven. It places a gift into empty hands and welcomes us with love that is patient, steady, and overflowing.

Mercy is compassion we do not deserve but are given anyway. It is kindness shown to someone who has fallen short or caused pain, offered by the one who has every right to respond with judgment. Mercy steps into the moment where consequences are warranted and chooses healing instead of punishment. It is like warm light breaking through clouds of anger, softening what justice alone could never restore.

To appreciate the transforming power of grace and mercy, we need to see them against the backdrop of what our human nature naturally desires: retribution and justice.

Retribution and Punishment

Retribution reflects our natural longing for justice when a wrong has been committed. The word itself means "to pay back," expressing the truth that every action carries a consequence. This principle is clearly seen throughout the Old Testament law, "an eye for an eye, a tooth for a tooth" (Exodus 21:24). At its heart, retribution reflects fairness and the desire to restore moral order;

it is not necessarily an act of cruelty. It acknowledges that when something is broken, it must be made right.

In the same way, punishment bears a serious weight. It upholds accountability, yet its true purpose should be correction, not destruction. When punishment is properly administered, it can be a form of discipline. Just as a loving parent disciplines a child to shape the heart rather than wound it, Scripture reminds us that divine discipline flows from love, not anger: "For the Lord reproves him whom he loves" (Proverbs 3:12). When rooted in love, discipline shapes character and restores what was lost.

Retribution addresses justice, balancing the moral scales; while punishment can shape the heart through discipline.

The Transforming Power of Grace and Mercy

Extending grace and mercy through forgiveness changes everything. Mercy spares us from what we deserve, while grace offers what we could never earn. Grace turns failure into favor and rejection into belonging. It's been said that God's grace is "perfect acceptance, not a shade of rejection" — which eliminates fear.

Scripture shows that both grace and mercy are essential to forgiveness. Paul writes, "Be kind to one another, tenderhearted, forgiving one another, as God in Christ forgave us" (Ephesians 4:32). Here kindness and tenderheartedness reflect grace, while forgiveness expresses mercy shaped by that grace. Paul's linking these qualities significantly mirrors how God has forgiven us through Jesus Christ. God's grace was displayed by enduring the cross, giving us what we did not merit; and his mercy through Jesus' accomplishment there, sparing us from the judgment we deserved.

In the same way, our forgiveness of others begins with grace and is carried out through mercy—with grace remaining even after forgiveness is complete to free us from negative thoughts and words that unforgiveness once controlled. Grace provides the foundation for extending mercy, and mercy withholds what is deserved. Continuing its work, grace offers undeserved kindness, patience, and favor instead of bitterness or resentment. Grace reminds us that restoration is possible and that love can grow again where pain once lived.

In family life, this difference is especially tangible. Grace softens things when wrongs occur and opens the way to genuine connection. It makes it easier to "speak the truth in love", with gracious speech "seasoned with salt [truth]". (Ephesians 4:15 and Colossians 4:6).

The Foundation for Our Forgiveness

Our ability to forgive others flows from hearts transformed by God's love, where grace and mercy work hand in hand. Paul reminds us of this truth in Titus, "When the goodness and loving kindness of God our Savior appeared, he saved us, not because of works done by us in righteousness, but according to his own mercy" (Titus 3:4-5).

Through his grace, we receive what we do not deserve: salvation and restoration. Through his mercy, we are spared the judgment that rightly belongs to us.

Scripture reveals both aspects of God's character, inviting us to follow his example. His mercy assures us, "He does not deal with us according to our sins, nor repay us according to our iniquities" (Psalm 103:10). His grace is just as abundant, for "The steadfast love of the Lord never ceases; his mercies never come to an end" (Lamentations 3:22).

This truth shines most clearly in Jesus. "But God shows his love for us in that while we were still sinners, Christ died for us" (Romans 5:8). Paul deepens this message in Ephesians: "In him we have redemption through his blood, the forgiveness of our trespasses, according to the riches of his grace that he lavished upon us" (Ephesians 1:7-8). Through Christ's sacrifice, God's grace and love overflow toward us, revealing the heart of divine forgiveness we are called to extend within our families.

When we choose to forgive within our families, we reflect God's pattern of kindness and mercy. Forgiveness becomes a living testimony of his love, freeing others from the weight of their offenses just as he has freed us. As we grasp the breadth of his mercy, we gradually learn to extend that same grace to others. With this foundation, we are able to continue to reflect on God's character and examine our own hearts, seeking a clearer understanding of true forgiveness.

Forgiveness Defined

Specifically, forgiveness is an unconditional act of kindness, a deliberate choice to release someone from the debt of wrongdoing. We do not forgive because others deserve it; we forgive because we choose to extend mercy, just as God has shown mercy to us.

Forgiveness starts as a decision of the heart, a quiet, inward act that often precedes reconciliation. It does not depend on another person's apology or acknowledgment of wrongdoing. An apology may open the way to healing, but it should never be the condition for forgiving. Forgiveness begins when we release the offense and place the burden into God's hands. When repentance or apology comes, forgiveness prepares the soil for reconciliation to take root and grow.

By its very nature, forgiveness is undeserved. If it could be earned, it would not be forgiveness but repayment. Here we see the beauty of divine balance: grace offers what is not deserved, and mercy withholds what is deserved. Forgiveness stands at the meeting point of both freely giving and graciously releasing. It is a gift that mirrors the heart of God and invites us to walk in the same grace he has shown to us.

Finally, forgiveness releases the debt; it does not deny the offense or minimize the pain it caused. It faces the wrong honestly while choosing the path of freedom, releasing the offender from the expectation of repayment. In this way, forgiveness becomes the harmony of mercy's compassion and grace's generosity working together.

Consider a simple illustration. Suppose we receive a speeding ticket and appear in court. The judge finds us guilty, and we pay the fine. In that case, we are not forgiven because we have satisfied the penalty that justice requires.

Now imagine a different scenario. The judge reviews the evidence and concludes that the citation was unjust, and we should never have been charged. Here, the fine is waived because innocence requires no forgiveness.

Finally, picture this: we stand before the judge fully guilty, with no excuse and no defense. Yet before the sentence is carried out, a friend steps forward and offers to pay the entire fine. The judge accepts what our friend provides and declares us forgiven.

Similarly, all who trust in Jesus receive divine forgiveness, which removes the record of our wrongdoing not by ignoring justice, but by fulfilling it through Christ's sacrifice. The debt was real, yet it was not released because we could repay it, but because Jesus carried it for us. Through his death on the cross, every charge against us was satisfied, and every debt was marked as forever paid in full. Scripture affirms this hope: "by canceling the record of debt that stood against us with its legal demands; this he set aside, nailing it to the cross" (Colossians 2:14). This promise touches every corner of our lives, embracing both the debts we recognize and those we fear are beyond forgiveness. In those places, God's mercy meets us fully, offering complete freedom.

C. S. Lewis captured the heart of forgiveness when he wrote, "To be a Christian means to forgive the inexcusable, because God has forgiven the inexcusable in you." [1] His words touch each of us. Sometimes, forgiveness does not repair a broken relationship, yet it always remains a conscious choice—a decision to release others from our personal demand for repayment or revenge and to entrust justice entirely to God.

Those who forgive consistently often display a maturity born from walking closely with the Lord. A. W. Tozer reminds us of the importance of perspective when he writes, "A Christian is spiritual when he sees everything from God's viewpoint." [2] As we learn to see life through God's eyes, forgiveness is more consistent and takes on a deeper meaning. Instead of dwelling on wounded pride or replaying hurtful words, we begin to view each offense as an opportunity to reflect on his love and character. Forgiveness shifts from focusing on what was done to us to recognizing what God has done for us.

This perspective gently draws our attention to everyday life, especially within our families, where forgiveness is most often tested and most deeply needed. In these close relationships, grace can either flourish or fade. To show us what this forgiveness looks like in practice, Jesus shared one of his most vivid and meaningful parables, a story that invites us to step into the heart of mercy and experience the beauty of forgiveness and reconciliation—reminding us that nowhere is forgiveness displayed more powerfully than within the home. In his story of a father and his two sons, Jesus paints a timeless portrait of love that restores, and grace that warmly welcomes us home.

The Prodigal Son

In this simple yet deeply moving account, Jesus reveals both the pain of fractured relationships and the astonishing grace of reconciliation. For readers unfamiliar with this account, the full parable can be found in Luke 15:11–32, where Jesus speaks of a father and his two sons. The younger son makes a bold and shocking request: he asks for his portion of the inheritance while his father is still living.

At first glance, the son's words may seem impulsive or immature. Yet in the ancient Middle Eastern world, such a request carried a far deeper wound. His plea was not merely about inheritance; it was a rejection of relationship. In essence, the son was saying, "Father, I want your wealth, but not your presence." With those words, he treated his father not as the giver of life and blessing, but as an obstacle to his own freedom.

Imagine hearing those words today. Picture a grown child saying, "I don't want a relationship with you anymore; but I'd like my inheritance now, so I can live my life without you." The emotional weight of such a statement would be devastating, an ache that cuts through both love and memory. Even so, the father granted his son's request. Without protest, he divided his estate between his two sons and watched the younger one gather his belongings and depart for a distant land.

What followed was inevitable. The younger son squandered his inheritance through reckless living until nothing was left. When a severe famine struck the land, he found himself penniless, hungry, and utterly alone. In desperation, he accepted the only work he could find: feeding pigs, a task no devout Jewish man would ever willingly choose. For a Jewish son, this was the lowest point imaginable. Pigs were considered unclean, and tending them brought deep humiliation. Yet hunger silenced his pride. Even the food meant for the pigs began to look appealing. The stench of the pigsty clung to his clothes, a bitter reminder of how far he had fallen and how empty his pursuit of freedom apart from his father had become.

Then came the turning point: "He came to his senses."

This was more than the realization of financial ruin; it was a moment of spiritual awakening, a clear-eyed awareness of all he had truly lost. He had not only wasted his wealth; he had turned his back on the relationship. He had not only left comfort behind; he had abandoned his place of belonging and the identity that came with it. Perhaps, in that quiet moment, a memory stirred something as simple as the warmth of home or the sound of laughter drifting from the kitchen. Against the harshness of the pigpen before him, those memories rekindled an awareness of the goodness he had once known and the grace he had forsaken.

As A. W. Tozer wisely observed, "God never greatly uses anyone until he tests them deeply." [3] The prodigal son's painful experience in that distant land became the fertile soil where repentance took root. In much the same way, our deepest wounds, whether self-inflicted or caused by others, often become the very ground God cultivates to transform our hearts.

His confession showed how deeply repentance had worked within him. He said, "Father, I have sinned against heaven and before you. I am no longer worthy to be called your son. Treat me as one of your hired servants" (Luke 15:18-19). His words showed no attempt to justify his actions or escape their consequences. He was ready to return in humility, fully aware of the grace he did not deserve.

What happened next would have astonished everyone listening to Jesus. While the son was still a long way off, the father saw him coming. Instead of waiting with dignified restraint for his son to approach and beg for mercy, the father did something unimaginable for a man of his standing: he ran to meet him! This meant lifting his robes and exposing his legs, an act considered deeply shameful for a man of his age and honor. Yet the father cared nothing for appearances. Moved by compassion, he set aside all concern for dignity and hurried toward the son who had once broken his heart. Before the young man could finish his rehearsed apology, the father wrapped him in a loving embrace.

In that moment, mercy outran judgment. This is the essence of forgiveness: grace overcoming shame, love conquering pride, and compassion covering failure rather than exposing it. With tender urgency, the father interrupted his son's unfinished confession and called for a joyful celebration. "Bring quickly the best robe, and put it on him, and put a ring on his hand, and shoes on his feet. Bring the fattened calf and kill it, and let us eat and celebrate. For this my son was dead, and is alive again. He was lost and is found" (Luke 15:22-24). In that moment, grace triumphed over guilt. The father's response revealed the very heart of God, a love that restores dignity, renews relationships, and rejoices over repentance.

Every action the father took carried profound meaning; each gesture reflected a unique aspect of restoration and genuine forgiveness. First, the father called for the best robe, a powerful symbol of renewed honor and complete acceptance. In that culture, such a robe was reserved for the most distinguished guests. By placing it around his son, the father made a public declaration of his son's restored place in the family. "This is not a servant. This is my son, fully restored." [4]

Then the father commanded his servants to bring a ring for his son's hand. In biblical times, a ring symbolized authority, identity, and trust, often engraved with the family seal. Placing it on his son's finger was a public declaration of full restoration. The son was not merely forgiven; he was reinstated as a true member of the household. Though his inheritance was gone, his place in the family was secure. No longer an outsider, he was once again a beloved son. [5]

The father also ordered sandals for his feet. In that culture, servants and slaves went barefoot, while sons wore sandals. By restoring his footwear, the father made it unmistakably clear: this was not a servant's return, but a son's homecoming. The welcome was not marked by shame but by dignity and freedom. The father's embrace sealed his son's complete restoration. [6]

Then came the fattened calf. In village life, the slaughter of such an animal was rare, reserved only for moments of great joy. Meat was a luxury, and the fattened calf was kept for occasions that called the whole community to celebrate. When the father ordered it to be prepared, he made a public and costly declaration of love and restoration. "My son is home, and we will rejoice." His generosity was extravagant, and his love was unconditional. [7]

The feast was far more than a simple family meal; it became a joyful community celebration. Music and dancing carried across the fields, and the father's invitation to his older son revealed that not only the household but also the neighbors had come to share in the joy. The air was alive with song, laughter, and heartfelt gratitude, honoring the homecoming of one who had been lost but was now found. Jesus emphasized this truth when he said, "Just so, I tell you, there will be more joy in heaven over one sinner who repents than over ninety-nine righteous persons who need no repentance" (Luke 15:7).

But the story does not end there. When the older brother returned from the field and heard the music and celebration, he hesitated to join in. His response revealed the true condition of his heart: "But he answered his father, 'Look, these many years I have served you, and I never disobeyed your command, yet you never gave me a young goat, that I might celebrate with my friends.'" (Luke 15:29). This response revealed deep roots of resentment. He exaggerated his own faithfulness and saw his relationship with his father as a duty rather than love. Comparing himself to his brother, he kept a mental record of sacrifices and replayed old wounds. He diminished his brother's repentance by saying, "this son of yours" instead of "my brother," and he withheld joy, remaining outside the celebration of grace—reactions exposing a heart trapped in pride and comparison, struggling to rejoice in mercy.

The older brother's posture reminds us how easily any of us can stand outside the joy God offers when bitterness clouds our perspective; and the father's gentle reply speaks not only to his son but to each of us: "And he said to him, 'Son, you are always with me, and all that is mine is yours'" (Luke 15:31). God's forgiveness does not take away what he has entrusted to us. Instead, it invites us into a celebration of mercy that restores both prodigals and elder siblings with equal grace. The father's compassion and the older brother's resentment show us that forgiveness is needed on both sides. The one who repents requires mercy, and the one who has been hurt needs freedom from bitterness. In their own ways, both sons needed the transforming love of their father.

This same truth applies to our families today. Every home has moments when one of us feels like the prodigal—ashamed, broken, and uncertain of our welcome; while another feels like the elder brother, outwardly faithful yet quietly harboring resentment. Parents may carry pain from children who have wandered. Children may struggle with the problems a wandering sibling creates, or comparisons that slowly erode affection. Spouses may feel burdened, growing distant just when forgiveness is most needed. Yet Paul urges us to "present your bodies as a living sacrifice, holy and acceptable to God, which is your spiritual worship" (Romans 12:1). When we become a living sacrifice, we maintain steadfast love for our families.

The father in Jesus' story mirrors our heavenly Father, whose love is so extravagant that he runs to meet us even while we are still far away. Scripture reminds us of our shared need for God's grace. "If we say we have no sin, we deceive ourselves, and the truth is not in us." (1 John 1:8). Every one of us depends on the forgiveness our Heavenly Father freely offers. A simple question invites reflection: Where do we find ourselves in this story today? Are we like the prodigal, longing for restoration, or perhaps the elder brother, hoping to be free from resentment? Perhaps we carry elements of both, seeking the father's love to transform us from within.

This parable encourages us to look beyond a family and into the heart of God's greater narrative. The father's forgiveness, as Jesus reveals it, mirrors the mercy and reconciliation woven throughout Scripture. It is the story of a loving God who restores what has been lost and draws us back to himself through Jesus. To grasp why this parable matters so deeply, we step back and see that forgiveness lies at the very center of God's plan of redemption. It is the thread connecting the Father's compassion, our human need, and the hope Jesus brings to every wounded heart.

The Big Picture

Forgiveness is profoundly significant and must be viewed within a broader perspective. As the saying goes, "cannot see the forest for the trees," we sometimes overlook the whole when we focus only on the parts. Forgiveness is no different. Before examining how it shapes our daily lives, we have to step back to consider the larger story of Scripture. Seen through the lens of the entire Bible, forgiveness takes on a richer, more profound meaning.

If someone asked us to summarize the Bible's central message in a single sentence, how might we respond? While believers may express it in different ways, most would affirm this essential truth: the Bible reveals God's plan of forgiveness and reconciliation for all who place their trust in Jesus. It tells the story of a God who pursues us, restores us, and invites us into a relationship marked by grace. From the very beginning, God created a perfect world and placed the first humans in a paradise free from sin and death. Yet Adam and Eve's disobedience brought sin into the world, separating humanity from the Creator. Without God's forgiveness, every person would face judgment and eternal separation. But God, rich in mercy and overflowing with grace, chose a different path. He sent his Son, who took on human flesh, lived a sinless life, and willingly suffered on the cross to bear the penalty for our sins. He died, was buried, and rose again so that all who trust in him might be forgiven and reconciled to God forever.

Through the cross, God shows himself as both perfectly just and fully forgiving. Psalm 85 beautifully captures this union of justice and mercy: "Steadfast love and faithfulness meet; righteousness and peace kiss each other" (Psalm 85:10). At the cross, this divine meeting becomes a reality. Paul describes it this way: "And you, who were dead in your trespasses and the uncircumcision of your flesh, God made alive together with him, having forgiven us all our trespasses, by canceling the record of debt that stood against us with its legal demands. This he set aside, nailing it to the cross" (Colossians 2:13-14). This is not merely a theological background. It is the foundation that makes human forgiveness possible. When we begin to grasp the depth of God's forgiveness toward us, we discover both the motivation and the strength to extend that same forgiveness to others.

Seen in this light, forgiveness is not optional. It becomes the natural overflow of God's mercy at work within us. And if this is true, an important question follows. What might forgiveness look like when it is lived out in the rhythms of our daily family life?

Practicing Forgiveness

In answer to that question, Scripture offers guidance with both clarity and compassion. First, we are reminded that God calls us to love even those who have deeply wounded us. Jesus taught, "You have heard that it was said, 'You shall love your neighbor and hate your enemy.' But I say to you, love your enemies and pray for those who persecute you, so that you may be sons of your Father who is in heaven" (Matthew 5:43-45). This command speaks directly to our homes. When a brother breaks our trust, a parent repeatedly disappoints us, or a child turns away from biblical values, Jesus invites us to respond with love. Loving in this way does not mean excusing harmful behavior or allowing ourselves to be mistreated. Rather, it means choosing love over bitterness and entrusting our pain to God, who alone can heal our hearts and bring lasting restoration.

Forgiveness also replaces condemnation. Left to our own devices, we often step into the role of judge, determining what others deserve for the pain they have caused. Yet Jesus calls us to a higher path: "Judge not, and you will not be judged; condemn not, and you will not be condemned; forgive, and you will be forgiven" (Luke 6:37). This, of course, does not apply to loving parental judgment of their own children. With that said, what would it look like to release our family members from the courtroom of our minds? Instead of replaying their mistakes over and over, can we choose to trust God enough to free them from the silent judgments we hold inside? Scripture reminds us that "mercy triumphs over judgment" (James 2:13).

Forgiveness is an ongoing journey, especially within families, where old wounds may resurface and familiar hurts can reappear. Jesus provides clear guidance for this path. "Pay attention to yourselves! If your brother sins, rebuke him, and if he repents, forgive him, and if he sins against you seven times in a day, and turns to you seven times, saying, 'I repent,' you must forgive him" (Luke 17:3-4). In this call, Jesus shows us that forgiveness is not a single moment but a rhythm of grace, reflecting the patience God extends to us each day. Jesus emphasizes continual forgiveness, even when the same offences recur. This does not mean allowing harmful behavior to continue unchecked. Rather, it invites us to cultivate hearts that remain open to reconciliation and ready to forgive whenever genuine repentance appears.

Ultimately, we forgive because God has forgiven us. As Paul reminds us, "Be kind to one another, tenderhearted, forgiving one another, as God in Christ forgave you" (Ephesians 4:32). Our forgiveness toward others flows from the forgiveness we ourselves have received. When we feel the temptation to withhold grace or mercy, we remember the immeasurable cost of the forgiveness given to us through Jesus. Forgiveness is not a single act; it becomes a way of life, shaped by the cross that is a result of following him: "If anyone wants to follow after me, let him deny himself, take up his cross daily and follow me" (Luke 9:23). We must be willing to embrace the cost of obedience. This forgiveness is complete and all-encompassing. It reaches beyond every boundary of race, background, belief, and even the severity of the wrong. Scripture calls us to forgive all people, at all times, including those who are no longer with us. Such forgiveness frees our hearts and opens space for healing. Forgiving those who have passed may seem abstract, yet it brings profound healing. Even when reconciliation in this life is impossible, forgiveness remains essential for our own peace. It is a deliberate choice to release resentment and surrender anger to God. Scripture gives us no reason to hold grudges, even against those who cannot respond. In choosing forgiveness in these situations, we reflect the grace we have received, extend mercy where none can be returned, and allow our hearts to experience true freedom.

Understanding what forgiveness truly means begins with recognizing what it is not. Many of us struggle to forgive because we try to follow a version of forgiveness that differs from the biblical model. Forgiveness does not mean denying our pain. True forgiveness never dismisses hurt by saying, "It was not that bad," or "I am probably overreacting." Genuine forgiveness faces the offense honestly and acknowledges its full weight. When we minimize an offense, we are not truly forgiving; we are avoiding reality. Denial cannot bring healing; only truth brings freedom.

Forgiveness is also not the same as the familiar phrase "forgive and forget." Scripture never uses this expression. Only God promises to "remember [our] sins no more" (Hebrews 8:12), an act of divine mercy that lies beyond human ability. While we cannot erase painful memories, we can choose not to revisit them in bitterness or use them as weapons during moments of frustration or conflict.

Forgiveness is not the same as trust. We may choose to forgive in a single moment, yet trust often grows slowly through consistent, reliable actions. It is possible to forgive sincerely while still saying, "I need to see change before trust can be rebuilt." This distinction matters and will be explored more fully in the next chapter.

Forgiveness does not mean allowing others to harm us. Some of us have been taught that forgiving requires tolerating continued hurt, but that is not biblical forgiveness. True forgiveness does not ask us to accept abuse or voluntarily enable destructive behavior. Love may require boundaries, consequences, and protection, even as our hearts remain free from bitterness and resentment.

Bitterness and hatred are closely related, but they are not the same. Bitterness often begins as quiet resentment, taking root in the heart when pain or injustice remains unresolved. It lingers beneath the surface, slowly poisoning our thoughts and emotions. Hatred, by contrast, is the fruit that bitterness bears when it hardens into open hostility.

Bitterness quietly resents; hatred strikes openly. One grows silently beneath the soil, while the other produces visible and destructive fruit. Scripture warns us, "See to it that no one fails to obtain the grace of God; that no "root of bitterness" springs up and causes trouble, and by it many became defiled" (Hebrews 12:15). The cure for both is forgiveness. It uproots bitterness before it can harden into hatred and replaces resentment with grace and mercy.

Forgiveness is not based on feelings. Many of us wait until we feel ready before taking the first step, yet forgiveness is an act of obedience rather than emotion. We choose to forgive because God calls us to walk in his grace and mercy, trusting that, in time, our hearts and emotions will follow our decision.

Forgiveness is not the same as a pardon. When we forgive others, we are not declaring them innocent, nor are we excusing their actions. Our forgiveness does not remove their responsibility before God. Instead, it frees us from bitterness and the exhausting desire for revenge. True forgiveness releases the personal debt we believe someone owes us while still recognizing that every person remains spiritually accountable to God. Only God can truly forgive sin. A president might pardon a criminal, but no human authority can erase sin itself. Similarly, we can forgive those who have wronged us, yet their guilt before God remains. Each person is ultimately responsible for seeking his forgiveness. King David recognized this truth when he prayed, "Against you, you only, have I sinned and done what is evil in your sight, so that you may be justified in your words and blameless in your judgment" (Psalm 51:4). Although David's actions deeply harmed others, including Bathsheba, her husband Uriah, and the nation he led, he ultimately recognized that sin, at its core, is rebellion against God. This truth lies at the heart of the gospel: only God can forgive sin, and he offers that forgiveness freely through Jesus. We cannot earn it; it is a gift of pure grace, given to all who place their trust in him. Scripture reminds us, "If we confess our sins, he is faithful and just to forgive us our sins and to cleanse us from all unrighteousness" (1 John 1:9).

Yet forgiveness is not only for others; it is also a gift we must learn to receive and embrace within our own hearts.

Receiving Forgiveness

Forgiveness begins with humility, which is shown in the willingness to acknowledge our sins honestly and to accept forgiveness when it is freely offered.

Many struggle to receive forgiveness because pride, shame, or denial hold us back. A guarded heart often seeks self-protection instead of surrender. When forgiveness is resisted, the one offering it may feel unheard, and true reconciliation cannot take root. Healing is hindered when grace is present but not embraced.

The story of Zacchaeus illustrates this beautifully. The wealthy tax collector did not merely voice acceptance of Jesus' grace—his actions revealed a transformed life: "Behold, Lord, the half of my goods I give to the poor. And if I have defrauded anyone of anything, I restore it fourfold." (Luke 19:8). His encounter with divine mercy led him to repentance, generosity, and lasting transformation. Zacchaeus reminds us that forgiveness is not only a gift we receive but also a power that reshapes our hearts and guides our actions.

When we truly accept forgiveness, whether from God or

from others, it begins to transform us from the inside out. We no longer feel the need to cling to pride, make excuses, or justify ourselves. Forgiveness frees us to heal, to grow, and to walk forward in God's grace with renewed humility.

Forgiveness opens the door to reconciliation, but true restoration requires the willing participation of both hearts. One person can offer forgiveness, yet rebuilding trust needs two who are ready to engage in the process. As we continue our journey, the next chapter will explore how reconciliation differs from forgiveness and why both are vital in restoring and healing our relationships.

Closing Remarks

Understanding what forgiveness truly is and what it is not prepares us for the journey ahead. Like an artist who first studies the properties of paint, canvas, and light before creating a masterpiece, we must grasp the foundations of forgiveness. What we learn here will shape everything that follows in our lives.

Forgiveness is not the finish line; it is the gateway. But what lies beyond it? If forgiveness frees us from the prison of bitterness, how do we begin restoring the relationship itself? How can we move beyond merely letting go of the past to building a future shaped by hope?

It is essential to distinguish between forgiving someone and trusting them again, a challenge that often causes the most struggle within families. We may know forgiveness is the right path, yet still wrestle with discerning when reconciliation is wise.

How can we tell when it is safe to open our hearts? What signs reveal genuine change rather than momentary regret?

As we move forward, remember that forgiveness and reconciliation, though closely connected, are not the same. Forgiveness clears the path, while reconciliation involves carefully rebuilding trust over time, guided by humility, patience, and mutual commitment. The next chapter will explore reconciliation more deeply, showing how forgiveness meets the ongoing work of restoring trust, and how families can begin writing a new story together.

Questions for Personal Reflection or Group Discussion

1. When Grace Is Confused with Conditions

"I'll forgive you when you apologize."

"I'll forgive you when you change."

"I'll forgive you when you prove you deserve it."

Grace doesn't have conditions, but we often keep adding them anyway. Think of someone specific right now who you've struggled to forgive. What conditions have you been waiting for them to meet? What if today you chose to release them, not because they've earned it, but because grace doesn't require them to?

2. The Lie That Forgiveness Means Forgetting

Some people think forgiveness means saying, "It's okay. It wasn't that bad. No big deal."

But if you have to minimize the hurt to forgive, you haven't actually forgiven. True forgiveness faces the full weight of the wound and says, "This mattered. It hurt deeply. And I'm releasing you anyway." Is there someone you are trying to forgive by pretending it didn't hurt as much as it did? And what would it look like to name the real hurt and forgive anyway?

3. What Bitterness Costs You

Bitterness is heavy. It steals your sleep. It poisons your prayers. It changes how you talk about them when they're not around. You know this. You've felt it. What has unforgiveness cost you, now or in the past? Your peace? Your joy? Your connection with God? Name it.

4. Forgiveness Frees You First

You've been waiting for them to apologize. To change. To see what they did. They haven't, and they might never. But what if forgiveness is the key to *your* freedom, not theirs? You can walk free today. Whether they ever change or not. Is there someone you need to forgive to be set free? Say their name. Forgive them.

CHAPTER 2
What Is Reconciliation?

When Japan surrendered at the end of World War II in 1945, many Japanese citizens feared the worst, and with good reason. History often showed that defeated nations were stripped of their resources, humiliated, or forced to make overwhelming reparations.

After World War I, for example, the Treaty of Versailles imposed heavy burdens on Germany. It required Germany to pay 132 billion gold marks in reparations, equivalent to several trillion dollars in today's value. It stripped the nation of thirteen per cent of its European territory, as well as all of its overseas colonies. Even more painful was the requirement that Germany accept sole responsibility for starting the war, although historians agree that the causes of World War I were far more complex and involved multiple nations.

The result was humiliation and deep resentment. Many Germans used that resentment to seek revenge, and scholars widely agree that the harsh terms of the treaty worsened economic hardship and helped create the conditions that led to the rise of Adolf Hitler and outbreak of World War II. [8]

Japan braced for severe retribution. Yet when General Douglas MacArthur arrived to oversee the Allied occupation, he took a remarkably different approach. Rather than punishing the nation, he treated its people with dignity and respect, insisting that Emperor Hirohito remain as a symbolic figurehead, a decision that helped preserve Japan's sense of unity and national identity. [9]

MacArthur collaborated with Japanese leaders to draft a constitution that protected civil liberties and expanded women's rights [10] Instead of dismantling Japan's industry, he helped rebuild it, reformed schools, strengthened democratic institutions, and released political prisoners. [11]

At the same time, he recognized Japan's deep spiritual need. He invited Christian organizations to send missionaries and provide Scriptures in Japanese. Churches responded eagerly by printing and distributing millions of Bibles, and sending missionaries to live among the Japanese people. This spiritual awakening, together with political and economic reforms, opened the door to renewal in a nation that had previously resisted such transformation. [12]

Under General MacArthur's leadership, former enemies became partners, and the postwar occupation grew into a true alliance. Within a single generation, Japan was transformed from a defeated nation into a thriving democracy and one of America's closest allies. The Japanese people did more than tolerate MacArthur; over time, they came to respect and even revere him. Crowds often gathered just to catch a glimpse of him, showing that reconciliation had become mutual, not one-sided. His approach was extraordinary: a nation that once faced defeat came to honor the leader who had guided its occupation.

MacArthur's decision to pursue reconciliation rather than revenge stands as one of history's most striking examples of true restoration. Reconciliation is not a sign of weakness; it reflects courageous leadership, capable of transforming hostility into trust and shaping a hopeful future.

Just as reconciliation can restore a fractured nation, it can also bring healing to a hurting home. The principles are the same: we choose restoration over retaliation, cultivate space for trust to flourish, and take patient steps toward a renewed, peaceful life.

An Overview of How Forgiveness Differs from Reconciliation

Reconciliation and forgiveness are closely related, but not the same; and understanding the difference is essential for healthy family relationships.

Forgiveness	Reconciliation
Involves one person	Involves all parties
A unilateral decision	A relational process
Commanded by God	Desired by God, but not always possible
Can happen immediately	Can be immediate or progressive
Does not require the other person's participation	Requires mutual participation
Cancels the debt	Restores the relationship
Frees the forgiver from bitterness	Rebuilds trust and closeness
Does not require apology or repentance	Requires repentance and trust

Forgiveness prepares the heart. Reconciliation restores the relationship.

Joseph and His Brothers:
A Family Story of Brokenness and Healing

Like many families today weighed down by favoritism and rivalry, Jacob's household was fragile and easily wounded. His open preference for Rachel's firstborn, Joseph, created an atmosphere thick with tension. Jacob did not hide his affection; he expressed it through an ornate, multicolored robe far more extravagant than anything he had given his other sons.

Joseph, still a teenager, unintentionally deepened his brothers' resentment when he shared the dreams God had given him—night visions that foretold he would one day rise to honor, even above his brothers and parents. Though these dreams were true revelations from God, his words sounded prideful to brothers already stung by their father's belittling and favoritism. Resentment quietly took root and jealousy grew, eventually hardening into betrayal. Their wounded hearts set the stage for a moment of cruelty that would forever change their family.

At just seventeen, Joseph suffered a devastating betrayal by the very brothers who should have loved and protected him. They seized him, tore off his cherished robe, and threw him into an empty pit. Then, at Judah's urging, they pulled him out not to save him, but to sell him to passing traders, condemning him to a life of hardship and slavery. In that moment, they not only wronged their brother but also planted years of hidden guilt within their family.

Joseph was taken as a slave to Egypt, far from all that was familiar. By the age of thirty, he had faced years of hardship, betrayal, false accusations, unjust imprisonment, and the deep loneliness of being separated from his family. Yet, through every painful trial, Scripture says "the Lord was with Joseph" (Genesis 39:2, 21). His awareness and acknowledgement of God's steady presence sustained him, shaped his character, and prepared him for a purpose he could not yet see.

In time, the same God who allowed Joseph's trials raised him to a position of remarkable influence, second only to Pharaoh. His journey shows how God can work through the darkest chapters of our lives to prepare us for what lies ahead.

Through divine wisdom, Joseph interpreted Pharaoh's dreams, revealing that seven years of abundance would be followed by seven years of famine. Guided by God's insight, he led Egypt to store grain during the fruitful years, preparing the nation for significant hardship to come.

When famine spread across the surrounding regions, families traveled to Egypt seeking relief. Among them were Joseph's brothers, arriving more than twenty years after the day they betrayed him. As they bowed before him, they unknowingly fulfilled the very dreams that had once stirred their jealousy. They did not recognize Joseph, but he recognized them immediately. Before him stood the same brothers who had torn his robe, thrown him into a pit, and sold him into slavery. If there was ever a moment where revenge would have seemed justified, it was this one.

Yet Joseph chose a different path. Instead of reacting hastily or letting old wounds dictate his actions, he paused. He took time to discern whether true reconciliation and restored trust were possible. His restraint reminds us that while forgiveness can be immediate, genuine reconciliation often requires wisdom, patience, and spiritual discernment.

Joseph's Wise Path to Reconciliation

Modern parents sometimes face a difficult question: when an adult child returns home after years of harmful choices, how can we tell whether their change is genuine or deceptively born out of desperation? Similarly, when someone who has deeply wounded us expresses a desire to reconcile, we need wisdom to discern whether their repentance is true transformation, temporary regret, or even deception.

It is easy to overlook the intentional process Joseph followed before reopening the door to trust. Scripture shows that he did not rush reconciliation. Guided by divine wisdom, Joseph carefully observed the state of his brothers' hearts— paying attention not only to their words but also to their actions, especially under pressure. He allowed time to reveal whether genuine repentance had taken root.

His example reminds us that we can seek peace while still exercising discernment. We can forgive sincerely, yet patiently watch for signs of true change. Joseph teaches that reconciliation grows not from impulse but from humility, integrity, and the courage to let God reveal the truth in his time.

Test One: Allegation of Spies
Genesis 42:1–17

As famine spread across the land of Canaan, Jacob sent ten of his sons to Egypt to buy grain, keeping Benjamin, the youngest, at home. Rachel had given Jacob two sons, Joseph and Benjamin; and after losing Joseph years earlier, Jacob could not bear to risk Benjamin's safety. So the ten older brothers embarked on the long journey to Egypt, while Benjamin, Joseph's only full brother, stayed behind with their father.

When the brothers arrived in Egypt, they stood before the powerful governor, unaware that the man before them was their long-lost brother. Joseph recognized them immediately. Memories from years past must have surged through his mind: the cold emptiness of the pit, the silver coins exchanged for his life, and the distant faces of his brothers as he was carried away by the slave caravan.

Yet Joseph did not reveal himself. Instead, he chose a path that would test the condition of their hearts. He concealed his identity and addressed his brothers as strangers. With calm authority, he accused them of being spies who had come to probe Egypt's defenses.

Startled and afraid, the brothers quickly defended themselves. "And they said, 'We, your servants, are twelve brothers, the sons of one man in the land of Canaan, and behold, the youngest is this day with our father, and one is no more'" (Genesis 42:13). The irony was striking: the very brother they had believed lost forever now stood before them, clothed in the garments of Egyptian authority.

Joseph pressed the matter further, insisting they prove the truth of their words. Yet even in their fear, a new tone began to emerge: humility, honesty, and a quiet sorrow for the brother they once thought gone—the very qualities absent in the young men who had mocked Joseph and sold him into slavery. Their words now revealed the first signs of the change Joseph longed to see.

Still cautious, Joseph continued to conceal his identity and test them. Through this trial, a faint light of transformation began to appear, their responses showing a humility that had not been evident for many years.

Test Two: Prison
Genesis 42:18-24

Joseph's next test reached even deeper into his brothers' hearts. He ordered all ten to remain in prison for three days. We can imagine their fear during those long hours—cold, hungry, uncertain, and trapped in the very land where they had once sold their brother into slavery.

On the third day, Joseph softened his command. Nine of the brothers could return home with grain for their families, but Simeon would remain in custody as a pledge until they brought back Benjamin. This became a defining moment: would they risk themselves to rescue a brother, or turn away as they had years before with Joseph?

Then something remarkable happened. Speaking in their own language, not realizing Joseph understood, the brothers began to confess their guilt. They said to one another, "In truth we are guilty concerning our brother, in that we saw the distress of his soul, when he begged us and we did not listen. That is why this distress has come upon us" (Genesis 42:21). Their words revealed what Joseph needed to know. The seeds of repentance were finally taking root. What they had once dismissed with hardened hearts was now acknowledged as sin. The very men who had ignored Joseph's cries were awakening to their own need for mercy. Reuben reminded them, "Did I not tell you not to sin against the boy? But you did not listen. So now there comes a reckoning for his blood" (v. 22).

Their words revealed that the memory of their sin had never truly faded. Even after many years, remorse weighed heavily on their hearts. Joseph must have felt a deep stirring within as he recognized that his brothers were beginning to grasp the full weight of their betrayal. He quietly listened as their confession broke the silence. These were the same brothers who had once mocked him, their hearts closed to compassion, yet now they spoke with honesty and sorrow. Overwhelmed, Joseph stepped aside and wept, his tears carrying both old pain and a renewed sense of hope. This second test had revealed more than fear; it uncovered the beginnings of genuine repentance, showing that God was already at work softening their hearts.

Test Three: Money in the Sacks
Genesis 42:25-28; 43:15-23

Joseph's third test revealed the integrity of his brothers. Secretly, he instructed his steward to return their silver, placing it back in their sacks along with the grain—along with telling them not to return to Egypt for more food without their youngest brother. The brothers departed for home, unaware of the hidden treasure. When one of them opened his sack and discovered the silver, fear seized their hearts. "What is this that God has done to us" (Genesis 42:28). The brothers were anxious not just about potential punishment in Egypt, but because they felt the weight of their past sin against Joseph. It seemed to them that God was holding them accountable for what they had done.

In Canaan, Jacob struggled to let Benjamin go. His grief for Joseph was still deep, and he clung to Rachel's last son. Yet, as the famine worsened, the brothers pleaded persistently, and Jacob finally relented. He sent them back to Egypt with Benjamin, providing double the silver and "a little balm and a little honey, gum, myrrh, pistachio nuts, and almonds" (Genesis 43:11). These humble gifts, precious in a land struggling with famine, reflected genuine sincerity and goodwill. They conveyed honesty, respect, and a quiet yet meaningful hope for peace.

Upon their arrival, Joseph's steward welcomed them with unexpected warmth. "Peace to you, do not be afraid. Your God and the God of your father has put treasure in your sacks for you" (Genesis 43:23). Simeon was released, and all eleven brothers were led into Joseph's house.

When Benjamin appeared, Joseph's composure faltered. His heart swelled with emotion, and he stepped away to weep in private. Yet even in that tender moment, the test was not complete. Joseph longed for reconciliation, but he also needed assurance that their repentance was genuine and enduring.

Test Four: Benjamin Favored at Banquet
Genesis 43:29-34

After regaining his composure, Joseph presented a banquet for his brothers. They were seated in perfect order, from oldest to youngest, a sight that astonished them and stirred questions they could not answer. How could this powerful Egyptian leader know their ages with such precision? Then Joseph introduced the heart of the test. Benjamin, the youngest and most beloved of Jacob, received a serving five times larger than the others. Years before, parental favoritism had sparked jealousy that led them to betray Joseph. Would the same envy now rise against Benjamin?

Joseph watched them closely, and this time their hearts responded differently. Scripture records, "They drank and were merry with him" (Genesis 43:34). Jealousy had vanished. In its place, joy and fellowship filled the room. The envy that once fractured their unity no longer held sway. For Joseph, this moment confirmed the change he had longed to see. Their hearts had softened, and the shadow of jealousy was gone. The transformation among them was unmistakable.

Test Five: The Silver Cup
Genesis 44:1–13

Before revealing himself, Joseph arranged a fifth test. He instructed his steward to refill the brothers' sacks with grain and secretly place his silver cup in Benjamin's sack. When the brothers had gone, the steward caught up with them and accused them of stealing. Shocked and deeply distressed, they protested their innocence, boldly declaring, "Whichever of your servants is found with it shall die, and the rest of us will become my lord's slaves" (Genesis 44:9).

When the cup was discovered in Benjamin's sack, devastation swept over them. In anguish, they tore their garments, the ancient sign of grief. Years earlier, they had watched Joseph taken away without sorrow or compassion; their hearts hardened. But now, standing on the brink of losing Benjamin, their grief was immediate and overwhelming, revealing how much they had changed. Their unity shone through, and their love for their youngest brother was real.

What happened next marked a true turning point. Instead of abandoning Benjamin, the brothers returned together to Joseph's house, united in loyalty and love. This final test revealed a complete transformation of their hearts. The same brothers who once betrayed Joseph now stood side by side, willing to share Benjamin's fate. Their repentance was no longer spoken in promises but demonstrated through costly, selfless action. In that moment, Joseph saw what he had long hoped for: the door to reconciliation was no longer closed; it was beginning to open.

Test Six: Benjamin's Enslavement
Genesis 44:14-34

Back in Joseph's house, the brothers fell before him once more. Joseph announced that Benjamin would stay as his servant while the others were free to return home. With those words, he set before them the same choice they had failed to make years earlier: Would they abandon a brother again, or would they stand together and risk everything to save him?

Then Judah stepped forward. This was the same brother who had once suggested selling Joseph for silver, but his heart now spoke with humility and deep compassion. He pleaded, "Please let your servant remain instead of the boy...For how can I go back to my father if the boy is not with me?" (Genesis 44:33–34). Judah stepped forward as a substitute, offering to take Benjamin's place, so their father would not have to endure the crushing pain of another loss. His words revealed a love forged through hardship, a love willing to sacrifice for the sake of others.

This was the true turning point. Repentance was no longer just a concept; it was made visible through sacrificial love. The same men who had once sold a brother for profit were now prepared to lay down their lives for one another. As Dwight L. Moody noted, "Repentance is not being sorry for sin. It is being sorry enough to quit." [13] Judah had turned away from the old path of selfishness and embraced the costly way of love. Seeing this transformation, Joseph could no longer hold back his emotions. The trials were over, his brothers had truly changed, and the moment of reconciliation was finally at hand.

A Lesson for Families Today

Have we ever wronged someone deeply and wondered if trust could ever be restored? Judah's story reminds us that genuine repentance is possible not through empty promises, but through a transformed heart and a willingness to make meaningful, sometimes costly, amends.

And when we are the ones who have been hurt, as Joseph was, are we willing to look for signs of change in those who wronged us? Or have we quietly decided they could never change? God calls us to walk with humility and discernment, extending grace without abandoning wisdom.

Joseph saw more than regret in his brothers; he saw repentance shown through their actions. The final test had been met, and the time for reconciliation had come.

Reconciliation Within Joseph's Family

At that pivotal moment, Joseph could no longer hold back his emotions. He asked everyone to leave the room and wept so deeply that even Pharaoh's household could hear him behind the closed doors. When he finally spoke, he said words that his brothers would never have expected: "I am Joseph! Is my father still alive?" (Genesis 45:3)

His brothers stood in stunned silence, gripped by fear and disbelief. Yet Joseph did not condemn them; he gently invited them closer, saying, "Come near to me, please" (Genesis 45:4) The years of testing, waiting, and hidden identity had fulfilled their purpose. The moment for revelation and restoration had finally arrived.

He said to them, "I am your brother, Joseph, whom you sold into Egypt. And now do not be distressed or angry with yourselves because you sold me here, for God sent me before you to preserve life. For the famine has been in the land these two years, and there are yet five years in which there will be neither plowing nor harvest. And God sent me before you to preserve for you a remnant on earth, and to keep alive for you many survivors. So it was not you who sent me here, but God. He has made me a father to Pharaoh, and lord of all his house, and ruler over all the land of Egypt.

Hurry and go up to my father and say to him, 'Thus says your son Joseph, God has made me lord of all Egypt. Come down to me; do not tarry. You shall dwell in the land of Goshen, and you shall be near me, you and your children and your children's children, and your flocks, your herds, and all that you have. There I will provide for you, for there are yet five years of famine to come, so that you and your household, and all that you have, do not come to poverty.' And now your eyes see, and the eyes of my brother Benjamin see, that it is my mouth that speaks to you. You must tell my father of all my honor in Egypt, and of all that you have seen. Hurry and bring my father down here" (Genesis 45:4-13).

Joseph's words carried both truth and tenderness. He did not excuse or minimize his brothers' sin, yet he framed their actions within the greater story of God's redemptive work. What they had intended for harm, God had used for good to preserve life, restore their individual lives and family, and shape the destiny of a nation.

Tears and grace intertwined in that sacred moment. Joseph recognized repentance in his brothers and saw God's redemption at work. Forgiveness had come full circle, not as forgetfulness, but as trust in the sovereign goodness of God. Scripture tells us, "Then he fell upon his brother Benjamin's neck and wept, and Benjamin wept upon his neck. And he kissed all his brothers and wept upon them. After that his brothers talked with him" (Genesis 45:14-15). There is a gentle and meaningful progression in this scene: revelation, reassurance, weeping, embracing, then conversation. True reconciliation restores more than peace; it rebuilds relationships and allows the heart to speak again where silence once lived.

In Joseph's story, reconciliation unfolded slowly and thoughtfully. Joseph, deeply wronged, had to open his heart to the very people who had caused him pain. His choice to forgive was neither immediate nor impulsive; it rested on clear evidence of genuine change in his brothers. At the same time, his brothers demonstrated a sincere desire to rebuild the relationship they had once broken. Their move to Egypt, together with their father Jacob, became a living picture of grace renewed: a family restored through trust and love.

Joseph's forgiveness sprang from his steadfast trust in God's sovereign plan. He looked beyond the pain and betrayal of his past and saw God's redemptive work transforming loss into purpose and suffering into deliverance.

Comparing Forgiveness and Reconciliation

Building on Joseph's example, reconciliation can be understood as the act of repairing a relationship that has been harmed. It is the work of restoring fellowship after conflict, disappointment, or distance. In its purest form, reconciliation turns hostility into friendship and renews peace where tension once lived.

Yet reconciliation is not the same as forgiveness, and understanding the distinction between them is essential for nurturing healthy family relationships. Although closely related, they are not identical.

Forgiveness is a personal act. It is the deliberate choice to release anger and resentment, freeing the heart of the one who forgives. Forgiveness does not depend on the participation of the one who caused the harm, nor does it automatically restore trust. It stands on its own as an act of obedience to God—a response to his command and an expression of his grace working within us. Forgiveness can happen in a single moment. It is offered without delay and without expectation, an act of grace that begins in the heart.

Reconciliation requires both parties. While forgiveness is a solo decision, reconciliation is a shared journey. A broken relationship cannot be restored unless both hearts are willing to engage in the process. Reconciliation typically unfolds gradually as trust is tested, proven, and strengthened over time. It often begins with small, cautious steps. With grace, honesty, and patience, those steps can grow into renewed fellowship built on trust. [14] When trust has been violated, reconciliation may proceed with care; but where trust remains intact, fellowship can resume without delay.

Joseph's heart had clearly softened toward his brothers before he revealed his identity, yet he did not rush into reconciliation. Instead, he carefully observed whether their repentance was genuine and whether trust could be rebuilt. Even with a forgiving heart, he pursued reconciliation wisely and deliberately.

Whether the relationship involves spouses, siblings, parents, or children, reconciliation becomes the bridge that heals and strengthens families. Forgiveness prepares the heart. Reconciliation restores the relationship. Both are essential, yet each serves a distinct purpose in God's design for healing broken bonds.

Timeless Lessons from Joseph's Story

The story of Joseph offers timeless wisdom for families today as we learn to walk in forgiveness, rebuild trust, and seek reconciliation.

1. The Power of Transformation:

Joseph's brothers remind us that genuine change is possible. Many of us have witnessed transformation through recovery, counseling, or deep spiritual renewal. Among them, Judah stands out as one of Scripture's clearest examples of a redeemed heart. The same man who once urged his brothers to sell Joseph into slavery later stepped forward with humility and love to protect Benjamin. His willingness to offer himself in Benjamin's place revealed that his heart had been truly transformed.

Judah's change foreshadows the greater redemption that Jesus would bring. Just as Judah offered himself for another, Jesus offered his life to reconcile us to God, becoming our substitute so that we might live. It is no coincidence that both King David and Jesus came from Judah's line, the promised "Lion of the tribe of Judah" (Revelation 5:5). Judah's journey reminds us that God can completely transform a life and use it to fulfill his purposes.

2. God's Presence in Suffering:

Many of us have walked through seasons of pain and asked,

where is God in this? Joseph's story offers a powerful answer: God is present in the pit, in the prison, and in every moment of our suffering. Joseph's journey shows a man whose character was shaped by unwavering confidence in God's presence. His trust in the Lord gave him the strength to release bitterness and to look upon his brothers with compassion rather than resentment. What sustained Joseph was not perfect circumstances, but God's unchanging faithfulness.

Scripture emphasizes this truth repeatedly. While serving as a slave in Potiphar's house, we read that, "The Lord was with Joseph, and he became a successful man" (Genesis 39:2). Later, when Joseph was unjustly thrown into prison, Scripture tells us, "The Lord was with Joseph and showed him steadfast love" (Genesis 39:21). These verses carry profound meaning. They don't speak of seasons of comfort or ease but of slavery and imprisonment. Yet even in those painful places, Joseph was never alone. God was with him, shaping his heart, protecting his life, and guiding his steps.

These words bring the same assurance or us today. God does not measure success by our position, achievements, or circumstances, but in our trust in him, especially in times of trial. His presence may not spare us from suffering, but it strengthens us in the midst of it. Joseph's story reminds us that God is near, even in our darkest moments.

3. Faith in God's Sovereignty:
Faith in God's sovereignty transforms the way we view trials, disappointments, and even the pain of family betrayal. Rather than focusing solely on the hurt within our stories, faith invites

us to trust that God is at work in our wounds, bringing healing, redemption, and restoration.

Joseph endured profound suffering, yet his hardship did not harden his heart. Instead, it refined his character as he continued to walk closely with God. This spiritual maturity was revealed most clearly when he stood before the very brothers who had once betrayed him. Because Joseph's confidence rested in God's purpose, he was able to treat his brothers with mercy. When he finally revealed his identity, his words overflowed with compassion and unwavering trust in God's plan. "For God sent me before you to preserve life" (Genesis 45:5).

Years later, after their father, Jacob's death, Joseph's brothers once again feared what happens in many families— that he might seek revenge. Yet Joseph responded with humility and a spirit of peace: "Do not fear, for am I in the place of God? As for you, you meant evil against me, but God meant it for good...So do not fear; I will provide for you and your little ones" (Genesis 50:19-21). Joseph's posture invites us to reflect on how trusting God's sovereignty can gently soften our own responses to those who have caused us pain.

4. Patience in the Process:
Like Joseph, we are called to resist the urge to force reconciliation before trust has been rebuilt. True wisdom invites us to hold both grace and discernment close as we navigate the pain of broken relationships. God worked even through Joseph's betrayal to bring healing and restoration to his family. Joseph's forgiveness was not sentimental or impulsive;

it was grounded in confidence in God's sovereign plan. Joseph's close walk with the living God enabled him to seek reconciliation with a steady heart and a clear, discerning mind.

These same truths guide us today. Trusting God's sovereignty, avoiding unnecessary conflict, discerning hearts with care, waiting patiently for real transformation, and seeking lasting change rather than temporary remorse all shape the journey from forgiveness to reconciliation. Patience allows us to move forward thoughtfully, giving God room to work in ways we may not yet see.

Why This Story Matters for Today

Like Joseph and his brothers, we also face moments when family members who have been distant or estranged seek a path toward reconciliation. This story in Scripture shows how love and discernment can work together when we are invited into those moments.

Nearly every family carries some measure of brokenness. For some, it may be the quiet tension of an unresolved disagreement. For others, the wounds run deeper: a child trapped in addiction, a son-in-law whose behavior causes harm, or a spouse wrestling with hidden struggles. These situations remind us that reconciliation is often complex, yet God's wisdom meets us in the midst of that complexity.

This story calls us to reflect on what it looks like to walk toward healing with patience, courage, and trust in God's guidance. It reminds us that even in the most painful circumstances, grace and mercy can bring transformation.

Forgiveness and reconciliation are not signs of weakness but demonstrations of divine strength, a powerful testimony that God can redeem even the darkest chapters of family life.

The principles that guided Joseph still apply to us: we are called to trust God's sovereignty and goodness, as Joseph did, which grounded his capacity to forgive and reconcile. We are also called to avoid provoking conflict, remembering Joseph's words to his brothers: "Do not quarrel on the way" (Genesis 45:24). Rebuilding relationships requires careful evaluation and discernment. Like Joseph, we look for clear evidence of genuine change before restoring trust. Some relationships may heal quickly, while others take longer. Wisdom, prayerful reflection, and guidance from the Holy Spirit help us discern when to move forward and when to wait patiently. True reconciliation takes time, and healing requires the willing participation of everyone involved. Sometimes, we wait for God to prepare another person's heart or to transform our own.

Deep, sincere love triumphed over Joseph's pain. Reconciliation often demands extraordinary patience, especially after deep betrayal. Joseph could have ignored his brothers, imprisoned them, or sought revenge. Instead, he gave them multiple opportunities to demonstrate their sincerity. His restraint and discernment serve as a timeless example of grace in action. Like Joseph, we are called to persevere. Courageous trust in God's providence, combined with careful observation of another's repentance, allows us to restore broken lives and transform pain into peace.

When Reconciliation Must Wait

There is an important truth to remember: forgiveness can be extended immediately, but reconciliation often takes time. Forgiveness lifts the burden from our hearts, yet re-entering a relationship should only happen when trust has been rebuilt through consistent, demonstrable change. Reconciliation does not ask us to ignore abuse, betrayal, or harmful patterns. Rather, it invites careful discernment about whether a relationship has become safe, honest, and healthy again.

Joseph's story illustrates this wisdom. Though he forgave his brothers, he did not rush into restoring the relationship. He watched patiently for humility, repentance, honesty, and sacrificial concern for one another (Genesis 42-44). Only when he recognized genuine transformation did he reveal his identity and welcome his brothers back into relationship with him (Genesis 45:4-15). His example reminds us that reconciliation is not automatic; it grows where real change has occurred and trust can be rebuilt.

Reconciliation should be postponed when an offender shows no genuine remorse; when patterns of manipulation or abuse continue; when promises are repeated, but real change is absent; or when restoring the relationship would endanger vulnerable family members. In some cases, professional counseling may be necessary before any safe reunion can occur. Sometimes reconciliation may not be possible at all because the person remains unrepentant. In these situations, firm but loving boundaries help protect us and those we care for, even as our hearts remain open to reconciliation if genuine change ever happens. Forgiveness keeps the door unlocked, but wisdom guides us in deciding when it is safe to walk through.

Although this chapter focuses on reconciliation within families, God also invites us to seek peace within our church family. Just as Joseph's careful discernment protected his life and the lives of others, we are called to practice grace and wisdom in every relationship, trusting God to guide both the timing and the process of restoration.

Philemon and Onesimus

Paul's brief letter to Philemon presents one of the Bible's most compelling portrayals of reconciliation within the church. Unlike his other letters, it is deeply personal, demonstrating how the gospel can transform even the most fractured relationships.

Philemon had a slave named Onesimus, who had likely stolen from him and then fled. While Paul was in prison, Onesimus encountered the gospel and became a Christian. Paul then sent him back to Philemon with these remarkable words: "No longer as a bondservant, but more than a bondservant, as a beloved brother, especially to me, but how much more to you, both in the flesh and in the Lord" (Philemon 1:16).

In this single verse, Paul reframes the entire relationship. He does not erase the past but points toward a new future in Jesus. What was once a broken bond between master and slave is now transformed into brotherhood. This illustrates the heart of gospel reconciliation: our new identity in Jesus surpasses every offense, injury, or division.

Paul also models gospel-centered forgiveness in action as he writes to Philemon, "If he has wronged you at all, or owes you anything, charge that to my account" (Philemon 1:18). Onesimus' wrongs are fully restored to Philemon, illustrating reconciliation rooted not in fairness but in grace. The gospel reconciliation Paul modeled between Philemon and Onesimus remains profoundly relevant for churches today.

This brief letter provides a timeless model for the church: when believers wound one another, we are called to see each other not through the lens of offense but through the lens of Jesus' redeeming work. In our families, friendships, and congregations, gospel-centered reconciliation invites us to view one another as brothers and sisters, each redeemed by the same blood, and to bear personal cost when necessary for the sake of unity.

Though we live in a fallen world marked by conflict, misunderstanding, and sin, we can move forward with hope. Every act of reconciliation offers a glimpse of what is to come, a foretaste of the day when Jesus will make all things new, when his people will be perfectly united, and when love triumphs over every division.

Love That Endures

As our lives draw to a close, we will no longer be concerned with wealth, status, or the petty grievances that once kept us from forgiving others. What will truly matter is whether we loved God and loved people well. While we may forget how often we were wronged, we will remember the moments when we chose forgiveness and sought reconciliation through the guidance of the Holy Spirit.

The path to reconciliation varies with the depth of the wound. Minor misunderstandings can often be resolved quickly, but cases of betrayal, abuse, or repeated harm must be approached deliberately, with prayer, wise counsel, and discernment. Rushing reconciliation in such situations can be unwise or even dangerous. It is essential to protect ourselves and our loved ones from further harm. Scripture calls us to forgive from the heart, yet true reconciliation must wait until trust is genuinely restored. While we maintain healthy boundaries, we are still called to uphold a posture of love.

Even when reconciliation is paused, love can endure, as we continue to hope, and pray. Sustained by the Holy Spirit, love keeps the door open, waiting not only for hearts to soften but also for trust to be rebuilt.

Closing Remarks

Joseph's journey from pit to palace, from betrayal to blessing, reveals how God redeems even our deepest wounds. His story unfolds like a masterwork painted over many years, with each painful stroke contributing to a portrait of love. Layer by patient layer, mercy covered betrayal, grace transformed suffering, and God's sovereign hand was evident in every moment.

Joseph's life reminds us that reconciliation, while beautiful, requires wisdom, patience, and genuine change from both parties. It cannot be rushed, nor can it be one-sided. His careful approach demonstrates that love can coexist with discernment, and that hope can flourish alongside healthy boundaries as trust gradually develops.

Yet a deeper question arises: if reconciliation is complex and requires mutual participation, what happens when restoration is not possible? In such moments, forgiveness prepares the heart for eventual reconciliation, even if the relationship cannot yet be restored. Forgiveness keeps the door open, allowing love to wait with hope and act with wisdom until trust is established.

Questions for Personal Reflection or Group Discussion

1. The Most Freeing Truth About Reconciliation

You can forgive someone who never apologizes. You can forgive someone who's no longer in your life. You can even forgive someone who's died. But reconciliation? That takes two. For some, this truth is a relief: I can forgive and move on, even if they never change. For others, it's a heartbreak: I want reconciliation but they won't come back.

Which one is it for you right now? Relief or heartbreak? And why?

2. Trust Is a Slow Rebuild

"Just trust me."

"Can't you give me another chance?"

"I said I'm sorry, what more do you want?"

When trust has been deeply broken, it isn't built by asking for it. It's often rebuilt brick by brick, over time, through consistent righteous action. What's one brick you're looking for before you're willing to trust again? And if you're the one asking to be trusted, what brick can you lay today?

3. The Difference Between 'I'm Sorry' and Repentance

Some people are sorry they hurt you. Others are sorry they got caught.

True repentance doesn't just say, "I'm sorry." It says: "I was wrong in sinning against you in that way. I see the damage I caused. Here's what I'm doing to change."

When have you heard both versions? What was the difference between the words and the actions that followed? And which one have you typically offered when you've been the one apologizing?

4. Boundaries Are Gates, Not Walls

Boundaries aren't walls designed to keep someone out forever. They're gates that can open again when it's safe.

Think of one relationship right now. Have you set a healthy boundary that protected you? Or have you failed to set one and are paying the price?

Where do you need a boundary today? And if you've already set one, what would need to change before that gate could open again?

CHAPTER 3
Why Forgive

Many people know the courageous story of the ten Boom family, who risked their lives to save nearly eight hundred Jewish people during World War II. Between 1943 and 1944, their modest home became a refuge, often sheltering up to six guests at a time. To protect them, they built a small hiding place behind a closet in daughter Corrie ten Boom's bedroom, and had a warning buzzer in the house that signaled danger during Nazi security sweeps. Each guest stayed only a few days before being moved to another safe house through the Dutch underground network.

Corrie, the youngest of the ten Boom children, played a vital leadership role in this resistance movement in Haarlem, the Netherlands. [15] But their brave mission came to a heartbreaking end when a Dutch informant betrayed them. On February 28, 1944, the Gestapo, Germany's secret police, raided their home and arrested everyone present. By nightfall, thirty people were in custody. Corrie, her sister Betsie, and their father were among them. They were sent to prison, where their father soon died. Later, Corrie and Betsie were transferred first to Vught, then to Ravensbrück concentration camps.

At Ravensbrück, Betsie fell gravely ill and died, as one of more than one hundred thousand women who perished there.

Twelve days later, a clerical error led to Corrie's release; and she walked out of that infernal place to spend the rest of her life sharing her family's extraordinary story of faith and forgiveness.

Life inside the camps was almost beyond description. The ten Boom family suffered starvation, freezing conditions, and cruel treatment at the hands of guards. Yet in the midst of such darkness, Corrie and Betsie continued to share the good news of Jesus. Through their unwavering faith, many fellow prisoners found courage and hope. [16] Even behind barbed wire, light shone in the deep darkness.

Corrie's Test

After the war, Corrie ten Boom spent years traveling the world, sharing her faith in Jesus Christ. On one occasion, she journeyed from Holland to Munich, determined to tell the German people that God's mercy extends even to the worst of sinners. During her message, she said, "When we confess our sins, God casts them into the deepest ocean, gone forever."

As the meeting ended, a man approached her. To her shock, she recognized him as one of the guards from the concentration camp. In an instant, memories flooded back of the fear, humiliation, and especially the moment she was forced to walk past him naked. Although he did not recognize her, he quietly admitted that he had served as a guard during the war and had since become a Christian. Standing face-to-face with someone tied to her deepest pain, Corrie felt her blood run cold.

The man explained that he knew God had forgiven him for his cruelty, but he longed to hear that Corrie could forgive him too. Then, as recognition seemed to dawn in his eyes, he reached out his hand and asked softly, "Will you forgive me?"

Corrie froze. The weight of her suffering pressed heavily on her heart. She thought of her sister Betsie, who had died in that very camp. Could such horror really be erased by a single request? Her heart cried out for justice; yet in that moment, she sensed the quiet stirring of God's Spirit within her. "Still, I stood there, coldness clutching my heart. But forgiveness is not an emotion. I knew that, too. It is an act of the will, and the will can move even when the heart feels frozen." Corrie prayed, "Jesus, help me." Then she reasoned, "I can lift my hand. I can do that much. You supply the feeling."

With effort, she extended her hand, and something extraordinary happened. "The current started in my shoulder, raced down my arm, and sprang into our joined hands. Then a healing warmth flooded my whole being, bringing tears to my eyes."

"I forgive you, brother, with all my heart," Corrie said as she and the former guard clasped hands. "I had never known God's love so intensely as I did then." [17]

Corrie's testimony reveals a profound truth: forgiveness is rarely accompanied by pleasant feelings, especially when wounds are still fresh. Yet, when we obey in faith, God meets us in the act itself, pouring his love where our strength ends. As C. S. Lewis observed, "Everyone says forgiveness is a lovely idea until they have something to forgive." [18] Corrie lived out this truth during the war, and in her obedience, she discovered that God's love meets us most deeply when we choose to forgive.

Her story captures the inner struggle many of us face when

forgiveness moves from principle to practice. Yet it also shows that when we forgive, especially amid pain and resistance, we step into a place where God's love can heal and transform us in ways we never expected.

Reasons to Forgive

The main reason we forgive is that it is a command from God. [19] When Peter asked Jesus how many times he should forgive someone, saying, "As many as seven times?"

Jesus replied, "I do not say to you seven times, but seventy-seven times" (Matthew 18:21-22). Peter's question revealed a sharp contrast to the customs of his time. In Jewish teaching, an offender was expected to seek forgiveness up to three times. After that, the person who had been wronged was no longer considered obligated to forgive. [20] But Jesus completely overturned this expectation. He shifted the focus from the offender's duty to the heart of the one who had been wronged, calling his followers to forgive without limit. When Peter suggested forgiving seven times, it sounded generous by cultural standards, but Jesus set a far higher standard. His phrase "seventy-seven times" was not meant to be taken literally but to show that forgiveness should know no limits, mirroring the boundless mercy of God.

Jesus also emphasized the posture of the heart. True forgiveness must be offered and received with humility, gratitude, and grace. To make this truth clear, He told a parable that vividly illustrated the transforming power of both forgiving and being forgiven.

The Parable About the Impossible Debt

To reveal the depth of God's call to forgiveness and to uncover the inconsistencies hidden within our own hearts, Jesus shared a profound parable:

Therefore, the kingdom of heaven may be compared to a king who wished to settle accounts with his servants. When he began to settle, one was brought to him who owed him ten thousand talents. And since he could not pay, his master ordered him to be sold, with his wife and children and all that he had, and payment to be made. So the servant fell on his knees, imploring him, "Have patience with me, and I will pay you everything." And out of pity for him, the master of that servant released him and forgave him the debt.

But when that same servant went out, he found one of his fellow servants who owed him a hundred denarii, and seizing him, he began to choke him, saying, "Pay what you owe." So his fellow servant fell down and pleaded with him, "Have patience with me, and I will pay you." He refused and went and put him in prison until he should pay the debt.

When his fellow servants saw what had taken place, they were greatly distressed, and they went and reported to their master all that had taken place. Then his master summoned him and said to him, "You wicked servant! I forgave you all that debt because you pleaded with me. And should not you have had mercy on your fellow servant, as I had mercy on you?" And in anger, his master delivered him to the jailers until he should pay all his debt (Matthew 18:23-34).

The figures in this parable are deliberately astonishing,

designed to capture our attention and expose the depth of human inconsistency. The unforgiving servant owed ten thousand talents—or about sixty million denarii, representing roughly 160,000 to 200,000 years of wages for a common laborer! It was an utterly unpayable debt, equivalent to nearly $6 billion in today's currency. [21]

Yet moments later, that same servant refused to extend mercy to a fellow servant who owed him one hundred denarii— about three to four months of wages, or roughly $10-12,000. [22] Although the second debt was not insignificant, it was tiny by comparison and could have been repaid with time and patience.

Commentators often emphasize the exaggerated scale of the first debt and the vivid contrast it creates. [23] The comparison reveals a heart eager to receive mercy but reluctant to extend it. [24] Despite being forgiven an unimaginable sum, the servant could not bring himself to forgive a minor one.

The second servant pleaded earnestly for more time, recognizing that repayment would require patience and sacrifice. Yet the forgiven man hardened his heart and demanded immediate payment. When the master learned what had happened, he was deeply grieved by the servant's cruelty and ordered him imprisoned until the entire debt was repaid, an impossible sentence that underscores the tragedy of an unmerciful heart.

Heart Transformation

Jesus told this parable to reveal the hardness of the human heart and to show how God's mercy is meant to soften and transform it. The story speaks on several levels, displaying both the vastness of divine grace and the limits of human forgiveness. When we place ourselves within the parable, Jesus is the master, we are the unforgiving servant, and those who have wronged us are the fellow servants. The message is clear: the debt we owe to God because of sin is infinitely greater than anything another person could ever owe us. When we understand this, our hearts are reshaped, and God's forgiveness becomes the foundation of how we relate to others.

Without God's mercy, we remain imprisoned in spiritual debt, cut off from true freedom. Yet through Jesus, that debt has been completely forgiven. Because of this immeasurable gift, we are called to forgive others with the same mercy we have received, no matter how hard it may be.

This parable also reminds us that no one can earn their way out of debt to God. The master forgave his servant precisely because repayment was impossible. In the same way, we stand before God owing a debt we could never repay. But Jesus took that debt upon himself, doing what no number of good deeds could ever accomplish.

The unforgiving servant's attitude exposed a faith that had lost its vitality, quick to receive mercy yet reluctant to extend it to others. Scripture reminds us, "Faith by itself, if it does not have works, is dead" (James 2:17). Genuine saving faith bears the fruit of forgiveness, while a heart untouched by God's grace remains indifferent to the needs of others. God calls us to mirror his mercy by forgiving those who wrong us, even when it feels difficult or undeserved.

Withholding forgiveness carries a serious consequence: it damages our fellowship with God. Jesus concluded the parable with a sobering reminder: "Should you not also have had mercy on your fellow servant, as I had mercy on you?" In his anger, the master handed the servant over to the jailers until the entire debt was paid. Jesus then added this warning: "So also my heavenly Father will do to every one of you, if you do not forgive your brother from your heart" (Matthew 18:33-35).

This warning exposes the true condition of the heart. It is not a threat that believers might lose their salvation; rather, it encourages us to reflect on the authenticity of our faith. Matthew 18:35 urges us to reflect on whether our belief is genuine, for true faith produces visible fruit, and forgiveness is one of the clearest expressions of that. As Jesus taught in prayer, "forgive us our debts, as we also have forgiven our debtors" (Matthew 6:12), he shows how our experience of God's forgiveness is closely connected to our willingness to forgive others. While salvation is received by grace through faith, the presence of good works reflects the reality of that faith.

In Ephesians 2:8-10, the apostle Paul says not only that salvation comes by grace through faith, not by our own efforts, but also that this gift of grace carries a purpose: "For we are his workmanship, created in Christ Jesus for good works, which God prepared beforehand that we should walk in them" (Ephesians 2:10). In other words, we are saved for good works, not by them.

The parable of the unforgiving servant illustrates this truth beautifully. It both encourages and warns, assuring us of God's complete forgiveness while calling us to extend the same grace to others. When we receive God's forgiveness freely, it naturally begins to shape the way we live and how we relate to those around us.

The Cost of Bitterness

A biblical understanding of forgiveness correctly orders our daily lives. When we are wronged, anger often arises first; and if left unchecked, can harden into bitterness. The old saying, "Sticks and stones may break my bones, but words will never hurt me," is misleading. Words have the power to wound deeply and leave lasting scars. Yet Scripture assures us, "There is one whose rash words are like sword thrusts, but the tongue of the wise brings healing." (Proverbs 12:18). This verse teaches that words can wound, but they also have the power to restore and heal.

Revisiting our wounds only deepens the pain. Refusing to forgive can feel like watching the same painful video over and over, each replay intensifying our anger toward the wrong done to us. We may find ourselves imagining revenge, replaying old conversations, or dwelling on times when we wish we had spoken differently. In fact, modern neuroscience confirms what Scripture has long taught: when we continually dwell on hurtful memories, the brain strengthens pathways of anger and resentment, making forgiveness feel even harder. Holding on to bitterness is like clutching a small snowball that gradually grows into an avalanche, burying us beneath our own emotions. Unforgiveness traps the heart and slowly robs us of peace and joy.

The effects of resentment also ripple outward. Broken

relationships, divided families, and strained workplaces often grow from one individual's unforgiving spirit. Many marriages could be healed if the one who caused the hurt truly repented and the wounded spouse chose to forgive. Forgiveness transforms the atmosphere of a home, restoring warmth where coldness once lingered. As Proverbs 17:1 reminds us, "Better is a dry morsel with quiet than a house full of feasting with strife." True peace and joy, not financial abundance, is what makes a home blessed.

Effective Prayer

It is sobering to realize that harboring unforgiveness can block our prayers. Isaiah illustrated how Israel's sin interrupted their fellowship with God: "Behold, the Lord's hand is not shortened, that it cannot save, or his ear dull, that it cannot hear; but your iniquities have made a separation between you and your God, and your sins have hidden his face from you so that he does not hear" (Isaiah 59:1-2). Thus, our sin of unforgiveness can create barriers in our relationship with God, hindering open and heartfelt communication with him.

In contrast, those who pursue righteousness experience the blessing of effective prayer. As James reminds us, "The prayer of a righteous person has great power as it is working." (James 5:16). The apostle John also affirms this: "Beloved, if our heart does not condemn us, we have confidence before God; and whatever we ask we receive from him, because we keep his commandments and do what pleases him" (1 John 3:21-22).

When our hearts are aligned with God, our prayers flow freely, strengthened by obedience and trust in his will. As we follow his commandments, we draw closer to Jesus and bear fruit that reflects his character. Jesus promised that when we remain in him and let his words guide us, our prayers align with his will, and he provides everything we truly need. "If you abide in me, and my words abide in you, ask whatever you wish, and it will be done for you. By this My Father is glorified, that you bear much fruit and so prove to be my disciples." (John 15:7-8).

When we reflect God's character in our daily lives, especially by forgiving others, we bear fruit that honors him. Offering forgiveness is one of the clearest ways to demonstrate his love and glorify his name.

Measurable Benefits for Our Health

Forgiveness nurtures both the body and the mind. Scripture has long taught that bitterness harms us, while forgiveness brings healing; and modern science now confirms this. Research has identified common barriers to giving and receiving forgiveness, along with the profound benefits that come when we release resentment. Studies show that choosing to forgive others leads to noticeable improvements in both mental and physical health. [25]

The offences we endure often evoke deep emotions, such as anger, resentment, and bitterness, which can significantly impact our overall well-being. A comprehensive meta-analysis published in the Journal of the American College of Cardiology examined forty-four studies showing that anger and hostility increase the risk of coronary heart disease by 19% in healthy individuals and lead to a 24% poorer outcome among those already living with heart disease. [26]

Unresolved anger can also draw us into patterns that harm both our bodies and our relationships. We might turn to excessive drinking, overeating, or smoking in an attempt to soothe the unrest within us—or experience disrupted sleep. These habits place our bodies under constant strain, raising cortisol levels and increasing inflammation. When we cling to resentment, we remain trapped in cycles of anger and bitterness, leaving our hearts restless and our minds burdened.

Forgiveness offers a different path. It leads to freedom and provides a healthy, God-honoring response to the brokenness we encounter in this world. Again, modern research affirms what Scripture has long taught. Studies on forgiveness show measurable benefits for emotional and psychological health. Everett Worthington Jr., a leading scholar in forgiveness research, observes that forgiveness interventions consistently improve mental well-being, including reducing anxiety, depression, and post-traumatic stress. [27] Research also indicates that forgiveness can meaningfully support individuals who have experienced trauma from abusive or deeply painful relationships. [28]

Studies from Johns Hopkins Medicine also report that forgiveness supports healthier living by lowering the risk of heart attack; improving cholesterol levels and sleep; and reducing anxiety, blood pressure, depression, pain, and stress.

It is clear that when we choose to forgive, we release bitterness and experience real benefits for both our physical and mental health.

Forgiveness Is Time Sensitive

We've all heard the saying that time heals all wounds, but forgiveness is urgent. In truth, time can sometimes deepen our pain, if we dwell on the offense or harbor a desire for justice or revenge. What begins as hurt can quietly harden our hearts, giving pride and bitterness room to grow. Hebrews 12:15 cautions, "See to it that no one fails to obtain the grace of God; that no 'root of bitterness' springs up and causes trouble, and by it many become defiled." Withholding forgiveness places a heavy burden on the heart. When left unresolved, that weight grows—fostering resentment, deepening bitterness, and creating distance from God. Unforgiveness saps our emotional strength and gradually isolates us spiritually.

To avoid these consequences, we are called to forgive promptly. Lingering resentment embeds itself more deeply in our hearts and minds. What begins as legitimate pain can take root as destructive bitterness, harming our relationships and disrupting our fellowship with God. Forgiveness lifts this weight and opens the way to healing. The sooner we forgive, the sooner we step out of the shadows of resentment and walk in the freedom and peace God intends and graciously provides.

Closing Remarks

Understanding why we forgive lays an important foundation, yet it naturally leads to another question: if forgiveness matters so much, what about reconciliation? Forgiveness, as we have seen, can be something we offer unilaterally—a grace we extend by choice, whether the offender repents or not. Reconciliation, however, requires something more—the participation of both parties and a mutual desire to rebuild what was damaged.

When reconciliation becomes possible, its blessings reach far beyond individual healing, bringing a sense of wholeness and joy that forgiveness alone, though essential, does not fully provide. Still, we might wonder how far we should go in seeking reconciliation. What cost is worth bearing to restore a fractured relationship?

The answer may surprise us. It is found in its quiet simplicity and in the extraordinary lengths one man was willing to go for the sake of the love he had for his brother.

Questions for Personal Reflection
or Group Discussion

1. How Much Have You Been Forgiven?

In Matthew 18, the servant owed his king 10,000 talents—roughly 200,000 years of wages. Unpayable. Impossible. Yet the king forgave it all. Then the servant went and choked a man who owed him 100 denarii—about 100 days of wages.

How much have you been forgiven? Who are you refusing to forgive—or who have you refused to forgive in the past?

2. Forgiveness as Obedience

Jesus doesn't suggest forgiveness. He commands it (Matthew 6:14-15). But here's the surprising part: He commands it because he knows forgiveness sets *you* free.

Is there someone you need to forgive? If so, does the thought of forgiving them feel like a grinding duty—or like relief? Be honest: If you forgive, are you obeying because you "have to," or are you beginning to see that forgiveness might actually set you free? What would change if you believed God's command is for your good, not just his glory?

3. The Prison Cell You're Locked In

Corrie ten Boom forgave the Nazi guard who had abused her. Not because he deserved it. Not because she felt like it. But because God called her to and gave her the strength. She couldn't forgive him in her own strength. But she didn't have to.

What prison cell of bitterness are you locked in? And what if the key isn't your strength, it's his?

4. Forgiveness Transforms Relationships

Unforgiveness doesn't just poison you; it often poisons others. Children sense it. Friends feel it. The whole atmosphere shifts.

But when forgiveness breaks through? It doesn't just free you. It changes the entire relational climate. Peace returns. Hope grows. Others breathe easier.

Tell a story: Where have you seen forgiveness ripple through a family or friend group, transforming more than just the two people involved? How did things change?

CHAPTER 4
Why Reconcile

How far would we go to make peace with someone we love? One summer, Alvin Straight embarked on a 240-mile journey from his home in Iowa to reconcile with his brother Henry in Wisconsin. What made his story unforgettable was not just the distance, but the quiet determination and humility with which he traveled, and the extraordinary effort it required.

Years of estrangement had grown from a quarrel that seemed increasingly trivial with each passing year. Then Alvin learned that his eighty-year-old brother had suffered a stroke. The news came one heavy July evening through the hesitant voice of a neighbor: "Alvin, I thought you should know about Henry." In that moment, the pride and stubbornness that had kept the brothers apart for a decade began to crumble like dry leaves in the wind.

Determined to make peace before it was too late, Alvin faced a daunting challenge. At seventy-three, his health was failing; diabetes had dimmed most of his sight, and his legs struggled to carry him across a room. His driver's license had long been revoked, and he knew he could not travel by car. Too proud to ask for help and determined to go on his own terms, Alvin stood at his kitchen window, gazing at the old riding mower parked beside his garden shed. An idea began to form, one that many would have dismissed as impossible.

The next morning, the sharp clang of metal echoed across his backyard as Alvin welded together a small trailer with nothing but scrap iron, patience, and quiet determination. Curious neighbors watched through their windows as he packed camping gear, canned food, and enough supplies for what he hoped would be a six-week journey. His plan was simple, even if it seemed unwise: he would travel ten hours a day at the mower's top speed of five miles per hour and sleep wherever he was when daylight ended.

The first attempt lasted only twenty-five miles. The old Craftsman mower sputtered to a stop on a hill outside of town, black smoke curling from its engine like a small funeral pyre. Alvin stayed seated on the worn vinyl seat, hands resting on the steering wheel, sweat gathering beneath his John Deere cap. Before long, a passerby in a pickup truck pulled over, offered help, and towed the disabled mower back home. Later that day, Alvin sold it for parts without complaint, accepting the setback as part of the journey.

Three days later, hope arrived in the form of an old John Deere tractor at a local farm auction. Its once-bright green paint had faded, and the seat was cracked, but when Alvin turned the key, the engine rumbled to life with a steady, confident purr, a promise of strength that matched his determination. He hitched his homemade trailer to the back, reloaded his supplies, and set out again toward the northeast, moving slowly through the corn-lined heartland of America.

The tractor's engine puttered like an old airplane, its steady rhythm becoming the soundtrack of Alvin's unlikely pilgrimage. Mile after mile, the aging machine carried him through Iowa's endless cornfields, the late summer sun pressing down on his weathered face. The deck rattled over every crack in the asphalt, sending vibrations up through the torn vinyl seat and into his aching spine.

Five miles per hour was all it could manage, a mechanical turtle inching toward reconciliation. Cars and trucks thundered past, their drivers slowing to stare at the old man who had chosen the world's slowest vehicle for a two hundred forty-mile journey. Some honked, perhaps in encouragement or amusement; Alvin could not tell, and he did not dwell on it. He had miles ahead to consider what he might say to Henry, and for once, he was grateful for the time to do it.

When the first storm hit near Clermont, the sky darkened to the color of tarnished pewter, and heavy raindrops spattered his glasses. Lightning tore across the horizon, and thunder rolled over the prairie like a distant freight train. Alvin pulled his rain slicker tightly around him, pressing on, the mower's single headlight cutting a narrow tunnel of light through the downpour that turned the road into a shallow river.

That night, after the storm moved eastward, he set up camp by the roadside. Lying in his sleeping bag, he gazed at stars that seemed close enough to touch, their quiet shimmer offering a comfort words could not capture.

Breakdowns became routine: a flat tire outside Prairie du Chien, a thrown belt that left him stranded until a farm boy with grease-stained hands patched together a temporary fix. Each setback tested his endurance, yet Alvin pressed on, carried by something stronger than his aging body, a deep need to make peace and say he was sorry before the chance slipped away forever.

After six weeks of steady travel, Alvin finally puttered into Henry's driveway in Wisconsin. The John Deere's engine clicked softly as it cooled in the quiet evening air. Henry stepped onto the porch, leaning on his walker, his face marked by disbelief and the gentle rise of long-buried joy.

"Hello, Henry," Alvin called, his voice carrying across years of silence.

"Hello, Alvin," Henry replied, shaking his head in wonder. "You came all this way on that thing?"

"Had to," Alvin said with a faint smile. "You're my brother."

What followed was a reconciliation both simple and profound. Within a few months, Henry moved to Iowa to be near Alvin, and the two brothers spent their remaining years slowly rebuilding what time had taken from them. When Alvin passed away two years later, his funeral procession included a John Deere mower, like the one he had ridden on his journey toward peace, a humble symbol of love that refuses to give up. [29]

Alvin's journey illustrates what reconciliation truly asks of us: determination to endure setbacks, humility to lay aside pride, and love steady enough to travel two hundred forty miles, five miles at a time.

As noted in the previous chapter, forgiveness frees us from the prison of anger and bitterness, allowing our minds, bodies, and spirits to breathe again. Reconciliation takes us a step further. A family cannot experience lasting wholeness until its members move beyond forgiveness and actively pursue restored relationships. For this reason, reconciliation remains a central priority for anyone seeking genuine peace.

Reconciliation as a Priority

Reconciliation is profoundly important to God, who calls us to seek it whenever restoration is possible. Healing broken relationships, particularly among believers, is a divine priority that runs throughout Scripture. Jesus made this clear when he taught that reconciliation should take precedence even before worship: "So if you are offering your gift at the altar and there remember that your brother has something against you, leave your gift there before the altar and go. First be reconciled to your brother, and then come and offer your gift" (Matthew 5:23-24).

This teaching reflects God's heart: offering him a gift while neglecting a broken relationship is empty worship. Scripture repeatedly emphasizes this truth: "To obey is better than sacrifice" (1 Samuel 15:22), and "To do righteousness and justice is more acceptable to the Lord than sacrifice" (Proverbs 21:3). God cares far more about the posture of our hearts than the outward appearance of our worship. Our attitudes, motives, and relationships matter deeply to him. True worship begins not with ceremony, but with humility before God and a sincere willingness to pursue peace with others.

The Cost of Delayed Reconciliation

One of the greatest blessings of reconciliation is the chance to rebuild trust and renew relationships. For parents estranged from their adult children, the pain carries a unique grief marked by ambiguity and quiet isolation. These ruptures often arise from betrayal, conflicting values, or years of emotional distance. Such sorrow can be difficult even to name. It feels like mourning someone who is still alive, grieving a bond that is broken yet ever-present beneath the surface of everyday life. Counsellors often describe this ache as disenfranchised grief: real and heavy; yet unseen, unspoken, and misunderstood. [30]

Some carry this lingering sorrow for years. Others face a sharper pain that comes too late, losing a parent before there was a chance to reconcile, or watching time slip away while relationships remained unfinished. Reconciliation, like forgiveness, has a window of opportunity. When we reach out to restore a broken relationship, especially within our families, we spare ourselves years of unhealed pain and the weight of regret that cannot be undone. This is why Jesus calls us to be peacemakers, faithfully pursuing reconciliation whenever it is possible.

Peacemakers and Reconciliation

When was the last time we truly experienced joy? Was it holding a newborn after hours of labor, turning off our work phones to ride a bike through the quiet countryside, or sitting on a beach with a good book? Or perhaps it was in the quiet, tender moment of reconciliation with someone we love.

Jesus not only encouraged peacemaking; he also elevated it as a mark of spiritual maturity. Reconciliation opens the door to peace and invites us to embrace the calling of peacemakers, a truth Jesus affirmed when he said, "Blessed are the peacemakers, for they shall be called sons of God" (Matthew 5:9).

It is important to remember that Jesus offered this teaching not as a burden, but as part of the Beatitudes, a declaration of divine blessing. In Scripture, a beatitude describes the joy and favor given to those who walk in alignment with God's will. When we pursue reconciliation, we are not only doing what is right, but also stepping into the blessing Jesus promised to those who make peace.

Today, many people think of blessing only in terms of material wealth or outward success. Yet Jesus pointed to something far deeper: the joy of living under God's favor; the delight of drawing near to his presence; and the privilege of experiencing, even now, the goodness of his coming Kingdom. The apostle Peter emphasized the importance of blessing others when he wrote, "Do not repay evil for evil or reviling for reviling, but on the contrary, bless, for to this you were called, that you may obtain a blessing" (1 Peter 3:9).

Reconciliation's Impact on Families

While Scripture calls us to forgive, it also shows us that reconciliation, when possible, can have a profound impact on the health of a family. Both Scripture and our lived experience confirm that rejection can cut as deeply as a physical wound. Relational pain affects more than our emotions. It touches our bodies, our minds, and our sense of belonging. Within families, emotional rejection is rarely limited to a single relationship. Often, one strained relationship spills over, affecting and complicating others that might otherwise remain healthy and whole. [31]

For instance, marital conflict rarely affects only a husband and wife. Children, extended family members, and even close friends often feel its ripple effects. Children who grow up in unstable home environments often face increased behavioral, academic, and emotional challenges. [32] This wider circle of pain becomes especially visible in divorce. Those who initiate separation, as well as those who endure it, may experience a mixture of anger, anxiety, grief, and deep sadness. These experiences remind us that marriage is far more than a legal or social bond. It is a covenant created by God to unite two lives in mutual love, trust, and faithfulness. When that covenant is broken, the wound reaches beyond the couple and touches everyone connected to them.

A home where forgiveness and reconciliation have taken root, however, becomes a place of safety and growth. Trust is rebuilt, peace returns, and the family gains a foundation that nurtures emotional and spiritual health. Children who grow up in such homes are better equipped to navigate life's challenges with confidence and resilience.

Validation of Trust

Repentance can grow deeper and more stable over time. Proverbs reminds us that "the path of the righteous is like the light of dawn, which shines brighter and brighter until full day" (Proverbs 4:18). In the same way, reconciliation often unfolds gradually as repentance grows and trustworthiness can be validated.

While reconciliation can sometimes happen immediately, there are times when patience, careful observation, and prayerful discernment are necessary. Scripture reminds us to walk in wisdom rather than offering blind trust. Hesitation to reconcile with someone who has genuinely repented may reveal that forgiveness has not yet taken root in our hearts; but guided by the Holy Spirit, reconciliation becomes a living expression of forgiveness, creating space for wounds to heal, relationships to mend, and families to experience the peace that flows from grace.

When reconciliation is possible and safe, it brings deep healing through God's grace. Research shows that divorced individuals often face poorer health than those who remain married—effects that continue even after remarriage; but a restored marriage can renew emotional, spiritual, and even physical well-being. Most importantly, reconciliation within marriage testifies to the redemptive power of Christ. The same grace that restores sinners to fellowship with God can also restore broken relationships when hearts are humble before him. [33]

When Reconciliation Should be Avoided

It is also important to recognize that reconciliation is not always possible. Scripture allows for divorce in cases of sexual immorality, abandonment, or ongoing abuse. In recent years, respected theologians, including Wayne Grudem, have affirmed that certain forms of abuse may provide a biblically valid reason for divorce. Grudem maintains that in 1 Corinthians 7:15, Paul allows separation when an unbelieving spouse chooses to leave—highlighting the Greek phrase *en tois toioutois*, meaning "in such cases". This phrase suggests a broader application—that the principle is not limited to sexual immorality or physical abandonment, but can also include other serious violations that break the covenantal bond of marriage, such as persistent, unrepentant abuse. [34]

Abuse can be understood as a form of covenant abandonment, releasing the victim from the binding responsibilities of marriage. Research indicates that over 40% of divorces occur for what is described as life-saving reasons, including infidelity, physical or emotional abuse, and substance addiction. In destructive relationships, reconciliation without genuine repentance is neither realistic nor safe. Scripture teaches that reconciliation should never be pursued if it places anyone in physical, emotional, or spiritual danger. Yet when repentance is sincere and trust begins to grow again, reconciliation can become a path of grace and healing once more.

Hope in a Broken World

Some of the thoughts explored in this chapter may be difficult to read. Many of us carry the pain of a broken home or the deep scars of betrayal. Others grieve the loss of a marriage that ended despite our best efforts, or feel regret over choices we wish we could change. We live in a world marked by grief and sorrow, and some wounds may not fully heal until Jesus returns.

Conversations about reconciliation often bring tender emotions to the surface. They can awaken memories we thought were settled or revive aches we had hoped would remain quiet. Because these truths can be heavy, this chapter closes with reflections intended to bring comfort, steady our hope, and remind us of God's nearness in every season of life.

Even when reconciliation feels out of reach, we are not left in despair. Through God's grace, we can still grow, flourish, and experience joy. The research explored earlier gives us caution, but does not remove hope. There is always a path forward. Many have found strength and healing through wise pastors, Christian counsellors, and trusted believers who walk with us through the grief of unresolved relationships.

We can also take comfort in knowing that when trust is genuinely rebuilt, reconciliation can be deeply transformative. Those who courageously walk the difficult path of forgiveness and reconciliation often discover God's blessings in unexpected and beautiful ways. While strained relationships can wound the heart, reconciled relationships nurture healing, spiritual growth, and lasting joy.

This is part of the glorious hope of the gospel. Jesus meets us in our sin and suffering. When we repent and place our trust in his atoning death and resurrection, he completely forgives even our gravest sins. The cross quiets shame, offers perspective on our regrets, and lifts the burden of guilt. One day, Jesus will return to renew all things, and God will wipe away every tear from our eyes.

Closing Remarks

Alvin Straight's 240-mile journey on a riding mower reveals something profound about the human heart. We were created for relationships; and deep within us, we recognize when those bonds have been broken. His determination to reconcile before it was too late reflected a truth woven into the very fabric of our being: reconciliation is rarely easy and often costly, yet always worth pursuing.

Questions for Personal Reflection
or Group Discussion

1. What If You Made the First Move?

Alvin Straight drove 240 miles on a lawn mower to reconcile with his brother. At 73 years old. Unable to legally drive a car. Six weeks on the road. Because reconciliation mattered more than pride.

What if you made the first move toward reconciliation even though they're the one who hurt you? What terrifies you most about taking that step? And what if God is calling you to do it anyway?

2. Your Part, Not Theirs

"If possible, so far as it depends on you, live peaceably with all" (Romans 12:18). You can't control their response. You can't make them forgive you. You can't force reconciliation.

But something *does* depend on you. What's your part in this broken relationship? What can you do even if they never do theirs? And have you done it?

3. When God Calls, and They Don't Answer

You reached out. They didn't respond. You apologized. They rejected it. You tried to reconcile. They refused.

God doesn't measure your obedience by their response. What if faithfulness is enough even when reconciliation never comes? Have you ever had to choose obedience when the door stayed closed? What was that like?

4. The Blessing of Making Peace

"Blessed are the peacemakers, for they shall be called sons of God" (Matthew 5:9). Blessed. Not burdened. Not obligated. *Blessed*.

When have you experienced peacemaking as a blessing, either when you made peace, or when someone made peace with you? What made it feel like a gift instead of a duty? And where do you need to believe that blessing is waiting not just on the other side of reconciliation, but in the very act of pursuing it?

CHAPTER 5
Love and Humility

In 1948, Pastor Richard Wurmbrand was imprisoned in Romania for courageously preaching the gospel. Over the next fourteen years, he endured suffering few of us can imagine: freezing isolation, starvation, and repeated beatings that left his ribs cracked and his bones broken. His body weakened, but his faith did not.

At one point, Richard asked his torturers if they ever felt pity. Their replies were chilling: "You can't make an omelet without breaking a few eggs," some said. Others replied, "You can't cut wood without making the chips fly." To them, prisoners were only eggshells and splintered objects to be broken in the process of their cruel work—a mindset that allowed them to inflict pain without remorse. [35]

Richard later described several methods of torture used against Christians. One of the most horrific was to force prisoners to stand inside a narrow wooden box lined with nails. They could not move without being pierced; and as exhaustion set in, even a small tremor would drive the nails into their flesh. [36] Another was to be hung upside down and beaten simply for believing in Jesus. [37] Prisoners were sometimes locked in ice-cold cells until they were near death; and guards released rats into the cells to deprive them of sleep for days. Some believers were forced to watch their children being beaten; and one woman even witnessed her husband's execution. His final words still echo through history: "You must know that I die loving those who kill me. They do not know what they are doing, and my last request is this: love them." [38]

Richard's long season of suffering and cruelty revealed the true depth of virtue within his heart. From that place of pain and perseverance, he offered a gentle yet profound reminder: "God will judge us not by how much we endured, but by how well we loved." [39] Love lies at the very foundation of forgiveness and reconciliation. Richard's awareness that even his enemies were to be loved reflected a heart refined by humility. His example reminds us that love and humility are inseparable companions on the path toward forgiveness and the restoration of broken relationships.

Love is the Foundation of Forgiveness

Genuine love is the foundation of forgiveness and reconciliation. Unconditional love holds a quiet strength; it draws hearts together and nurtures the harmony that leads to lasting peace. Scripture reminds us of this truth: "And above all these put on love, which binds everything together in perfect harmony (Colossians 3:14). This verse reminds us that love is the binding force in every relationship. Without love, even our best intentions can wound rather than heal. Pride and arrogance often lie at the heart of conflict, as seen in Joseph's story. His royal coat and prophetic dreams, though not sinful, intensified the tension within his family. Each person contributed to the fracture in some way. Yet in the end, it was loving patience, redemptive and enduring, that reunited Joseph and his brothers in grace and restored unity.

The Greatest Commandments

Jesus proclaimed that the greatest commandments are to love both God and our neighbor, saying, "You shall love the Lord your God with all your heart and with all your soul and with all your mind. This is the great and first commandment. And a second is like it: You shall love your neighbor as yourself" (Matthew 22:37-39).

In the New Testament, seven passages repeat the command to love our neighbors as ourselves. [40] This repeated call invites us to pause and reflect on two vital questions: What is love, and who is my neighbor? Understanding both through a biblical lens helps us recognize the kind of love that makes forgiveness possible and sustains genuine reconciliation.

The Good Samaritan

A deeper understanding of biblical love is obtained through Jesus' teaching in the parable of the good Samaritan. While studying the Hebrew and Greek terms for love can enrich our insight, Jesus' story reveals its meaning with simple, unmistakable power. He shared this parable with the Jewish lawyer who sought to test him, yet his words continue to search our hearts today.

In the parable, a man traveling alone was attacked, beaten, and left half dead on the dangerous road between Jerusalem and Jericho. A priest came by, saw the wounded man, and crossed to the other side. Soon after, a Levite approached, noticed the injured traveler, and did the same. Both were respected spiritual leaders, devoted to temple service and religious duty—yet they failed to show compassion. Through their neglect, Jesus reminds us that true love is not proven by status or knowledge but by mercy in action.

Finally, a Samaritan came along. Unlike the others who passed by, he stopped when he saw the wounded man. Kneeling in the dust, he poured wine and oil on the man's wounds, then gently lifted him onto his own donkey. He brought him to an inn, cared for him through the night, and left money for his continued care.

Jesus ended the parable by asking, "Which of these three do you think proved to be a neighbor?" Then he said, "Go, and do likewise" (Luke 10:37).

The Samaritan showed compassion to a complete stranger by tending his wounds, ensuring his safety, and providing for his recovery. Jesus purposely chose a Samaritan, someone despised by the Jews, to reveal that love transcends every boundary of ethnicity, religion, and social status. Through this story, Jesus teaches that genuine love is self-sacrificial; and that our neighbor is anyone in need, whether we know them or not.

The Nature of Love

Paul beautifully describes this kind of love in 1 Corinthians 13: "If I give away all I have, and if I deliver up my body to be burned, but have not love, I gain nothing. Love is patient and kind; love does not envy or boast; it is not arrogant or rude. It does not insist on its own way; it is not irritable or resentful; it does not rejoice at wrongdoing, but rejoices with the truth. Love bears all things, believes all things, hopes all things, endures all things" (1 Corinthians 13:3-7). This passage reveals the selfless and enduring nature of Christlike love, a love that mirrors the very heart of God. It calls us to reflect on how patience, kindness, humility, and perseverance can transform our relationships and shape the way we live with others.

Jesus also broadened the meaning of "neighbor," teaching that it includes not only those near us but also anyone we encounter in the ordinary rhythms of life: classmates, coworkers, fellow believers, and even strangers.

Love Expressed Through Humility

What does it truly mean to be humble? Humility, as a virtue, reflects a heart that is gentle, modest, and willing to submit to God and to others, rather than one dominated by arrogance or pride. [41] In every circumstance, humility proves to be more honorable and ultimately more powerful than pride. Throughout Scripture, God consistently shows favor to those who walk in humility, granting them his grace. This truth is evident in passages such as: "Clothe yourselves, all of you, with humility toward one another, for 'God opposes the proud but gives grace to the humble'" (1 Peter 5:5).

When we encounter someone who truly embodies love and humility, we naturally feel seen, accepted, and valued. The apostle Paul affirms this attitude when he writes, "Do nothing from selfish ambition or conceit, but in humility count others more significant than yourselves. Let each of you look not only to your own interests, but also to the interests of others" (Philippians 2:3 4).

Humility shifts our focus from ourselves to others. It invites us to look beyond our own desires so that we can love our neighbors with genuine compassion and sincerity. By resisting the urge to overestimate our own importance, humility helps us understand ourselves more clearly and, in turn, to recognize God more fully. Paul expresses this truth beautifully in Romans: "For by the grace given to me I say to everyone among you not to think of himself more highly than he ought to think, but to think with sober judgment, each according to the measure of faith that God has assigned" (Romans 12:3).

What True Humility Looks Like

One of the clearest marks of humility is a genuine willingness to apologize. A humble heart readily admits mistakes and recognizes the hurt words or actions may have caused. Humility helps us see how our own behavior can contribute to misunderstanding or division. A sincere apology, offered without excuses or expectations, often opens the door to reconciliation.

True humility also protects us from undervaluing ourselves. It does not mean thinking less of who we are, but thinking rightly about ourselves in light of God's greatness. When humility takes root, our focus shifts from seeking personal recognition to honoring God in all we do. In the New Testament, humility begins with surrendering to the Lordship of Jesus Christ. The International Standard Bible Encyclopedia explains it this way: "The humble person acknowledges that he has no claim on God, but that

God has a total claim on him." [42]

True and False Humility

Jesus offered profound and challenging guidance on humility. When we are wronged, should we retaliate or choose instead to turn the other cheek? Should we insist on repayment, or generously help those in need? In calling his followers to a life of radical humility, Jesus said, "Whoever has two tunics is to share with him who has none, and whoever has food is to do likewise" (Luke 3:11). He also taught, "You have heard that it was said, 'An eye for an eye and a tooth for a tooth.' But I say to you, do not resist the one who is evil. But if anyone slaps you on the right cheek, turn to him the other also" (Matthew 5:38-39).

Another sign of true humility is a heart that serves others. Jesus perfectly exemplified this when he washed his disciples' feet: "If I then, your Lord and Teacher, have washed your feet, you also ought to wash one another's feet. For I have given you an example, that you also should do just as I have done to you" (John 13:14-15). The Creator of all humbled himself to serve. Similarly, humility is so central to God's nature that he sometimes allows us to experience suffering, shaping our hearts and cultivating genuine humility within us.

To grasp true humility more clearly, it helps to contrast it with false humility. Like master chefs distinguishing between artificial and genuine flavors, true and false humility are revealed by seeing the difference:

False Humility	True Humility
Arrogant and proud	Shuns arrogance and pride
No remorse for sin	Exhibits repentance from sin
Places personal needs first	Considers others' needs as more important
Considers oneself superior to others	Maintains a balanced view of self and honors others
Denies or pridefully accepts compliments	Receives compliments with gratitude and gives glory to God
Defies or dishonors authority	Respects and submits to authority unless it contradicts Scripture
Is impatient, easily offended, or inattentive	Is patient, not easily offended, and listens carefully
Relies on oneself to succeed	Depends on God for success

True humility blossoms from complete dependence on God. It grows in hearts willing to walk the lowly path, and is meek rather than self-assertive and surrendered rather than self-seeking. Genuine humility is rooted in our identity in Jesus, not in comparison with others. We express it not through self-promotion but through quiet acts of service and a heart willing to love. A truly humble spirit naturally pursues reconciliation, valuing relationship above pride.

The Fruit of True Humility

When we contrast false humility with genuine humility, the difference is unmistakable. Those whose worth and identity are rooted in Jesus do not need to belittle others to feel significant. Freed from pride, they recognize the God-given value in every person and resist the temptation to use others merely as a means to an end.

Humility allows us to acknowledge our mistakes, confess our sins, and seek forgiveness with sincerity. It also strengthens our willingness to forgive others quickly and wholeheartedly, valuing their well-being as much as, if not more than, our own. Genuine humility dispels anger, resentment, and bitterness, paving the way for peace and healing where division once existed.

Without love and humility, our efforts at reconciliation fall flat like bread without yeast or dessert without sweetness. But when these virtues are carefully blended, they produce something beautiful: relationships that reflect God's love and bring glory to his name.

The Ultimate Example of Humility

While imprisoned for proclaiming the gospel of Jesus Christ, Paul wrote to the believers in Philippi, inspired by the Holy Spirit to share some of the most profound teachings on humility ever recorded: "Have this mind among yourselves, which is yours in Christ Jesus, who, though he was in the form of God, did not count equality with God a thing to be grasped, but emptied himself, by taking the form of a servant, being born in the likeness of men. And being found in human form, he humbled himself by becoming obedient to the point of death, even death on a cross" (Philippians 2:5-8).

Though Jesus existed from all eternity and fully shared in the divine nature, he chose to humble himself. Taking on human form, he lived as a servant and willingly submitted to the shameful death of the cross. His humility flowed from perfect love, the love that sought to reconcile sinners who would repent and believe the gospel. As followers of Jesus, we are called to adopt his mindset and put the needs of others above our own. When we embrace the gospel and walk in his footsteps, love and humility naturally become the defining marks of our lives.

Closing Remarks

Richard Wurmbrand, whose reflections on love open this chapter, exemplifies what it truly means to follow Jesus. After enduring fourteen years of imprisonment and torture for his faith, he consistently chose love over bitterness and humility over pride. His life reminds us that the path of forgiveness and reconciliation grounded in love and humility is possible even in the harshest circumstances.

Having laid the foundations of forgiveness and reconciliation in Part One, Family Forgiveness and Reconciliation now turns to practical application in Part Two. The first topic is wisdom, which provides the insight needed to apply love and humility in everyday relationships.

Questions for Personal Reflection or Group Discussion

1. When Love Doesn't Feel Like Love

"Love is patient, love is kind" (1 Corinthians 13:4). Not "love *feels* patient, love *feels* kind." Love is something you do, not something you wait to feel.

Right now, today, where do you need to choose love, even though the feelings aren't there? Who needs your patience? Your kindness? Your forgiveness? Name them.

What's one thing you can do today?

2. What Humility Isn't

Jesus washed feet. But he also overturned tables. Humility isn't letting people walk all over you—it's strength under control. It's choosing not to demand your own way when love requires something different.

Where have you confused meekness with weakness? And where do you need to stand firm, not out of pride, but out of humble, loving strength?

3. How Well Have You Loved?

Richard Wurmbrand endured 14 years of torture in a Romanian prison. His body was broken, but his faith remained strong. At the end of his life, he said, "God will judge us not by how much we endured, but by how well we loved."

Not by how much you suffered. Not by how much you were wronged. But by how well you loved. In the relationships where you've been hurt, how well have you loved?

Tell a story: when have you seen someone love well in the face of deep hurt? What made it beautiful?

4. Love and Humility Are Inseparable

"Without love and humility, our efforts at reconciliation are like music without rhythm." You've seen it: someone says all the right words, but it feels hollow. They apologize, but you sense the pride underneath.

True reconciliation requires both love and humility. You can't fake either one. When have you experienced reconciliation that felt real, where both love and humility were genuinely present? What made it feel so different from a hollow apology?

And when have you seen (or offered) reconciliation attempts without love and humility, where the words were right but the heart wasn't? What was missing?

PART TWO

Forgiveness
and
Reconciliation
in Action

*The Bible is a portrait of love
painted on a canvas of forgiveness.*

PART TWO
Forgiveness and Reconciliation in Action

After the foundation is set, the artist begins to add color: a soft layer of warmth, gentle shadows, and the blending of cool blues with radiant golds. Slowly, the canvas transforms. What was once only preparation now gains depth and form, and the unseen picture begins to emerge with surprising beauty.

Part Two is where forgiveness and reconciliation take shape in real life. The truths learned earlier are now expressed through intentional choices and steps of faith. The hues deepen in the exploration of forgiveness in marriage, families, friendships, and in places where wounds have long awaited healing.

Wisdom becomes essential here, as each brushstroke is applied with care. The layers build, and the portrait becomes clearer. Light begins to penetrate places that once felt dark. As hearts soften, joy begins to shine. The tones grow warm and inviting as forgiveness restores depth and strengthens love.

Then, almost unexpectedly, a greater radiance appears with a heavenly glow suffusing the work: the radiance of Jesus himself shining upon us, illuminating the painting. What once seemed incomplete now reflects his presence. The portrait is no longer just about what we are doing; it reveals the One who has guided every stroke. Gradually it becomes clear: a masterful hand has been at work from the beginning. God is the artist, and we are the portrait upon which his love is revealed. Part Two invites us to watch the portrait unfold and to join him as he brings forgiveness and reconciliation to life, one brushstroke at a time.

CHAPTER 6
Wisdom in Action

L ucian and Eloise Smith were still basking in the fresh glow of newlywed life, only a few months past their wedding day. Every moment together felt wonderfully invigorating, the laughter they shared over dinner, the quiet conversations as the ship's lights shimmered across the dark Atlantic. Arm in arm, they strolled the promenade, dreaming aloud of the life they were beginning to build together.

Part of their peace came from what everyone had been told: this ship was a marvel of engineering, built to be unsinkable as far as human ingenuity could make it. [43] Its watertight compartments and advanced safety systems inspired confidence around the world. Passengers believed that no disaster could overcome them, not here, not on this voyage. But near midnight, the engines slowed and fell silent. The cabins grew still, and an uneasiness settled over everyone. Crewmen hurried past, and whispers spread that the ship had struck an iceberg. Soon came the call to prepare the lifeboats, accompanied by the terrifying realization that there were not enough boats for all aboard.

Lucian held Eloise's hand as they made their way to the boat deck. Crewmen were calling for the women to step forward. Eloise clung to her husband, pleading to stay. He promised she could, until the calls grew urgent: "Women and children first!" Lucian turned to her, his voice calm but firm. "This is the one time you must obey. [44] He lifted her into the lifeboat and stepped back. As the boat was lowered, Eloise's eyes remained fixed on him. She saw him standing there, calm and resolute, thinking not of himself but of her safety.

She would live to tell their story; Lucian would not.

That night, over fifteen hundred people tragically lost their lives. [45] Only, and only half of those aboard had access to lifeboats. Their story unfolded aboard the Titanic, the most infamous shipwreck in history, offering a powerful lesson in wisdom under pressure: not merely recognizing danger, but choosing what is right guided by love even when the cost is everything.

What Is Wisdom

The Old Testament makes this connection clear: "When pride comes, then comes disgrace, but with the humble is wisdom." (Proverbs 11:2). If humility guides us toward wisdom, it's worth pausing to consider what true wisdom really is and why Scripture calls it a treasure beyond all price. Scripture emphasizes the value of wisdom, urging us to pursue it wholeheartedly: "The beginning of wisdom is this: Get wisdom, and whatever you get, get insight." (Proverbs 4:7). We also read:

Blessed is those who find wisdom, and the one who gets understanding, for the gain from her is better than gain from silver and her profit better than gold. She is more precious than jewels, and nothing you desire can compare with her. Long life is in her right hand; in her left hand are riches and honor. Her ways are ways of pleasantness, and all her paths are peace. She is a tree of life to those who lay hold of her; those who hold her fast will be blessed (Proverbs 3:13-18).

The 1828 *American Dictionary of the English Language* defines wisdom as "the quality of being wise, knowledge coupled with the ability to use it well, understanding the best ends and the most effective means, discernment and judgment, discretion, sagacity, and skill." [46] This definition captures the heart of biblical wisdom: it is not simply acquiring knowledge, but applying it with discernment and intentionality.

The Hebrew word for wisdom, *chokhmah*, appears more than two hundred times in the Old Testament. Wisdom is not an abstract idea; it is a creative and practical gift from God, a capacity to live well and to order life according to his guidance. Scripture even portrays wisdom as present with God at creation, woven into the very fabric of the world: "The Lord by wisdom founded the earth; by understanding he established the heavens" (Proverbs 3:19).

People often describe wisdom as insight, prudence, discernment, or common sense. But biblical wisdom goes beyond cleverness or human intelligence. It is a God-given ability to apply knowledge and understanding in ways that honor God and bless others. Wisdom is moral, relational, spiritual, and creative. It guides us in responding to wrongs, letting go of pride, and acting with love even when we are hurt. We can see, as we define wisdom, that it is inseparable from forgiveness and reconciliation.

Proverbs reminds us, "The fear of the Lord is the beginning

of wisdom, and the knowledge of the Holy One is insight" (Proverbs 9:10). True wisdom begins with a deep reverence for God, not simply sharp intellect or clever strategy. James describes wisdom from above as "pure, peaceable, gentle, open to reason, full of mercy and good fruits, impartial and sincere" (James 3:17).

King Solomon understood that true wisdom comes from God. One night, God appeared to him and said, "Ask what I shall give you" (2 Chronicles 1:7). Solomon replied, "Give me now wisdom and knowledge to go out and come in before this people, for who can govern this people of yours, which is so great?" (2 Chronicles 1:10).

God's response to Solomon is remarkable: "God answered Solomon, "Because this was in your heart, and you have not asked for possessions, wealth, honor, or the life of those who hate you, and you have not even asked for long life, but have asked for wisdom and knowledge that you may govern my people over whom I have made you king, wisdom and knowledge are granted to you. I will also give you riches, possessions, and honor, such as none of the kings before you had, and none after you shall have the like" (2 Chronicles 1:11-12).

Wisdom brings both insight and understanding. Insight is the ability to perceive and discern to see beneath the surface and grasp the deeper meaning in a situation. Understanding allows us to distinguish truth, clarify its significance, and see how various truths fit together within God's design. At its heart, wisdom is inseparable from love, as Paul reminds us: "If I have prophetic powers, and understand all mysteries and all

118

knowledge, and if I have all faith, to remove mountains, but do not have love, I am nothing" (1 Corinthians 13:2). Love ensures that wisdom does not serve pride or self-interest but seeks the good of others.

Wisdom is not a single quality; it is a rich tapestry that begins with reverence for God and grows as we apply knowledge and love with insight, understanding, humility, patience, and discernment. It unfolds in fresh ways through creativity and thoughtful action. This kind of wisdom is essential for forgiveness and reconciliation, enabling us to perceive clearly and respond with love, even amid painful situations.

Worldly vs. Divine Wisdom

Even the story of the Titanic illustrates the contrast between worldly wisdom and divine wisdom. The shipbuilders and owners relied on the most advanced knowledge of their time, yet their decisions were clouded by pride and misplaced confidence. They created a ship believed to be unsinkable but provided lifeboats for only half the passengers, prioritizing appearance and comfort over preparation. Worldly wisdom may seem impressive until it is tested.

Scripture draws a clear line between human wisdom and the wisdom that comes from God. We are reminded that "For the wisdom of this world is folly with God" (1 Corinthians 3:19). James describes this same kind of wisdom as "earthly, unspiritual, demonic" (James 3:15). Worldly wisdom depends on human strength, seeks shortcuts, and trusts appearances rather than God. In our relationships, it often whispers: "Protect yourself, hold on to the grudge, make them pay, or choose comfort over righteousness."

Divine wisdom follows a different path. It honors God, rises above pride, and seeks the good of others. In our relationships, it gently invites us to release debts, pursue peace, and walk in love. Divine wisdom leads us toward forgiveness, reconciliation, and lasting harmony. Lucian Smith's choice on that cold April night provides a vivid example of divine wisdom in action. Like every man on deck, he faced fear and urgency, yet instead of seeking his own safety, he used his final moments to secure his wife's place in a lifeboat. He recognized what was right and acted with love that valued her life above his own. At its heart, divine wisdom is the ability to see clearly, act humbly, and seek the good of others, even at great personal cost.

If we are to choose between these two kinds of wisdom, we naturally ask: how can we recognize and pursue the wisdom that comes from God? Scripture answers: the foundation of all true wisdom is the fear of the Lord.

The Fear of the Lord is a Fountain of Life

True wisdom begins with reverence for God. The Hebrew word for fear, *yir'ah*, conveys awe, profound respect, and a deep awareness of God's holiness and majesty, which stirs our hearts toward obedience. In the New Testament, the Greek word *phobos* similarly refers to reverent awe, while *eusebeia* describes godly devotion. Together, these terms reveal that "the fear of the Lord" is not a fear that drives us away, but a holy reverence that draws us near—in worship, trust, and faithful obedience.

This fear also encompasses a reverent respect for God's perfect judgment, as the psalmist declares: "The fear of the Lord is clean, enduring forever; the rules of the Lord are true, and righteous altogether" (Psalm 19:9). Jesus reminded his disciples not to fear those who can harm only the body, but to cultivate a deep reverence and awe for God alone. "And do not fear those who kill the body but cannot kill the soul. Rather, fear him who can destroy both soul and body in hell" (Matthew 10:28).

The fear of the Lord is deeply intertwined with divine discipline. As the writer of Hebrews reminds us, even God's correction springs from his boundless love: "My son, do not regard lightly the discipline of the Lord, nor be weary when reproved by him. For the Lord disciplines the one he loves, and chastises every son he receives" (Hebrews 12:5-6). Proverbs 14:27 tells us, "The fear of the Lord is a fountain of life, turning one away from the snares of death." Far from being a burden, the fear of the Lord is a life-giving gift. It humbles us, steadies our hearts, and guides our steps along the path of righteousness.

Charles Spurgeon beautifully captures the depth of this truth. He wrote, "The fear of the Lord, which is the beginning of wisdom, fills the heart, and the goodness of the Lord becomes the source and fountain of that fear in the hearts of all whom the Lord has blessed with his grace." [47] His words remind us that true reverence for God arises not from fear, but from recognizing his goodness and resting in his grace.

A. W. Tozer cautioned us about the danger that arises when we lose our reverence for God. He observed, "When men no longer fear God, they transgress his laws without hesitation."

Yet Tozer also pointed to a beautiful paradox: "The greatness of God rouses fear within us, but his goodness encourages us not to be afraid of him. To fear and not be afraid, that is the paradox of faith." [48] This reverent fear, rooted in wisdom, directs our steps on the path of godly living and provides guidance and protection. As Proverbs teaches, "For wisdom will come into your heart, and knowledge will be pleasant to your soul; discretion will watch over you, understanding will guard you, delivering you from the way of evil..." (Proverbs 2:10-14).

The benefits of wisdom are unmistakable: it is priceless, life-giving, and overflowing with blessings. These gifts become even clearer as we journey along the challenging path of forgiveness and reconciliation. To grasp the fullness of wisdom, our hearts must turn to its ultimate source, Jesus Christ.

Wisdom Is a Person

The heart of wisdom is not an abstract concept; it is a Person. Jesus himself reveals the wisdom of God. This means that wisdom is not merely something we strive to obtain, but Someone we are called to know intimately. As Paul reminds us, Jesus is "the power of God and the wisdom of God" (1 Corinthians 1:24). In him "are hidden all the treasures of wisdom and knowledge" (Colossians 2:3). Even as a child, Jesus "increased in wisdom and in stature and in favor with God and man" (Luke 2:52). His life shows us that discipleship is a journey of continual growth. Walking with him shapes us, giving us the wisdom to forgive, the desire to reconcile, and the strength to love even when our understanding feels limited.

The wonderful news is that this wisdom is not reserved for

a select few; God offers it freely to all who come to him with open hearts. As James assures us, "If any of you lacks wisdom, let him ask God, who gives generously to all without reproach, and it will be given him" (James 1:5).

The Wisdom to Forgive

All of the qualities of true wisdom—reverence for God, knowledge, insight, understanding, love, humility, and creativity—are revealed in how we respond to those who have wronged us. Unlike worldly wisdom, which may encourage retaliation or quietly nurture resentment, divine wisdom guides us to forgive, release debts, and seek reconciliation whenever possible.

True wisdom does not suppress our emotions. Even Jesus wept at Lazarus's tomb and mourned over Jerusalem. Rather, it places our feelings under the guidance of God's truth, allowing them to serve his purposes instead of controlling our hearts. Elisabeth Elliot expressed this beautifully when she said, "Feelings are important in many ways, but they do not define the truth. The ultimate truth is found in the Word of God." [49] Wisdom helps us acknowledge grief, anger, and anxiety without letting these emotions overwhelm us. It gently leads us toward forgiveness as we trust in God's purposes in the midst of our pain.

Forgiveness and Reconciliation

As noted in Chapter 2, forgiveness and reconciliation are not the same. Forgiveness can be extended from the heart even when the other person never asks for it. Reconciliation, however, requires genuine repentance, honesty, and trust.

Romans 12:18 offers wise guidance for the tension we often feel: "If it is possible, as far as it depends on you, live at peace with everyone." This instruction carries both invitation and realism. We are encouraged to do everything within our ability to pursue peace; yet the words "if it is possible" remind us that some relationships may not be fully restored in this life. Forgiveness does not always result in reconciliation, but it gently keeps the door open should restoration one day become possible.

Jesus spoke directly about reconciliation when he said, "If your brother sins against you, go and tell him his fault, between you and him alone. If he listens to you, you have gained your brother" (Matthew 18:15). In this teaching, forgiveness softens the heart, and reconciliation rebuilds the relationship. Both matter deeply, yet they follow different rhythms and require different steps. Paul expands this theme in 2 Corinthians 5:18-19: "All this is from God, who reconciled us to himself through Christ and gave us the ministry of reconciliation: that God was reconciling the world to himself in Christ, not counting people's sins against them. And he has committed to us the message of reconciliation." Just as God reconciled believers through Jesus, we are invited to pursue reconciliation with others.

Pursuing reconciliation requires careful discernment. Trust is typically not rebuilt in a moment. While forgiveness can often be extended quickly, true restoration usually unfolds gradually as honesty, humility, and changed behavior begin to repair what was broken. There are situations where reconciliation must be postponed. We should never return to relationships that are unsafe or abusive. Forgiveness does not mean enabling sin or accepting harm. We seek peace wherever possible, yet when reconciliation cannot occur, we entrust the offender to God and guard our hearts against bitterness.

This understanding prepares our hearts for the practical steps ahead. Wisdom becomes most visible when it is expressed through our daily choices; and in the often-complex realities of family life, we learn how forgiveness and reconciliation take shape through actions guided by God's truth.

As we saw in Chapter 2 through Joseph's story, genuine reconciliation becomes possible only when the offender sincerely repents. Forgiveness can be extended by one person, but reconciliation requires the participation of both. It is built on honest acknowledgment of wrongdoing and a sincere desire to make things right.

Trying to restore a relationship without genuine change can be emotionally unhealthy and even unsafe, especially when patterns of abuse, deception, or unhealthy control remain unaddressed. Without true repentance, any sense of peace may feel real for a moment but will not have the foundation to endure. Reconciliation also depends on trust, a quality and attribute that reaches beyond repentance.

The Foundation of Trust

Trust becomes the essential foundation for restoring any relationship. A marriage, for example, cannot experience true depth without mutual trust. Scripture highlights this truth from both sides of the relationship: "The heart of her husband trusts in her" (Proverbs 31:11), and husbands are instructed to "love your wives, as Christ loved the church and gave himself up for her" (Ephesians 5:25). This shared posture of trust and sacrificial love creates the security where intimacy can flourish.

As we walk toward reconciliation, we learn to extend trust with discernment, remembering that our ultimate security rests in the Lord. The Bible teaches, "It is better to take refuge in the Lord than to trust in man" (Psalm 118:8). While wisdom may lead us to offer relational trust to others, our confidence ultimately rests in God. Because we trust him, we can extend trust to others when it is wise to do so.

Our willingness to trust others grows not only from their repentance but also from our confidence in God's power to transform hearts. Joseph's story gives us a beautiful example of this balance between repentance and restored trust. Before embracing his brothers, Joseph observed the sincerity of their change, gently testing their hearts. Only when he saw genuine repentance did he extend trust again.

Restoring Trust

Trust can grow deeper and more stable over time. Proverbs reveals that "the path of the righteous is like the light of dawn, which shines brighter and brighter until full day" (Proverbs 4:18). In a similar way, reconciliation often develops gradually as a person demonstrates trustworthiness through consistent actions and sincere effort.

While reconciliation can occur immediately, most often patience, careful observation, and prayerful discernment are needed. Scripture calls us to walk in wisdom rather than offering blind trust. On the other hand, when we hesitate to reconcile with someone who has genuinely repented and seeks restoration, it may reveal that forgiveness has not yet taken root in our hearts.

The Digital Barrier to Reconciliation

Social media creates real challenges for reconciliation. Online conversations often magnify small offenses, reward quick judgment, and encourage people to take sides before they understand the situation. Instead of gently addressing conflict in private, disagreements become public, emotional, and permanent. Once something is posted, it can feel impossible to repair.

Cancel culture adds to the problem. People are publicly shamed or discarded without space for repentance, clarification, or growth. Even sincere apologies can be mocked or rejected. These patterns make reconciliation harder, because they remove the privacy, patience, and compassion needed for healing.

Scripture calls us to a different way—one that restores rather than destroys. Paul writes that those who are spiritual should "restore him in a spirit of gentleness" (Galatians 6:1), reminding us that reconciliation grows best in humility, honesty, and quiet conversations—not public outrage. In a world that reacts quickly and forgives slowly, Christians are called to keep the door of restoration open.

Putting Wisdom into Practice

Wisdom is never meant to remain merely an idea in the mind or a feeling in the heart. Without action, knowledge accomplishes little. We may understand that a boat is sinking, but wisdom urges us to put on a life jacket. In the same way, someone may know that Jesus is the Savior, yet pride can still hold the heart back from receiving him.

Forgiveness and reconciliation follow a similar pattern. They are not abstract concepts or distant ideals; they invite us to live out what we believe through deliberate, thoughtful choices. Divine wisdom helps us translate knowledge into the way we speak, respond, and build peace with others. The saying, "It is easier said than done," reminds us how challenging it can be to put wisdom into practice. Yet as followers of Jesus, we are called to move beyond intentions and walk in obedience, step by step. Forgiveness becomes a deliberate act of the will, and reconciliation grows more attainable when guided by godly wisdom.

Sometimes, wisdom calls us to speak the truth with gentleness. We might picture a parent lovingly correcting a child rather than allowing a harmful pattern to continue. At other times, wisdom prompts compassion toward someone who has wounded us, or patience as we wait for God to soften a heart before taking the next step. There are also moments when wisdom leads us to remain silent, especially when a heated argument needs a pause for prayer rather than another sharp word. Each response is an expression of discernment rooted in love.

Among all the ways wisdom expresses itself, prayer may be the most vital and yet the most easily overlooked. When we are wounded, our first instinct is often to react. We may want to defend ourselves, release our frustration, or find a way to even the score. Yet wisdom gently invites us to pause, breathe, and bring the matter before God. Prayer steadies the heart, aligns our emotions with his truth, and opens space for the Holy Spirit to guide our next step.

A prayer does not need to be elaborate. Even a simple, honest plea becomes a doorway for grace. We may pause and whisper, "Holy Spirit, transform my heart. Soften what is hardened within me, and grant me the wisdom to choose forgiveness. I cannot do this on my own. Amen." Scripture reassures us of God's promise to help us with this. James writes, "If any of you lacks wisdom, let him ask God, who gives generously to all without reproach, and it will be given to him" (James 1:5). We never approach God in vain. He delights in granting wisdom to those who seek him with sincere hearts and steadfast trust.

Prayer holds the power to transform our hearts, and Scripture reassures us that it will. Philippians 4:6-7 teaches, "Do not be anxious about anything, but in everything, by prayer and supplication with thanksgiving, let your requests be made known to God. And the peace of God, which surpasses all understanding, will guard your hearts and your minds in Christ Jesus. Prayer soothes our worries and opens space for God's peace to steady our minds.

Jesus taught us to pray daily, seeking forgiveness through the prayer commonly called the Lord's Prayer. He said, "Pray then like this: 'Our Father in heaven, hallowed be your name. Your kingdom come, your will be done, on earth as it is in heaven.'" He continued, "'Give us this day our daily bread, and forgive us our debts, as we also have forgiven our debtors. And lead us not into temptation, but deliver us from evil'" (Matthew 6:9-13). This prayer is familiar to many of us, yet its profound emphasis on forgiveness can be easily overlooked. In just fifty-two words, five essential themes emerge: honoring God's name, longing for his will to be done on earth, depending on him for daily provision, receiving forgiveness as we extend forgiveness, and seeking his protection from temptation and evil. A central focus of this prayer is forgiveness. Jesus reminds us to first approach God for his forgiveness of our own sins; then, following his example, to extend that same forgiveness to others. Prayer teaches us to receive grace before we give it, moving forgiveness from an intellectual idea to a posture of the heart.

Prayer also guides us toward reconciliation. When Jesus instructed us to pray that God's will be "done on earth as it is in heaven," he invited us to imagine relationships as they will be in heaven where every barrier is removed and every relationship fully reconciled. As we pray, we begin that process here and now. Prayer softens the heart, invites God's presence, and fosters genuine peace. Whenever possible, praying with the person who has offended us becomes a powerful act of unity, opening a door for God to work in both hearts.

Finally, prayer reshapes how we respond to those who hurt us. Jesus instructed his followers, "But I say to you who hear, love your enemies, do good to those who hate you, bless those who curse you, pray for those who abuse you" (Luke 6:27-28). These words do not minimize pain, but they reveal a path where bitterness loses its grip and love begins to lead.

A. W. Tozer once wrote, "It is well that we accept the hard truth now: The man who would know God must give time to him. He must count no time wasted which is spent in the cultivation of his acquaintance with God." [50] His words speak profoundly to the times when conflict and pain weigh heavily on our hearts. True wisdom rarely comes in the midst of strong emotions, especially when we are angry. We can read about this in James 1:19–20 "Let every person be quick to hear, slow to speak, slow to anger, for the anger of man does not produce the righteousness of God." More often, it is found in the quiet stillness of God's presence, where our thoughts settle, and our hearts become open and teachable once again. Proverbs 3:5-6 speaks of this: "Trust in the Lord with all your heart, and do not lean on your own understanding. In all your ways acknowledge him, and he will make straight your paths"—words that guide us away from reacting in the moment and toward relying on God's steady wisdom.

Prayer should never be our last resort; it is meant to be our first response. Without prayer, forgiveness can falter under the weight of pain, frustration, or fear. But through prayer, forgiveness and reconciliation become divine works, not merely human efforts. The Holy Spirit strengthens what is weak within us and enables us to walk paths we could never navigate on our own. It steadies our hearts before God and brings clarity to what truly matters. Sometimes, wisdom reveals that the best way to forgive is to quietly release an offence, letting it go without confrontation or debate and trusting God to bring peace in his time.

Overlooking Offenses

Not every wound requires confrontation. Some hurts are best

met with love, without lengthy discussions or explanations. This is not denial, nor is it pretending nothing happened. Rather, it is a conscious act of grace, a deliberate choice to release the offense rather than magnify it when a conversation would bring little or no healing. Proverbs 19:11 says, "Good sense makes one slow to anger, and it is his glory to overlook an offense." Overlooking an offense is not a sign of weakness but a reflection of spiritual maturity and godly wisdom.

The New Testament reinforces this truth. Paul exhorts believers in Ephesians 4:2: "Be completely humble and gentle; be patient, bearing with one another in love." This call to bear with one another acknowledges that life among family, friends, and fellow believers will naturally include irritations, misunderstandings, and hurt feelings. True wisdom does not demand repayment for wrongs; instead, it creates space for grace. It chooses patience over retaliation and gentleness over pride, reflecting the heart of Jesus in every relationship.

Bearing with one another is beautifully expressed in Colossians 3:13: "Bear with each other and forgive one another if any of you has a grievance against someone. Forgive as the Lord forgave you." This places forgiveness at the very heart of the gospel. We forgive not because others deserve it, but because we have already received God's undeserved grace and mercy. As we dwell on his forgiveness toward us, our hearts are gradually softened toward those who have hurt us.

Peter also strengthens this truth in 1 Peter 4:8, where he writes, "Above all, keep loving one another earnestly, since love covers a multitude of sins." This does not mean sin is excused or ignored but describes a love that is ready to release offences and trust God with what is beyond our control. Such love safeguards relationships and prevents bitterness from taking root. Overlooking an offense also means exercising restraint, choosing not to speak negatively about those who have wronged us. Proverbs 17:9 reminds us, "Whoever covers an offense seeks love, but he who repeats a matter separates close friends."

Dwelling on an offence, whether in conversation with others or even in our own thoughts, only deepens the wound. Yet when we choose silence over spreading hurt, and compassion over accusation, we nurture unity and strengthen the bonds of love. In this, we see the heart of God toward his people. Psalm 103:10-11 declares, "He does not deal with us according to our sins, nor repay us according to our iniquities. For as high as the heavens are above the earth, so great is his steadfast love toward those who fear him." When we overlook offences, we mirror divine love, imitating our Heavenly Father, who continually chooses compassion over condemnation.

Many of life's daily hurts are small and fleeting: an unkind word, a forgotten promise, or a careless remark. Wisdom teaches us to release these quickly rather than magnify them. Overlooking an offense does not mean pretending it never happened; it is a deliberate act of love that keeps short accounts, preserves unity, and nurtures peace. In responding this way, we reflect the heart of our Savior, who bore our offences on the cross. To overlook wrongdoing with love is not weakness; it is strength secured by grace.

Yet wisdom is discerning. Not every offense can or should be overlooked. Some wounds cut deeply, behaviors cause lasting harm, and certain patterns persist too long to ignore. In these cases, overlooking an offense is avoidance, not love. True wisdom calls us to confront sin with honesty, speak the truth in love, and, when necessary, take steps to protect ourselves and others while maintaining a forgiving heart.

When wounds run deep, our instinct may be to demand justice, seek repayment, or hope those who hurt us feel the pain they caused. But God's wisdom invites a higher path, one that reflects his mercy and restores peace to our hearts. As Paul writes with striking clarity in Romans 12:17-19, "Repay no one evil for evil, but give thought to do what is honorable in the sight of all. If possible, so far as it depends on you, live peaceably with all. Beloved, never avenge yourselves, but leave it to the wrath of God, for it is written, 'Vengeance is mine, I will repay, says the Lord.'" These verses remind us that only God has the right to bring justice. Our role is to seek peace, resist the urge to retaliate, and place our trust in his perfect and unfailing justice.

Paul's words echo the ancient wisdom found in Deuteronomy 32:35, where God declares, "It is mine to avenge; I will repay. In due time their foot will slip; their day of disaster is near, and their doom rushes upon them." When we take vengeance into our own hands, we step into a role that belongs to God alone. Proverbs also reinforces this truth: "Do not say, 'I will repay evil'; wait for the Lord, and he will deliver you" (Proverbs 20:22).

To release and forgive does not mean excusing the wrong or denying the pain. Rather, it means entrusting the matter to God's just and faithful hands. He sees everything with perfect understanding, judges with perfect righteousness, and acts in the perfect time. Psalm 37:7-9 provides this encouragement: "Be still before the Lord and wait patiently for him; do not fret when people succeed in their ways, when they carry out their wicked schemes. Refrain from anger and turn from wrath; do not fret, it leads only to evil. For those who are evil will be destroyed, but those who hope in the Lord will inherit the land." These words steady our hearts and remind us that God sees everything clearly, even when circumstances appear unjust.

A. W. Tozer once observed, "Justice is not something God has. Justice is something that God is." [51] This truth allows us to rest from the exhausting burden of seeking revenge, trusting that God's justice never fails. Our role is to trust him, wait patiently, and continue walking in his peace. Releasing vengeance does not mean ignoring justice. God has appointed civil authorities to uphold righteousness and restrain evil (Romans 13:1-2). [52] At times, legal or protective action is necessary to prevent further harm. Even then, our hearts must remain free from hatred or the desire for retaliation, resting in the certainty that God's justice is both perfect and complete.

When we release vengeance, we make room for peace. We follow the example of Jesus, who "when he was reviled, he did not revile in return; when he suffered, he did not threaten, but continued entrusting himself to him who judges justly" (1 Peter 2:23). This act of surrender releases us from bitterness and invites the Holy Spirit to bring healing into our hearts. Even after we choose forgiveness, the temptation to dwell on our pain may linger. Yet each time we resist that pull, we reaffirm our trust in God's justice and draw closer to the heart of Jesus.

Garding Our Thoughts

God is always aware of our thoughts, as David reminds us in Psalm 139:4, "Even before a word is on my tongue, behold, O Lord, you know it altogether." God's Word is also "living and active... discerning the thoughts and intentions of the heart" (Hebrews 4:12). He not only hears what we say but also understands the motives behind our words. This truth becomes even clearer in Psalm 139:23-24: "Search me, O God, and know my heart. Try me and know my thoughts. And see if there be any grievous way in me, and lead me in the way everlasting." The wonderful truth is that Jesus knows even the hidden evil in our hearts, yet he loves us abundantly and desires that we cultivate righteous thoughts for his glory and our good.

Our thoughts shape our emotions and, in turn, influence the choices we make. Proverbs 4:23 reminds us to guard our hearts, "for from it flow the springs of life." Our thoughts become the wellspring that nourishes our actions and directs the course of our lives. Paul gives us the standard for our thought life in Philippians 4:8: "Finally, brothers, whatever is true, whatever is honorable, whatever is just, whatever is pure, whatever is lovely, whatever is commendable, if there is any excellence, if there is anything worthy of praise, think about these things."

Our minds often linger on past hurts and replay old offenses, yet godly wisdom calls us to take every thought captive. As Scripture reminds us, "We destroy arguments and every lofty opinion raised against the knowledge of God, and take every thought captive to obey Christ" (2 Corinthians 10:5). Instead of dwelling on how we have been wronged, wisdom directs our hearts toward God's faithfulness, his justice, and his steadfast love, even for those who have hurt us. When our minds are fixed on his truth, our words follow naturally. Guarding our thoughts, then, becomes the first step toward speaking with grace and wisdom.

Guarding Our Words

James reminds us that "the tongue is a restless evil, full of deadly poison" (James 3:8). Our words carry great power. They can bring healing or cause harm, build others up or tear them down. But Ephesians 4:29 offers a clear standard: "Let no corrupting talk come out of your mouths, but only such as is good for building up, as fits the occasion, that it may give grace to those who hear." Forgiveness is not only a matter of the heart; it must also guide the words we speak and those we choose to hold back. The Psalmist prayed tenderly, "Set a guard, O Lord, over my mouth; keep watch over the door of my lips" (Psalm 141:3). His words remind us that controlling our speech is not just a matter of willpower; it is a grace we must earnestly seek from God. We rely on his Holy Spirit to guide our words and soften our tone, especially in moments of strong emotion.

Jesus also taught us how profoundly our words can impact others. In Matthew 12:36-37, he warned, "I tell you, on the day of judgment people will give account for every careless word they speak, for by your words you will be justified, and by your words you will be condemned." When we allow the Holy Spirit to shape our hearts and guide our words, what we speak can become an instrument of peace rather than division.

We cannot truly walk in forgiveness or remain reconciled

for long without learning to guard our speech. Gentle words open the door to healing and restore peace where pain once held sway. Proverbs 15:1 reminds us, "A soft answer turns away wrath, but a harsh word stirs up anger." In moments of tension, godly wisdom guides us to speak words that soothe rather than provoke, words that offer grace instead of resentment.

Often, the healthiest path toward healing a hurt is to address the person involved directly and with humility. Sharing our frustrations with others who are not part of the situation can create confusion and deepen the wound.

Going to the Person

Jesus gave us a loving and practical pattern for dealing with conflict: "If your brother sins against you, go and tell him his fault, between you and him alone. If he listens to you, you have gained your brother" (Matthew 18:15). If that first step does not bring resolution, he continues, "But if he does not listen, take one or two others along with you, that every charge may be established by the evidence of two or three witnesses" (Matthew 18:16). And if the conflict persists, Jesus instructs us to bring it before the wider faith community, allowing grace and accountability to work together to restore peace and unity (Matthew 18:17).

These steps are intended for believers, and many family and church conflicts have found healing when people humbly followed this process. Even when the other person is not a Christian, the first two steps, private conversation and the involvement of a few trusted witnesses, remain valuable. They uphold truth, protect discretion, and prevent gossip and heightened emotions.

At the same time, Scripture reminds us to exercise discernment in all matters. Proverbs 9:7-8 cautions that confronting a person who is unwilling to listen may only lead to harm: "Whoever corrects a scoffer gets himself abuse, and he who reproves a wicked man incurs injury. Do not reprove a scoffer, or he will hate you; reprove a wise man, and he will love you." Sometimes the wisest response is simply to pause, pray, and wait for the right moment or for the right person to step in and help.

If the situation involves any form of abuse—emotional, physical, or sexual, it is essential to reach out to someone trustworthy: a parent, pastor, counsellor, medical professional, or even the authorities. Seeking help is not an act of betrayal; it is an act of protection. True healing begins when we bring what has been hidden in darkness into the light.

Seek Wise Counsel

The journey toward forgiveness and reconciliation can feel uncertain. Deep wounds and complex family situations may leave us unsure how to take the next step. In these moments, the wisdom and guidance of mature believers is a precious gift from God. Colossians 3:16 encourages us, "Let the word of Christ dwell in you richly, teaching and admonishing one another in all wisdom." Likewise, Proverbs 11:14 says, "Where there is no guidance, a people fall, but in an abundance of counselors there is safety." Seeking counsel is not a sign of weakness but an act of wisdom. Pain and anger can cloud our perspective, yet the guidance of godly friends, mentors, and pastors helps us respond with clarity and love.

James 5:16 reminds us that we do not walk this road alone: "Therefore, confess your sins to one another and pray for one another, that you may be healed. The prayer of a righteous person has great power as it is working." Forgiveness can deepen through prayer, especially when others join us in interceding on our behalf. Proverbs 19:20 urges us: "Listen to advice and accept instruction, that you may gain wisdom in the future." Wise counsel may not always tell us what we want to hear, but it guides us toward the next faithful step on the path to peace and restoration.

Closing Remarks

When God's wisdom shapes our hearts, forgiveness becomes possible, healing takes root, and reconciliation begins to flourish. Yet wisdom is not just understood in theory; it must be practiced in the relationships where we live each day.

The movement from understanding to action is the focus of Part Two. Like an artist who has carefully prepared the canvas and now applies color, we move from foundation to visible work. What was learned in Part One takes shape through real choices in real relationships. Some strokes will be bold, while others require patient, gentle layering. With each one, the portrait of our lives and relationships begins to emerge.

This truth is especially evident in marriage, where two imperfect people promise to love one another for better or worse and discover that living wisely is essential for love to endure. The next chapter explores how God's wisdom can strengthen and sustain a marriage.

Questions for Personal Reflection
or Group Discussion

1. Wisdom vs. Urgency

Proverbs 29:11 says, "A fool gives full vent to his spirit, but a wise man quietly holds it back." Think of a recent conflict in your family. Did you respond immediately or did you pause? If you paused to pray and consider your words, what difference did it make? If you didn't pause what might have changed if you had?

2. Patterns of Reaction

When someone in your family hurts or frustrates you, what's your first instinct? Go silent? Escalate? Defend yourself? React immediately? Why does that response feel safer than pausing to pray?

Now look back: When have you seen wisdom change everything because you paused, or because you didn't?

3. Overlooking or Bringing It into the Light

"It is an honor to overlook an offense" (Proverbs 19:11). "If your brother sins, go and tell him" (Matthew 18:15). Both are biblical. Both are wise. So, what does wisdom call for here?

Think of a current tension in your family. Should you overlook it or bring it into the light? How do you know? And what will you do?

4. What Prayer Changes

You've rehearsed the conversation a hundred times. You know exactly what you're going to say. You're ready. But have you prayed?

Prayer doesn't always change others. But it should change you. When have you prayed before a hard conversation and found your words, your tone, or your heart shift? What changed?

What would it look like to pray before your next difficult conversation, asking God to change you first?

CHAPTER 7
Covenant Marriage

There was once a place untouched by sorrow or decay, a sanctuary where every breath carried peace. Morning light shimmered through branches heavy with fruit, and a gentle river wound through the land. The air hummed with divine love as a soft mist rose from the ground to nourish everything it touched. Flowers bloomed without effort, and no pest spoiled the harvest. Even the soil seemed to sing.

The married couple lived there in perfect unity with creation, with one another, and with God. Their hands shaped the soil not from need but from joy. Every task flowed with purpose and ease. Work was not a burden; it was a delight. The world around them was gentle. They needed neither clothing nor shelter, for every need was met before desire arose. They felt no fear, no shame, no sense of lack. Their openness with one another was as natural as their fellowship with God. Nothing threatened them, and even the animals lived peacefully under their care. In the cool of the day, the Lord walked among them, and his voice carried the calm of divine friendship.

But peace did not last. Disobedience shattered trust, and harmony gave way to hardship. The ground resisted their labor; the creatures drew back in fear. Joy gave way to toil, and sweetness turned bitter. Adam and Eve, the first husband and wife, lost more than a garden; they lost the perfect peace in which all things once flourished. Through their disobedience, that harmony was broken, and every marriage since has felt its echo.

Yet God did not abandon his creation. He set in motion a plan of redemption, a day when the Redeemer would crush evil's power, heal the wounds of separation, and reconcile all who trust in him. That promise still moves through history and touches the quiet struggles of every marriage today. Every act of forgiveness, every moment of reconciliation between husband and wife, parent and child, or friend and neighbor echoes that first harmony. Each time we choose to forgive, we help restore a small part of what was lost. When we seek reconciliation, we glimpse the peace that once filled the garden. Scripture promises that this peace, once lost, will one day be fully restored in heaven.

Imagine if our homes reflected the beauty of that first garden, free from power struggles, cold silences, and harsh words. Instead of tension, our lives could move to the rhythm of grace and understanding. The same peace that filled creation can begin to fill a marriage when forgiveness replaces blame and humility replaces pride. When a husband and wife choose to serve rather than be served, and to listen rather than accuse, they begin to rebuild what was broken. This is the heart of the marriage vow, for marriage is meant to reflect something far greater than two people. It is a divine covenant.

Marriage as a Divine Covenant

To understand why forgiveness is vital in marriage, we must

first distinguish between a contract and a covenant. A contract is conditional: "If you do this, I will do that." It depends on performance and can be broken when one party fails or wants to quit. A covenant, however, is a sacred, enduring promise. When we pledge, "for better or worse, in sickness and in health, till death do us part," we enter a covenant, not a contract. Genuine covenant love endures through forgiveness, for love that cannot forgive is not covenant love at all.

God is the perfect example of covenant love. He does not turn away when we stumble, or abandon us when we sin. Instead, he remains faithful even when we are unfaithful. As Scripture reminds us, "If we are faithless, he remains faithful, for he cannot deny himself" (2 Timothy 2:13). The cross did not signal a change in God's love; rather, it was the ultimate fulfillment of his covenant, a demonstration of how he chose to confront our sin without breaking his promise to redeem us. In the same way, a covenant marriage reshapes how we approach conflict. Instead of asking, "What have you done for me?" we begin to ask, "How can I honor my commitment to you?"

Maintaining a covenant marriage is where the wisdom principles discussed in Chapter 6 take root. In moments of irritation, wisdom teaches us to pause and pray instead of reacting impulsively. When conflicts arise, it helps us discern what to graciously overlook and what to address with gentle honesty. When sharp words threaten to escape, wisdom gives us pause and softens our speech with grace.

Forgiveness and reconciliation are essential to a lasting marriage. When a relationship is strained or wounded, it disturbs the peace of the home and inflicts deep emotional pain on everyone involved. As when a ship is struck by torpedoes, a fractured marriage can sink joy and weaken what was meant to be a lifelong covenant of love. Marriage is not merely a human agreement; it is a divine covenant established and sustained by God, meant to endure until death.

This covenant union is described in Genesis 2:24: "Therefore a man shall leave his father and his mother and hold fast to his wife, and they shall become one flesh." Jesus affirms this in Matthew 19:6: "So they are no longer two, but one. Therefore, what God has joined together, let no man separate." Scripture teaches that marriage is far more than emotion or physical attraction; it is a sacred and spiritual union established by God. The true strength of this bond lies not merely in affection or compatibility, but in a shared spiritual life that is continually nurtured through forgiveness and reconciliation.

When marriage functions as God intended, it becomes a living expression of self-giving love and lifelong devotion, a reflection of his covenant love for his people. While chemistry and compatibility have their place, the lasting foundation of a strong marriage is a couple's shared walk with Jesus. Only when husband and wife grow together in their relationship with God can they experience the fullness and joy that marriage was designed to offer.

As one scholar observes, "The conjugal union is a spiritual oneness, a vital communion of heart as well as of body in which it finds its consummation." This spiritual unity forms the foundation that strengthens marriage. It serves as a divine adhesive, holding the relationship firm even in the face of careless words or hurtful actions. When couples choose to practice forgiveness consistently and sincerely, their bond not only endures but also deepens. Such forgiveness is at the very heart of a covenant marriage.

Forgiveness Sustains Covenant Marriage

At the heart of every healthy marriage lies forgiveness. Without it, even the strongest bond can fracture under the weight of human weakness. Forgiveness in marriage is not merely a feeling; it is a conscious act of love and grace. Charles Spurgeon once said, "To be forgiven is such sweetness that honey is tasteless in comparison with it. But yet there is one thing sweeter still, and that is to forgive. As it is more blessed to give than to receive, so to forgive rises a stage higher in experience than to be forgiven." [53]

This sweetness is strengthened when married couples remember that their covenant was made before God. In Malachi 2:14, God describes marriage as "a covenant made before the Lord." Marriage is not simply a contract that ends when emotions waver; it is a sacred covenant designed to mirror God's enduring faithfulness. When couples forget this truth, their love weakens. But when they hold fast to it, their love becomes strong, steady, and enduring.

Scripture reminds us that forgiveness is the fullest expression of love, a love that restores peace and harmony. "Put on then, as God's chosen ones, holy and beloved, compassionate hearts, kindness, humility, meekness, and patience, bearing with one another and, if one has a complaint against another, forgiving each other; as the Lord has forgiven you, so you also must forgive. And above all these put on love, which binds everything together in perfect harmony" (Colossians 3:12-14).

When a husband and wife embrace this truth, forgiveness becomes the steady rhythm of their covenant, a continual posture of the heart rather than an occasional reaction to conflict. Letting go of grudges is essential for building a joyful, lasting marriage. We can choose to forgive immediately, even when hurtful words or actions are never acknowledged.

This kind of silent forgiveness happens when we release the need to correct, confront, or demand repayment, choosing instead to set our spouse free from lingering expectations or emotional debt. Yet silent forgiveness is not always wise, especially when it hides unresolved anger. Unresolved anger often appears in two main forms: aggressive and passive. Aggressive anger erupts visibly through shouting, harsh criticism, cutting remarks, or even abusive actions that leave deep and lasting scars. Passive anger, though quieter, can wound just as deeply. It hides behind silence or emotional withdrawal, showing up as stonewalling, distance, or the heavy chill of the silent treatment. Though less explosive, its quiet persistence slowly erodes trust and intimacy. Both forms of anger create separation rather than nurture love. A redemptive response takes a different path: instead of lashing out or shutting down, it chooses honesty wrapped in gentleness, seeking understanding rather than control.

In marriage, forgiveness is more than the resolution of conflict; it is a living reflection of Christ's love, the choice to love even in the face of disappointment or failure. As Elisabeth Elliot wisely observed, "A wife, if she is very generous, may admit that her husband has good qualities. But the greatest thing she can do is to forgive him and love him as Christ loved the

Church." [54] The same truth applies to a husband. His greatest strength is shown not only in protecting and providing for his family but in forgiving and loving as Jesus did, even when it is painful or undeserved. The apostle Paul expresses this beautifully in Ephesians 5:25: "Husbands, love your wives, as Christ loved the church and gave himself up for her." This kind of love is not weak or naïve; it is courageous, refining, and steadfast. True forgiveness is best offered without delay, even before the day comes to a close. Ephesians 4:26 speaks directly to this principle, especially within marriage: "Do not let the sun go down on your anger."

As noted in Chapter 6, the heart of covenant love grows stronger through both our thoughts and our words. When we learn to guide our thinking, blessings begin to flow naturally from within us. Our words, then, become clear streams of grace, refreshing those around us, beginning with our spouse. As we recognize the link between our inner meditations and the words we speak, we become wiser sowers, cultivating stronger marriages and families.

Sowing and Reaping in Marriage

The daily seeds of love, kindness, and forgiveness that we plant in our marriages grow into a harvest that extends far beyond our relationship. These seeds bless not only our spouse and children, but also everyone whose lives we touch.

The biblical principle of sowing and reaping, woven throughout Scripture, offers deep wisdom for how we think, speak, and act within marriage. The following three truths reveal both practical and spiritual insights into this principle.

We Reap What We Sow:

If we plant tomato seeds, we harvest tomatoes. If we scatter weed seeds, we reap weeds. The same principle applies to our thoughts and words. When we indulge the desires of the flesh through bitterness, selfishness, or careless speech, we ultimately reap destruction. But when we sow seeds of love, offering kind thoughts and gracious words, we cultivate a marriage that flourishes with joy and harmony. Paul affirms this truth in Galatians 6:7-8: "Do not be deceived: God is not mocked, for whatever one sows, that he will also reap. For the one who sows to his own flesh will from the flesh reap corruption, but the one who sows to the Spirit will from the Spirit reap eternal life." A joyful and lasting marriage begins by cultivating righteous thoughts and speaking words that lovingly uplift one another.

We Reap in Proportion to What We Sow:

Just as a farmer's harvest depends on how much seed he sows, the fruitfulness of a marriage reflects what we offer to one another. When we give only a little, the bond may remain shallow and fragile. But when we give generously through kind words, patient understanding, affectionate gestures, and thoughtful actions, we cultivate a deeper, more joyful connection. Paul highlights this truth in 2 Corinthians 9:6: "The point is this: whoever sows sparingly will also reap sparingly, and whoever sows bountifully will also reap bountifully." It's hard to imagine a husband saying, "I love you," on his wedding day and then never saying it again. A relationship like that would quickly wither. Just as seeds need to be nurtured to grow, words of love must be spoken consistently for a marriage to flourish.

Reaping Requires Patience:

Farmers do not scatter seed and expect a harvest the next morning. Likewise, nurturing healthy thoughts, kind words, and loving actions within marriage requires patience and steady commitment. The fruits of these efforts rarely appear overnight; yet when we consistently choose what is good and life-giving, blessings come in their proper time. Paul reminds us in Galatians 6:9, "And let us not grow weary of doing good, for in due season we will reap, if we do not give up." The wisdom of sowing and reaping often reveals itself in the quiet, everyday moments of marriage. Through simple words of kindness, gentle gestures of understanding, and ordinary acts of care, love takes root and flourishes.

Bookends of Each Day

In most marriages, love is strengthened not by grand gestures but through small, consistent acts of care and thoughtful words. The words we speak to our spouse at the beginning and end of each day often set the emotional tone of our home. These simple moments, the quiet bookends of daily life, carry far more influence than we may realize.

Start the morning with a warm, sincere, "Good morning. I'm so glad to see you." A gentle greeting like this can lift the spirit and create a positive atmosphere for the day. At night, closing the day with affection, "Good night. I love you. Sleep well," offers comfort, reassurance, and a sense of safety. While gracious speech should guide our conversations throughout the day, these brief greetings and farewells have a unique ability to nurture lasting joy and peace. Practiced consistently, they deepen intimacy and cultivate a sense of warmth and security within the home.

A strong marriage is sustained not by perfection but by daily expressions of love, kindness, forgiveness, and steady commitment. Resentment and neglect can create distance, which is why we should guard our hearts carefully. God designed the union between husband and wife to endure through every season, growing stronger as both partners choose to love faithfully. Forgiveness does not require us to pretend that hurt never happened or to silence our pain. Instead, it invites us to release resentment and extend grace, even when it is difficult. It mirrors the mercy God has shown us, a mercy freely given, undeserved, and anchored in his love.

Perhaps more than anywhere else, forgiveness is essential in marriage. In such a close relationship, wounds from harsh words, misunderstandings, or forgotten promises are inevitable; but if these hurts are ignored, they settle into the heart and begin to divide. Yet when forgiveness is offered, healing takes root. Trust can be rebuilt if it was lost, and intimacy restored. A marriage without forgiveness is like a house built on sand; a marriage shaped by forgiveness stands steady and secure on a firm foundation.

Elisabeth Elliot expressed this truth with great insight when she wrote, "Of all the things that can kill a marriage, a spouse's refusal to forgive may be the most deadly." [55]

Unforgiveness acts like a silent poison, gradually eroding love from within. What may begin as small grievances can grow into towering barriers, and minor frustrations can fester into deep resentment. Forgiveness, however, clears these obstacles and creates space for love to flourish once more.

To forgive is to follow the example of Jesus, who prayed even from the cross, "Father, forgive them, for they know not what they do" (Luke 23:34). If our Savior could forgive those who harmed him, we, too, can seek the grace to forgive our spouses when they fall short. Covenant love calls us to forgive not because it is easy, but because it reflects Christ's heart and honors the promises we have made.

Forgiveness opens the door, while reconciliation restores the relationship. Both are vital in a covenant marriage, where love is meant to heal rather than divide, to rebuild rather than retreat. When forgiveness softens the heart, reconciliation becomes possible, and peace can take root once more.

The Path to Reconciliation

Forgiveness and reconciliation work together, yet they are distinct. As explored in Chapter 2, forgiveness is a unilateral act that can be extended even when the other person does not acknowledge their wrongdoing. Reconciliation, however, is bilateral and requires both people to participate. Forgiveness steadies the heart of the one who was hurt, while reconciliation restores the relationship itself.

In marriage, both are essential. Forgiveness prevents bitterness from taking root, and reconciliation rebuilds what has been damaged. When both spouses humble themselves, listen with empathy, and seek genuine understanding, reconciliation unfolds gently, with time, patience, and grace. Reconciliation begins with honesty. The wounded spouse needs space to express pain without accusation, and the offending spouse must listen without defensiveness. This sacred exchange calls for humility, self-reflection, and a sincere desire to move together toward healing.

The next step is confession. Genuine reconciliation requires true repentance. The offending spouse must acknowledge their sin and ask for forgiveness—not a reluctant, "I'm sorry you feel that way," but a heartfelt admission: "I was wrong. What I did was sinful, and I know it hurt you. Will you forgive me?" Such honesty opens the door for God's healing work to begin.

Reconciliation also involves a commitment to change. Repentance is more than remorse; it is a decision to turn away from harmful patterns and walk in a new direction. The spouse who caused the hurt demonstrates sincerity through consistent actions, while the wounded spouse gradually opens their heart and allows trust to be rebuilt.

This process is rarely easy. Yet when both partners honor the covenant they made before God, reconciliation becomes not only possible but deeply redemptive. God delights in restoring what is broken; and when we cooperate with his grace, healing can take root, strengthening the marriage for years to come.

A Place Better than the Garden

Every time a husband and wife choose to forgive, they take a quiet step back toward the garden. Each act of grace restores something of what was lost, renewing trust, tenderness, and peace. Marriage becomes the soil where God makes two hearts grow together, where forgiveness flows like water and humility shines like sunlight. It is holy ground, not because it is free from struggle, but because God meets us in the midst of it.

When love bends instead of breaking, and when peace returns after pain, we begin to glimpse what God is restoring. We see hints of the unity, beauty, and joy that once filled Eden. Marriage, at its best, becomes the gentle work of love. It is ordinary yet sacred, fragile yet enduring. It is not a garden without weeds, but a place where grace is planted again and again, and where God brings new life in ways only he can. Every act of forgiveness and every gesture of humility becomes a seed of redemption, taking root in the soil of daily life. The same God who walked with Adam and Eve still walks with husbands and wives today, tending the places where love grows weary and hope begins to fade. When we choose to forgive, we step into God's ongoing story of restoration. Each time we decide to stay, to serve, and to trust again, we mirror the steadfast love of Jesus for his Church. Though every marriage bears the marks of a fallen world, each one also carries the potential to shine with the light of redemption.

Covenant love invites us to keep returning to grace, to cultivate peace, and to trust that even the smallest acts of faithfulness can give us a glimpse of paradise being restored. Yet the glimpses of renewal we experience now will one day give way to the fullness of God's glory. The story that began in a garden will reach its ultimate fulfillment when Jesus returns.

Revelation paints a breathtaking vision: a radiant city descending from heaven like a bride prepared for her husband, shining with the glory of God. There, the river of life flows as clear as crystal, the tree of life bears fruit in every season, and God's people will see his face. Scripture promises, "He will wipe away every tear from their eyes, and death shall be no more; neither shall there be mourning, nor crying, nor pain anymore" (Revelation 21:4). Heaven is not simply a return to Eden—it is Eden glorified, where what was lost through the first Adam is fully restored and beautifully enhanced in the second Adam, Jesus Christ.

Closing Remarks

Every married couple is called to make forgiveness and reconciliation a priority. These are not merely helpful virtues but covenant-sustaining commitments that enable love to endure. When husbands and wives choose to forgive and pursue reconciliation, their marriage reflects the heart of Jesus, who remains faithful to his covenant with us through steadfast, redeeming love.

Even with wisdom and sincere devotion, we sometimes fall short. Every relationship faces storms, moments when forgiveness and reconciliation feel painfully out of reach. In the next chapter, we will look at how to process painful memories and extend forgiveness successfully. Scripture offers clear and trustworthy guidance, almost like the wisest and most careful bookkeeper manages a financial ledger, making this sacred work both practical and dependable.

Questions for Personal Reflection or Group Discussion

1. Marriage Is Not a Transaction

God didn't say, "I'll be faithful to you as long as you're faithful to Me." He said, "I will never leave you nor forsake you" (Hebrews 13:5). Marriage is a covenant, not a contract. Be honest: Have you been keeping score? Mentally tallying who's done more, who's forgiven more, who owes whom? Covenant love doesn't keep score. It gives freely. Even when it's not returned.

What would change in your marriage if you stopped keeping score?

2. The Daily Bookends of Marriage

Every marriage has "daily bookends"—how you greet each other in the morning and how you say goodnight. These small moments shape the emotional climate of your entire home. What do your daily bookends look like right now? Warm? Cold? Rushed? Tender? Distracted? Resentful?

What would it look like to make tomorrow morning's greeting and tomorrow night's goodnight a deliberate choice to express love and put the other first?

3. "I'm Sorry You Feel That Way"

Genuine reconciliation cannot happen without true repentance. "I'm sorry you feel that way" isn't an apology. It's a dodge. Real repentance says: "I was wrong. What I did was sinful, and I know it wounded you. Will you forgive me?"

When have you heard (or offered) the fake version? What's the difference between those words and a real apology? And why is one so much harder to say than the other?

4. Better Than Eden

Adam and Eve walked with God in a perfect garden. No conflict. No sin. No hurt. But God's promise for your marriage isn't just to return to the garden. It's to grow your love toward the kind of restored wholeness God promises in heaven.

Think of a specific time when you forgave your spouse or they forgave you. Did something shift? Not just "we made up," but something deeper: more humility, more understanding, more grace than before? Those moments when forgiveness made you better—not just back together—are signs that God is building something more beautiful than Eden ever was.

CHAPTER 8

Mathematics and Forgiveness

Forgiveness becomes easier to grasp when we connect it to something familiar. In Scripture, it can be pictured as a ledger where debts are recorded, accounts are settled, and fellowship is restored. Just as financial records are reconciled, forgiveness releases another person's debt and opens the door to peace through love.

Forgiveness also follows what we might call spiritual mathematics. That is because we balance the books of the heart, our mental and spiritual ledgers. Payments are not made through financial repayment, but through grace and mercy. And just as an accountant trusts a reliable system, we learn to trust God's way of forgiveness rather than our own sense of fairness. The ledger of forgiveness does not follow human accounting; it is ruled by divine love. It may help to see how this "forgiveness ledger" works chronologically from the moment someone wrongs us to the freedom we find in forgiveness.

When Offense Is Recorded

When someone wrongs us, the offense is immediately recorded in our mental ledger. Perhaps they stole from us. Or they lied about us and caused great shame. Maybe there was an unwanted sexual advance or a betrayal of trust, or words were spoken that cut deeply. Whatever form the offense

163

takes, it goes into the ledger as a debt owed.

At this point, the bottom line is negative. We are in pain. The hurt is real. The loss or harm is real. We look at that ledger and see: "They owe me."

In time, we may try to make the pain go away by minimizing the offense. We tell ourselves it wasn't really that bad. We make excuses for the person who hurt us, perhaps they were intoxicated, or under stress, or going through a difficult season. We may even blame ourselves: "Maybe I'm too sensitive. Maybe I overreacted. Maybe I deserved it." But here's the problem: minimizing doesn't change the bottom line. Even when we convince ourselves the offense was smaller than it was, the ledger still shows a negative balance. The debt remains. We still suffer, even if we pretend we don't. Minimizing the offense is not forgiveness; it's denial. And denial never brings freedom.

Adding Grace and Mercy

True forgiveness happens when we take a different approach entirely. Instead of minimizing the offense or pretending it didn't happen, we do something counterintuitive: we acknowledge the offense at its full weight. We look honestly at what was done and refuse to diminish it. We face the truth: "Yes, that really happened. Yes, it really was that bad. Yes, it really hurt." As Psalm 62:8 says, we "pour out [our hearts] to God" about it.

Then, and this is the heart of forgiveness, as we find comfort in God, we add a positive entry of grace and mercy to the ledger. We release the person from the debt. Not because they deserve it. Not because they earned it. Not because the offense didn't matter. But because we choose to extend the same grace to them that God has extended to us. And when grace and mercy are added, something remarkable happens: the bottom-line changes. The offense is still there, recorded at its full value. But now, the account is balanced. The bottom line reads: "Paid in full." In some cases, grace is so abundant that it not only zeros out the debt but creates a positive balance, a reflection of the overflowing nature of God's redemptive love.

This understanding of the forgiveness ledger, that it requires adding grace and mercy rather than erasing or minimizing, can transform how we approach even the deepest wounds. The offense stays recorded at full value, but grace balances the account. But going back, how do we actually find the strength to add that grace? How do we move from understanding the mechanics to living them out?

Trusting God with the Ledger

When we turn to God in pouring out our hearts and truly trust him, we begin to experience the freedom that comes through forgiveness. At its heart, forgiveness is an expression of trust in him. It means relying on God to heal our pain, protect our hearts, and work in the lives of those who have wronged us. We pray for the understanding that forgiveness leads to lasting joy, even in the midst of pain. We ask God to fill our hearts with love for those who have hurt us and to grant us the grace to forgive, seeking reconciliation when it is wise and possible. As we learn to trust God fully, we become ready to balance the ledger of our hearts.

Canceling the Debt

In the same way God has forgiven us, we are called to release others from their debts and from the expectations we may place upon them. In the same way God has forgiven us, we are called to release others from their debts and from the expectations we may place upon them. But what does it really mean to "forgive" someone?

As we learn to trust God, we discover that forgiveness becomes an act of faith. Genuine, unconditional forgiveness depends on the guidance and power of the Holy Spirit, which is why prayer remains our constant lifeline. Through prayer, we come to understand that forgiveness brings freedom and joy, even amid pain. When we truly trust God, we begin to experience victory through forgiveness—which frees us from the burden of keeping accounts and allows us to release the ledger into God's hands.

As stated earlier, the Greek word *charizomai*, often translated as "to forgive," carries the meaning of releasing, pardoning, or canceling what is owed. [56] Paul used this word to describe the cancellation of sin's debt in Colossians 2:13-14: "[God] forgave [*charizomai*] us all our trespasses, by canceling the record of debt that stood against us with its legal demands. This he set aside, nailing it to the cross." In other words, God looked at the bottom line of our ledger, the debt we owed for our sin, added his grace and mercy, and proclaimed, "Paid in full!" In the same way, we are invited to release others from their debts and from the expectations we may have assigned to them. Just as financial debt can burden a household, unforgiven offenses can weigh heavily on the soul.

Most English translations capture the grace-filled meaning of *charizomai* in phrases like "freely forgave" or "graciously forgave," reminding us that forgiveness is never earned but is offered as a gift.[57] Luke, the Greek-speaking physician and Gospel writer, also used *charizomai* in a financial sense when telling Jesus' parable of the two debtors: "'A certain moneylender had two debtors. One owed five hundred denarii, and the other fifty. When they could not pay, he cancelled [*charizomai*] the debts of both. Now, which of them will love him more?' Simon answered, 'The one, I suppose, for whom he cancelled the larger debt.' And he said to him, 'You have judged rightly'" (Luke 7:41-43).

The cancellation of debt paints a vivid picture of forgiveness; a gracious act extended to someone who cannot repay. Just as forgiving a financial debt balances the ledger, extending relational forgiveness cancels the emotional debt, restoring harmony within our hearts.

Throughout this chapter, we have used financial language —accounts, debts, and ledgers—to illustrate the process of relational forgiveness. This metaphor helps us understand how grace and mercy work within families and relationships. However, readers often wonder: if forgiveness means canceling debt, does that also apply to actual financial obligations? This book focuses on relational debt, the emotional and spiritual accounts we keep in our hearts. Questions about financial debt, monetary disputes, and dealings with institutions involve additional considerations that are addressed separately in Appendix Two: Forgiveness Involving Financial Debt and Disputes.

Balancing the Ledger

The Greek word *logizomai*, meaning "to reckon", "to calculate", or "to keep account" appears frequently in the New Testament and classical Greek literature to describe bookkeeping. [58] When we keep an account, the focus is always on the bottom line. Paul uses *logizomai* in Romans 4:8 to illustrate the depth of God's forgiveness: "Blessed is the one whose sin the Lord will never count against him" (Romans 4:8). The cross made this possible. Through Jesus' sacrifice, God added grace to our ledger—so powerful, it paid the debt in full and ensured our sins would never be counted against us again.

When we choose to forgive others, we acknowledge that the offence was real, yet we refuse to let it dominate our thoughts. We add an entry of grace to the ledger so abundant that it balances the debt and changes the bottom line from negative to zero, or even to positive. Instead of clinging to the debt, we release it, for love has already covered it. True forgiveness restores balance not by denying the wrong, but because love has borne the cost and cancelled the debt. The record of the offence remains, yet it is no longer owed. The account has been settled. In forgiving, we are free to look upon the forgiven debt with peace, resting in the truth that love has fully covered the balance.

Are there debts we still revisit, wounds we continue to tally in our hearts? Perhaps it is time to open that mental ledger and quietly write across it, "Paid in full." This is what Jesus has done for us, and what he calls us to extend to others. Forgiveness does more than remove the negative; it writes love into the account and begins restoring the relationship. When we truly forgive, we release the emotional or mental record of another's wrongdoing. The pain may linger, like an old entry in the ledger, yet we choose to add a new entry of grace, bringing the balance back to zero. Sometimes, this grace even moves the account into a positive balance, reflecting the overflowing nature of redemptive love.

Paul provides a powerful example of God's transforming grace. Once a zealous persecutor of Christians, he humbly described himself as "a blasphemer, persecutor, and insolent opponent" (1 Timothy 1:13). Yet God did not merely overlook Paul's offences; he entrusted him with writing much of the New Testament through the guidance of the Holy Spirit. In Paul's ledger, the debt was significant, but grace was greater. God not only forgave the debt, but he also gave Paul a calling, a ministry, and opportunities to glorify him. Forgiveness does more than remove the wrong; it fills the space with love. This is the same truth Paul affirms in 1 Corinthians 13, where he reminds us that love keeps no record of wrongs.

Love Keeps No Record of Wrongs

Many translations of 1 Corinthians 13 use relational accounting language to convey this essential truth. For example, the Christian Standard Bible and the New International Version render it as, "love does not keep a record of wrongs." The Amplified Bible expands the idea to "love does not take into account a wrong endured," while the New American Standard Bible translates it as "love does not keep an account of a wrong suffered."[59]

Charles Spurgeon stated this with remarkable clarity when he wrote, "Love never keeps an account of wrongs; it blots them out and marks every offence with the cross of forgiving love." [60] When Spurgeon speaks of "blotting out," he does not mean erasing the record as if the offense never happened. He means the debt is no longer counted against the person. The offense remains in the ledger, but when we look at the bottom line, we see: Paid in full.

A. W. Tozer expressed the same truth in simple terms: "Forgiveness means refusing to keep score. Love holds no grudges and keeps no record of wrongs. It is the grace to let go again and again." [61] Tozer is describing what it looks like to check the bottom line of our forgiveness ledger. When he says love "keeps no record," he means we are not counting the debt against them anymore. The record exists, but the bottom-line reads: No debt remains.

Forgiveness does not mean the wrong is forgotten; it means its weight has been lifted. As Spurgeon observed, love cancels the debt at the foot of the cross, and as Tozer reminds us, grace continually sets us free. The offence no longer defines the relationship, because love has already paid the price.

When Memories Return

Even after we understand forgiveness and release a grievance, emotional pain can still surface. One of the most common struggles in the journey of forgiveness is this: what do we do if we truly forgave someone, yet months or even years later, the memory returns with the same anger or grief? Does that mean we have not forgiven? Do we need to begin the process all over again? When memories resurface, we face two possible paths, each shaped by our circumstances.

On the first path, if the offence has not been repeated but the memory resurfaces, we can gently remind ourselves that the debt has already been forgiven. When painful memories return, we may say, "I have released them. I will not reopen this case; the balance is zero." This spiritual reminder echoes Jesus' final words on the cross: "It is finished" (John 19:30). When old thoughts try to reclaim our attention, we follow Paul's counsel: "We take every thought captive to obey Christ" (2 Corinthians 10:5). Doing so prevents past offences from regaining emotional power in our hearts.

A second path appears when bitterness begins to resurface. If we find ourselves replaying the offence, longing for revenge, or withdrawing emotionally, it may be a sign that we need to forgive again. This does not mean our earlier forgiveness was insincere or ineffective; it simply shows that we have allowed the offence back into the ledger of our hearts.

Forgiveness is not merely a feeling; it is a deliberate choice we may need to renew again and again. Like careful bookkeepers, we examine the ledger of our hearts regularly, not to revisit old wounds but to confirm that love still balances the account. By entrusting every debt to God, choosing love, and refusing to dwell on the past, we learn to live out true forgiveness.

The Freedom of Forgiveness

As we reflect on the forgiveness ledger, we face a choice. Will we continue keeping careful records of every wrong? Will we minimize offences and pretend they don't hurt? Or will we balance the ledger with grace and mercy instead of resentment?

When we choose true forgiveness, acknowledging the full weight of the offense and adding grace to balance the account, transformation begins. The energy once spent keeping track of wrongs becomes energy devoted to gratitude and love. This is the redemptive power of the forgiveness ledger.

When Jesus cried, "It is finished," from the cross, he declared that the debt of sin had been paid in full. In our minds, the ledger of forgiveness may still hold entries of wrongs that feel too heavy to release. Some debts seem impossible to forgive, and some wounds too deep to cover with grace. Yet we can remember the parable of the two debtors: the one forgiven much, loved much. When we choose to write "Paid in full" across the pages of our hearts, we reflect the boundless love and mercy of God.

The question is simple but profound: Will we continue keeping careful records of every wrong, allowing bitterness to accumulate like interest in our hearts? Or will we follow God's divine accounting, where grace makes the final entry?

Perhaps it is time to open that mental ledger, the one we've kept hidden for so long and look honestly at the accounts that have remained unsettled. Our transformation from keepers of grievances to gracious forgivers begins the moment we stop trying to erase or minimize the offense, and instead choose to add grace that balances the account.

Closing Remarks

The forgiveness ledger provides a simple, practical way to navigate everyday hurts and ordinary conflicts. There are moments when betrayal feels overwhelming, when patterns of harm persist for years, or when the very thought of forgiving seems beyond our strength.

The next chapter examines how we face these moments when forgiveness feels out of reach. It shows how God's grace meets us in our hardest trials and how healing can begin, even when full restoration is not yet possible.

Questions for Personal Reflection
or Group Discussion

1. The Ledger and the Debt

"Love keeps no record of wrongs" (1 Corinthians 13:5). But forgiveness isn't pretending nothing happened. We need to name the real hurt not minimize it. So, a mental ledger can help: "Yes, this happened. It was wrong. It hurt." But that same ledger becomes poison when we use it to keep someone perpetually "in the red."

Think of someone you've forgiven or tried to. Are you using the ledger to name the truth? Or to hold them in debt? How can you tell the difference?

2. Absorbing the Cost

Forgiveness doesn't deny the debt. It cancels it by absorbing the cost. They owe you. And you know it. But mercy doesn't demand payment. Mercy says, "I'll carry this. You're free." Why does that feel so wrong? So unfair?

What does your resistance to absorbing the cost reveal about how you understand mercy or what you think you deserve?

3. Paid in Full

Your debt before God? Paid in full. Every sin. Every failure. Completely forgiven through Jesus. You believe that. You've received it. So why is it so hard to close the ledger for others?

Why can you accept that Jesus canceled your impossible debt—but you can't release the much smaller debt someone owes you? What does that reveal?

4. Trusting God with Justice

"Vengeance is mine, I will repay, says the Lord" (Romans 12:19). God doesn't need your help settling scores. He is a better judge than you are. So why is it so hard to let him handle it?

Do you fear that God's justice might include mercy that he might forgive in ways you find unfair? What would it look like to release your right to revenge and pray for a heart willing to trust God with both justice and mercy?

CHAPTER 9
When Forgiveness Seems Impossible

There are times in life when pain grows worse with each passing moment as offences continuously repeat, and reconciliation feels out of reach. Deepening hurt makes forgiving and restoring a broken relationship seem beyond our ability; and we may wonder how far we can go in forgiving someone who has been hurtful for years or caused a particularly grievous offense.

In this chapter, we share true stories of people who chose forgiveness and reconciliation in ways only God could have made possible. Their decisions echo the words of the psalmist: "Not to us, O Lord, not to us, but to your name give glory, for the sake of your steadfast love and your faithfulness!" (Psalm 115:1). Paul echoes this same truth, urging us to remember that "Whether you eat or drink, or whatever you do, do all to the glory of God" (1 Corinthians 10:31).

The first true story involves a pastor who interceded with George Washington on behalf of an adversary—when the tension of long-standing conflict, grudges, and pride set the stage for the events that unfolded during the Revolutionary War.

Washington Grants a Pardon

In 1775, a single gunshot ignited a conflict that lasted eight years and eventually gave rise to a new nation. Through George

Washington's steady leadership, the determination of the Continental soldiers, and the support of allies abroad, America gained the freedom declared in the Declaration of Independence. The United States War of Independence is filled with accounts of courageous men and women who risked everything for their convictions. One lesser-known story tells of an unexpected act of mercy by George Washington, offered in response to a request from his friend, Peter Miller.

Peter Miller had come to America to serve as pastor of the German Reformed Church in Ephrata, Pennsylvania. Among his congregation was a deacon named Michael Wittman, who became bitter when Peter later left to lead a Seventh-Day Baptist church. Although the disagreement happened years before the war, Michael's resentment only hardened with time. [62]

Their conflict had been intensely painful. Michael once struck Peter in the face and, on another occasion, spat on him. Yet Peter never retaliated, nor did he publicly shame Michael. By the time of the American Revolution, Peter, in his sixties, had become a respected pastor and scholar. Fluent in German, Latin, Greek, Hebrew, and several modern languages, his knowledge and wisdom earned the admiration of many leaders, including George Washington. [63]

Meanwhile, Michael ran a well-known tavern. One evening, two men stopped for dinner and rented a room. Not knowing who they were, Michael openly expressed support for the British and boasted that he had helped a British general. The two men were American agents who later reported him for treason. [64] Although Michael escaped through a window, he eventually surrendered after several days of cold and hunger.

He was convicted of treason and sentenced to hang. [65]

When Peter learned what had happened, he set out on foot, walking more than sixty miles through snow and bitter cold to plead with George Washington for mercy. Washington listened carefully but initially refused, explaining that he could not grant a pardon for Miller's "friend". "Friend?" Miller replied. "He is my worst enemy."

Washington was moved. "You mean you walked sixty miles to save the life of your enemy? That puts the matter in a different light. I will grant Wittman's pardon." [66] He signed the order and placed it in Peter's hands.

Peter then walked another fifteen miles to the execution site. As soldiers led Michael to the gallows, he sneered, "There is old Peter Miller. He walked all the way from Ephrata just to watch me hang." At that moment, Peter stepped forward, held up Washington's pardon, and stopped the execution. According to the account, the two men embraced and walked back to Ephrata together, finally reconciled. [67]

Could we do what Peter did? Could we forgive someone who mocked, humiliated, and even struck us; then go to great lengths to save that person's life?

This story shows forgiveness moving in both directions. Peter forgave Michael by refusing to retaliate, by not rehearsing his offences, and by risking his own safety in harsh weather to plead for mercy. After Peter's efforts saved him from the gallows, Michael's heart began to soften. Their embrace and shared walk home revealed a reconciliation that turned long-standing hostility into genuine friendship.

It is difficult to imagine walking seventy-five miles to save an enemy. Yet many of us know the weight of long-term resentment toward a friend who spread rumors, or a relative who repeatedly disrespected us. In those moments, the grace of God makes it possible for us to choose to follow Peter's example of not to dwelling on past wrongs, speaking kindly of those who have hurt us, and looking for ways to extend love. These small acts of grace protect our hearts and communities from bitterness.

A more recent and deeply heartbreaking account involves a mother who faced the devastating loss of her daughter, whose story shows us what forgiveness looks like in the midst of profound personal pain.

Losing a Daughter

Imagine beginning an ordinary, peaceful morning, finishing a hearty breakfast, when the doorbell suddenly rings. Renée opened the door to find her sister-in-law on the porch, her face filled with sorrow.

"There has been an accident," she quietly said. Then came the words that shattered Renée's world: "She didn't make it."

A drunk driver, someone who should never have been behind the wheel, had taken the life of her beloved twenty-year-old daughter, Meagan. In the face of such catastrophic loss, it would be understandable for Renée to feel anger and resentment toward the man responsible, Eric.

The court sentenced Eric to twenty-two years in prison for his actions. But even during the sentencing, Renée chose forgiveness. Instead of letting bitterness take root, she began traveling across the country, speaking about the dangers of drunk driving and hoping to spare others from the heartbreak she had endured.

The story did not end there, however. In time, Renée and her family returned to court to request a reduction in Eric's sentence. Moved by their appeal, the judge granted an eleven-year reduction. Two years before his release, Eric began joining Renée on tour. At churches, military bases, prisons, and schools, he stepped onto the stage in handcuffs, shackles, and chains. His presence became a powerful reminder of both the consequences of drunk driving and the transforming power of forgiveness. [68]

After his release, Eric continued traveling with Renée, sharing their remarkable story of redemption and grace. Forgiveness opened the door to a relationship that brought unexpected strength to many.

Anyone who has children understands how frightening it is to imagine outliving them. Losing a child is every parent's deepest fear. But what if that loss came through someone else's reckless decisions? Could we truly forgive the person responsible for such pain? And beyond forgiveness, could we ever imagine forming a friendship with that person, even standing beside them in shared work?

Not many people will experience the devastating loss of a son or daughter at the hands of a drunk driver. Yet there are moments in life when wrongs feel so great that forgiveness seems impossible—through a lie that leads to expulsion from school or loss of a job, a betrayal by a trusted partner who steals or deceives, or a similar wrong. Even in such painful circumstances,

God offers the peace and strength we need to forgive. Renée's story, though extreme, reminds us that God's grace empowers forgiveness even in the face of overwhelming wrongs.

Her story also gives us a modern picture of faith in action; but to see that such trust is not new, we can turn to Scripture and the testimonies of Old Testament believers who depended on God even in the face of injustice. If Renée's courage feels beyond what we could imagine, we can take heart: ordinary men and women in the Bible found extraordinary strength through faith in God.

Facing the Impossible

Hebrews 11 recounts the lives of men and women who demonstrated unwavering faith in the midst of great challenges. Abel, Enoch, Noah, Abraham, Sarah, Isaac, Jacob, Joseph, Moses, the Israelites who crossed the Red Sea, and those who marched around Jericho; along with Rahab, Gideon, Barak, Samson, Jephthah, David, Samuel, and the prophets are celebrated for their steadfast trust in God.

While the chapter cannot capture every detail of their lives, these believers continue to inspire us through their courageous devotion. The Bible tells us that these men and women:

...conquered kingdoms, enforced justice, obtained promises, stopped the mouths of lions, quenched the power of fire, escaped the edge of the sword, were made strong out of weakness, became mighty in war, put foreign armies to flight. Women received back their dead by resurrection. Some were tortured, refusing to accept release, so that they might rise again to a better life.

Others suffered mocking and flogging, and even chains and imprisonment. They were stoned, they were sawn in two, they were killed with the sword. They went about in skins of sheep and goats, destitute, afflicted, mistreated, of whom the world was not worthy, wandering about in deserts and mountains, and in dens and caves of the earth *(Hebrews 11:33-38).*

These Old Testament believers faced immense challenges, yet they triumphed through active faith. They truly lived by faith, trusting God and holding firmly to his promises, even when circumstances seemed impossible. Likewise, we are invited to run our own race with endurance, drawing strength and inspiration from their example as we navigate the trials of life.

We are encouraged by the words of Hebrews 12:1-2: "Therefore, since we are surrounded by so great a cloud of witnesses, let us also lay aside every weight, and sin which clings so closely, and let us run with endurance the race that is set before us, looking to Jesus, the founder and perfecter of our faith, who for the joy that was set before him endured the cross, despising the shame, and is seated at the right hand of the throne of God." We are called to run our race with endurance, trusting in God rather than relying on our emotions. This is what it means to live by faith.

Many heroes of the Old Testament experienced moments of failure: Noah became drunk, Samson fell into sexual sin, Jacob deceived, Rahab had been a prostitute, and David committed both adultery and murder. Yet God still counted each of them among the faithful. God sees our failures, too, but they do not disqualify us from his calling. Failure separates us only when we refuse to repent or learn from it. Often, our shortcomings become the very tools God uses to deepen our humility and strengthen our dependence on him. Through these moments, he shapes our character and leads us along paths of righteousness.

When we stumble, God's grace and mercy remain ever present, gently drawing us toward repentance and renewal. The call is to stay in his love, resist sin, and share in his divine nature. As we continue our race of faith, God himself will bring us to the finish line and into the glorious presence of his Son, Jesus Christ. On that day, we long to hear the words: "Well done, good and faithful servant." By his grace, if we do hear them, those words will carry even greater sweetness as we remember the suffering he endured on our behalf.

Part One of this book showed that Jesus' death and resurrection stand at the heart of the entire biblical story. His crucifixion remains the ultimate act of love, the supreme sacrifice for our forgiveness, a truth that becomes especially meaningful during seasons of hardship and when we are called to forgive others. Throughout his earthly life, even in the midst of suffering, Jesus walked by faith and taught his followers to take up their cross daily, surrender self-centered desires, and live in humble obedience. To follow him means extending forgiveness even to those who seem least deserving, and offering grace when the wounds inflicted by others feel unbearable.

As C. S. Lewis wrote, "To be a Christian means to forgive the inexcusable because God has forgiven the inexcusable in you." [69] Jesus taught that we are called to forgive, regardless of the character of the offender. We forgive even when the wrong seems irreparable or when the one who hurt us has become our enemy. In those moments, we remember that God will ultimately and perfectly judge all sin. His justice is flawless, and his mercy toward believers is secure, because their judgment has already fallen upon Jesus. God does not overlook unrepentant evil; instead, we pray for our enemies, asking him to lead them to repentance.

Jesus also calls us to pursue reconciliation. His death and resurrection had a central purpose: to reconcile us to God. Once dead in our sins, we are made alive through his redeeming love and restored to a right relationship with him.

Reconciliation is both vital and beautiful, yet Scripture also offers guidance for times when reconciliation may not be possible, appropriate, or safe. This truth prepares us for the next section on boundaries. At first, it may seem to conflict with the call to forgive. Yet Scripture and sound wisdom show that genuine forgiveness and healthy boundaries are not opposites; they often, and at times must, coexist.

The Wisdom of Boundaries

Earlier in this chapter, we saw Peter Miller forgive his enemy, walking miles through the snow to save the very man who had severely wronged him. His example shows how God can transform unbearably difficult circumstances into opportunities for reconciliation. Like Peter, we are called to pursue peace whenever we can.

At the same time, Scripture calls us to exercise discernment, especially when dealing with those who appear godly but show little evidence of true transformation. Paul warned Timothy about this very danger: "But understand this, that in the last days there will come times of difficulty. For people will be lovers of self, lovers of money, proud, arrogant, abusive, disobedient to their parents, ungrateful, unholy, heartless, unappeasable, slanderous, without self-control, brutal, not loving good, treacherous, reckless, swollen with conceit, lovers of pleasure rather than lovers of God, having the appearance of godliness, but denying its power. Avoid such people" (2 Timothy 3:1–5).

Paul's warning reminds us that it is unwise to pursue reconciliation with someone whose character consistently displays harmful patterns. While we are always called to forgive from the heart, wisdom calls us to exercise caution when a person shows harmful behavior and refuses to change. Reconciliation can be especially painful within the family where broken trust and unsafe dynamics make restoration difficult. When abuse is present, setting firm and protective boundaries is not only appropriate but essential.

One of the most common misconceptions about forgiveness is that it requires restoring a relationship to the way it was before the offense. In reality, forgiveness and boundaries can, and often must, exist together. We can release someone from the debt they owe while still protecting ourselves and others from further harm. Healthy boundaries often make genuine reconciliation possible, because they prevent repeated injury and create space for healing.

Jesus modeled the wise and healthy use of boundaries. When the Pharisees tried to trap him with questions, he did not always respond directly. Sometimes, he answered with a question of his own; other times, he redirected the conversation or quietly stepped away. Once, when an angry crowd tried to throw him off a cliff, he passed safely through their midst and continued on his way. [70] He also reminded his disciples to be "wise as serpents and innocent as doves." [71] Jesus taught, "Do not give dogs what is holy, and do not throw your pearls before pigs" (Matthew 7:6). His words encourage us to recognize unhealthy patterns, reminding us that genuine love sometimes requires setting healthy boundaries.

Paul offered similar guidance to the believers in Corinth, instructing them not to associate with anyone claiming to follow Jesus while continuing in deliberate, unrepentant sin. [72] These examples illustrate that love often calls for distance and protective boundaries.

Gates, Not Walls

Considering the analogy of a city with walls and gates, in biblical times walls offered safety, while gates allowed movement and connection. During peaceful seasons, gates remained open, welcoming trade and fellowship; in times of danger, they were wisely closed to protect those within. Healthy boundaries function like gates rather than walls; they protect while remaining flexible, closing when necessary but opening again as trust and safety are restored. A wall built from unforgiveness shuts people out completely, but a gate shaped by wisdom opens or closes according to the situation. Gates embody both protection and hope: they may remain closed temporarily while trust is renewed, but they are never meant to stay shut forever.

Consider how these contrasts help picture the difference:

- A wall declares, "There will be no more conversation." A gate responds, "Forgiveness is always available, yet the gate remains closed until genuine change takes root and peace can be restored."
- A wall says, "This relationship is over." A gate responds, "Love remains, but the gate stays closed while destructive behaviors continue. Steady commitment to sobriety and responsibility will open it again."
- A wall states, "The wrong will never be forgotten." A gate responds, "Forgiveness has been granted, but trust can open only through honest acknowledgment of sin and genuine transformation."

Several guiding principles can help us set healthy, God-honoring boundaries while maintaining a forgiving heart. Forgiveness releases the pain of the past, and boundaries protect against future harm. At times, boundaries must remain firm, yet they should also be flexible enough to respond to genuine repentance and lasting change, always guided by proven trust rather than words alone.

Setting healthy boundaries requires discernment and grace. What works in one season may need to change in another—which is why prayer, the guidance of the Holy Spirit, and wise counsel are so important. Love must always guide the establishment of boundaries, not revenge. The goal is restoration and safety, not punishment. In certain situations—especially when addiction, trauma, or mental illness are involved—seeking professional support or godly counsel is not a sign of weak faith but a demonstration of genuine trust in God's healing work. Healthy boundaries remind us that love is never careless; it protects and preserves what is good. Even as we guard the future with wisdom, we remember that forgiveness and boundaries are not opposites; they walk together in harmony under God's guidance.

Anger's False Promises

Perhaps we may genuinely want to forgive. We pray about it. We tell ourselves we are ready to let it go. Yet just when we think we have released the offense, anger resurfaces—quietly at first, then with familiar force. It pulls us back into secret thoughts and renewed bitterness.

What is anger? Webster's 1828 *American Dictionary of the English Language* defines it as "a violent passion of the mind excited by a real or supposed injury; usually accompanied with a propensity to take vengeance, or to obtain satisfaction from the offending party." This definition shows that when forgiveness feels inappropriate, it is likely because anger is active—quietly motivating us to seek satisfaction rather than release.

Anger often can make promises we do not recognize as false. Beneath the surface, we can hold mistaken beliefs about what anger does for us. Without consciously choosing to, we can begin to rely on anger—believing it protects us, empowers us, validates our pain, or ensures justice. These beliefs feel reasonable, even necessary. But though anger presents itself as a safeguard, it ultimately becomes an obstacle. Instead of leading us toward freedom, it quietly blocks forgiveness and makes reconciliation feel unsafe or unreachable.

One common belief is, *"I need the anger to protect me."* Anger feels like a shield. If we let it go, we fear we will be exposed to further harm. Anger keeps us alert, guarded, and emotionally braced for the next wound. Yet Scripture points us elsewhere for protection. "For God alone my soul waits in silence; from him comes my salvation. He alone is my rock and my salvation, my fortress; I shall not be greatly shaken" (Psalm 62:1–2). Anger does not protect the heart; it isolates it. It keeps us locked in vigilance, unable to rest or trust. Forgiveness, practiced with appropriate boundaries, frees us from the exhausting role of self-defense. We cannot forgive while believing anger is our protector. The two cannot exist together.

Another promise anger makes is, "I need the anger to empower me." Without it, we fear weakness or loss of control. Anger can feel energizing, even enlightening, especially when we have been wronged. But this strength is deceptive. Anger consumes more energy than it supplies. It drains us emotionally, spiritually, and relationally. Scripture reminds us where true strength is found: "But he said to me, 'My grace is sufficient for you, for my power is made perfect in weakness.' Therefore I will boast all the more gladly of my weaknesses, so that the power of Christ may rest upon me" (2 Corinthians 12:9). Forgiveness may feel like surrender, but in truth it is courage—a quiet confidence that God is sufficient to uphold us. Anger keeps us locked in a power struggle; forgiveness releases us from it.

Anger also whispers, *"I need this to validate the wrong."* If we release anger, it can feel as though we are minimizing what happened or excusing the offense. Anger seems to prove that the wound was real. But forgiveness does not deny the pain; it names it honestly. Forgiveness says, *"This mattered deeply. This* caused real harm. And I choose to release you anyway." Scripture assures us that God himself acknowledges our pain: "The Lord is near to the brokenhearted and saves the crushed in spirit" (Psalm 34:18). Our pain does not need anger to be legitimate. God sees it fully, and he draws near without anger as proof.

Finally, anger promises justice: "If I let this go, they get away with it." This belief is often the most persuasive. Anger feels like a moral stance, a way of holding someone accountable when no apology has come and no restitution has been made. Yet Scripture consistently reminds us that final justice does not rest in human hands. When we cling to anger as a form of justice, we assume a burden we were never meant to carry. Anger does not punish the offender; it binds the wounded. Forgiveness does not mean that the wrong no longer matters—it means we entrust judgment to the only righteous Judge.

These beliefs rarely announce themselves openly. They live quietly beneath the surface, shaping our reactions and sabotaging our attempts at forgiveness. Anger promises protection, power, validation, and justice—but delivers none of them. Instead, it binds us to the very offense we long to escape. When forgiveness feels impossible, it is often because we are still believing that anger is necessary for our survival or our righteousness.

Replacing Anger's Lies with God's Truth

Lasting change does not begin by suppressing anger or forcing ourselves to forgive before we are ready. It begins when we allow God to expose the beliefs that keep anger in place. Until those beliefs are confronted, forgiveness often feels like loss rather than freedom.

This process requires humility and patience. Many of us respond to anger by either indulging it or condemning ourselves for feeling it. Yet anger is often a signal pointing to something deeper. When we pause long enough to ask what we believe anger is doing for us, God often reveals the false promise beneath it. Scripture reminds us that our own hearts are not always reliable guides: "The heart is deceitful above all things, and desperately sick; who can understand it?" (Jeremiah 17:9). We need God's truth to uncover what we cannot clearly see on our own.

It is it helpful to take time for quiet, prayerful reflection when anger resurfaces. This is not a formula or technique, but a posture of honesty before God. In a quiet moment, we can allow the anger to surface without justifying it or pushing it away. Then we can name the belief beneath it.

If we wait without rushing, God often brings clarity—not always through dramatic insight, but through gentle conviction by the Holy Spirit, or, with a Scripture brought to mind. Writing down what we sense—a word, a verse, or a settled truth—can help anchor us when the old belief returns. Scripture consistently points us back to God as our refuge and strength: "The Lord is my rock and my fortress and my deliverer... my shield, and the horn of my salvation, my stronghold" (Psalm 18:2). In this way, anger becomes a reminder to talk with God, our real source of help.

This is rarely a one-time experience. Deep wounds produce deeply rooted beliefs, and those beliefs often resurface. Forgiveness, especially in painful family relationships, is frequently a process. Yet each time we bring the anger back to God and allow truth to confront the lie, the grip weakens. Over time, the anger fades—not because the offense disappeared or the other person changed, but because we stopped believing we needed the anger as we learned to trust God more fully.

Many have discovered that the turning point in forgiveness is not greater effort, but greater trust. When we stop relying on anger to do what only God can do, forgiveness no longer feels like loss. It begins to feel like release. We find ourselves less consumed, less guarded, and more free. One day, often quietly, we realize something has changed. The memory may still be there. The injustice may still be real. But the anger no longer rules our heart. We are free—not because the past was erased, but because we finally trusted God the way he intended us to. We no longer need the anger. He is faithful. We can let go.

Where Is Justice?

Forgiveness and justice are not enemies but companions. Forgiveness releases bitterness, while justice implemented by Godly authority protects the innocent and restrains wrongdoing. Personal forgiveness and public justice are not rivals; each serves a distinct purpose. Forgiveness heals the heart, while justice addresses the harm done to others and to the wider community. They work in harmony, not in conflict, as expressions of faithful discipleship. Yet even when justice is served, forgiveness can still feel out of reach. In those moments, Scripture directs us to the life of faith as the way forward.

Jesus teaches us to forgive not as a feeling, but as an act of obedience. Forgiveness does not excuse sin, erase consequences, or remove accountability; it speaks to the condition of the heart before God. At the same time, Scripture makes clear that justice belongs to God: "Beloved, never avenge yourselves, but leave it to the wrath of God, for it is written, 'Vengeance is mine, I will repay, says the Lord." (Romans 12:19).

God also appoints civil authority to "be the servant of God, an avenger who carries out God's wrath on the wrongdoer" (Romans 13:4). Scripture recognizes that discernment and righteous judgment are sometimes necessary because God delegates this responsibility. Parents are called to lovingly correct their children, teachers to guide and discipline their students, and leaders to uphold truth for the good of those they serve.

Jesus' warning against hypocritical judgment in Matthew 7:1-5 does not forbid wise evaluation; rather, it calls us to exercise judgment with humility and fairness. He taught, "Do not judge by appearances, but judge with right judgment." (John 7:24). God entrusts certain roles with the responsibility of moral and practical guidance, and even these judgments must be exercised in love, truth, and submission to his authority. True judgment, when rightly practiced, seeks correction rather than condemnation and reflects the character of a God, who is both just and merciful.

Reporting wrongdoing or cooperating with lawful authorities can honor God's justice. Forgiveness and justice are not opposed; they work together. One frees the heart from bitterness, while the other protects the innocent and restrains evil.

Yet even after justice has been served, the call to forgive can feel far beyond our strength. In such moments, the heart needs more than determination; it needs divine help. Scripture reminds us that the life of faith is the path forward, where grace accomplishes what human effort alone cannot.

Walking by Faith

Christians are called to undertake a journey of living by faith, as it is written, "The righteous shall live by faith" (Romans 1:17). Yet not all believers make this a daily pattern. Scripture gives us profound insight into what it truly means to walk by faith—which is to rely completely on Jesus, rather than depending on our own strength or seeking the approval of others. As Paul wrote: "I have been crucified with Christ. It is no longer I who live, but Christ who lives in me. And the life I now live in the flesh I live by faith in the Son of God, who loved me and gave himself for me" (Galatians 2:20).

This truth reminds us that our lives are no longer centered on ourselves. Jesus now dwells within his people, shaping their desires and guiding their steps. When his life is expressed in us, the natural result is a Spirit-led Walk, marked by the fruit of the Spirit and a growing resistance to the cravings of the flesh.

A powerful example of surrender and faith can be seen in the lives of Shadrach, Meshach, and Abednego. When King Nebuchadnezzar commanded everyone to bow before his golden image, they refused. Their steadfast response stands as one of the most remarkable declarations of trust in all Scripture: "Our God, whom we serve, is able to deliver us from the burning fiery furnace, and he will deliver us out of your hand, O king. But if not, be it known to you, O king, that we will not serve your gods or worship the golden image that you have set up" (Daniel 3:17-18). They trusted in God's power to save them, yet even if he chose otherwise, they remained steadfast in their devotion. This is the essence of walking by faith: obeying God even when the outcome is uncertain.

Galatians 5:16-24 describes the spiritual transformation that accompanies walking by the Spirit:

But I say, walk by the Spirit, and you will not gratify the desires of the flesh. For the desires of the flesh are against the Spirit, and the desires of the Spirit are against the flesh, for these are opposed to each other, to keep you from doing the things you want to do. But if you are led by the Spirit, you are not under the law. Now the works of the flesh are evident: sexual immorality, impurity, sensuality, idolatry, sorcery, enmity, strife, jealousy, fits of anger, rivalries, dissensions, divisions, envy, drunkenness, orgies, and things like these. I warn you, as I warned you before, that those who do such things will not inherit the kingdom of God. But the fruit of the Spirit is love, joy, peace, patience, kindness, goodness, faithfulness, gentleness, self-control; against such things there is no law. And those who belong to Christ Jesus have crucified the flesh with its passions and desires.

Walking by faith, as Shadrach, Meshach, and Abednego did, calls us to surrender our will to God, trust his guidance, and let the Spirit bear fruit in our lives, even amid trials. Many of the "works of the flesh", enmity, strife, jealousy, and fits of anger, create the very barriers that make forgiveness so difficult. In contrast, the fruit of the Spirit fosters love, patience, kindness, and self-control, the qualities needed to extend grace to others.

When we listen to the Holy Spirit, our decisions are no longer driven by fleeting perceptions or emotions but by God's

When Forgiveness Seems Impossible

wisdom and guidance. As Hebrews 11:1 teaches, "Faith is the assurance of things hoped for, the conviction of things not seen." This reminds us that the Christian life is lived by faith rather than by sight or human inclination, as affirmed in 2 Corinthians 5:7: "For we walk by faith, not by sight."

Walking in forgiveness means trusting God's promises, even when forgiving does not feel natural. It means believing that he is working all things together for good, even when the outcome is hidden from our sight. It means choosing obedience, even when our emotions pull our hearts toward bitterness. To walk by faith in forgiveness is to obey before the feelings arrive, to trust that God will provide the strength we lack, and to believe that he can redeem what we cannot restore. When we fully trust God, we embrace the wisdom of Proverbs 3:5-6: "Trust in the Lord with all your heart, and do not lean on your own understanding. In all your ways acknowledge him, and he will make straight your paths."

Reading, hearing, and singing Scripture also strengthen the desire to walk by faith: "So faith comes from hearing, and hearing through the word of Christ" (Romans 10:17).

The Faith to Forgive

When forgiveness feels difficult, we can turn to God's Word, which reveals his character and assures us of his promises. Our walk of faith profoundly shapes the way we pray. Scripture calls us to pray with confidence, trusting that God hears us and responds according to his perfect will. As James reminds us, believers should not waver in their faith: "But let him ask in faith, with no doubting, for the one who doubts is like a wave of the sea that is driven and tossed by the wind" (James 1:6).

Philippians 4:6-7 exhorts the church to trust God without doubting: "Do not be anxious about anything, but in everything by prayer and supplication with thanksgiving let your requests be made known to God. And the peace of God, which surpasses all understanding, will guard your hearts and your minds in Christ Jesus." This peace that surpasses all understanding is precisely what we need when forgiveness feels impossible. As we choose to walk by faith, our lives begin to reflect God's goodness through actions that honor him. Jesus taught: "I am the vine; you are the branches. Whoever abides in me and I in him, he it is that bears much fruit, for apart from me you can do nothing" (John 15:5). Paul affirms this truth: "For we are his workmanship, created in Christ Jesus for good works, which God prepared beforehand, that we should walk in them." (Ephesians 2:10). Forgiveness is a good work that God has prepared for his people to walk in. While we cannot accomplish it through our own strength, faith in Jesus empowers our hearts to bear its fruit.

As we conclude this reflection on walking by faith, may our hearts join the prayer of the disciples: "Increase our faith" (Luke 17:5). What does it truly mean to walk by faith, not just to understand it, but to live it daily within our families? Have there been times when we avoided difficult conversations, concealed our wounds instead of addressing them, or delayed obedience even when God was clearly prompting us to act? Let us seek God's guidance together and pray: "Lord, what step of faith would You have us take today and every day?"

Closing Remarks

We have seen how faith sustains us through circumstances that feel impossible, how healthy boundaries can coexist with genuine forgiveness, and how God's justice perfectly aligns with his mercy. We have also witnessed remarkable acts of grace: Peter Miller's long, frozen journey to save his enemy, and Renée's courageous choice to partner in ministry with the man responsible for her daughter's death.

These stories invite a more personal reflection: what if the hardest person to forgive is not someone else, but ourselves? Could the greatest barrier to the freedom described in this chapter be the quiet weight of guilt, shame, or regret? In the next chapter, we will explore these questions and discover how God's grace meets us even there.

Questions for Personal Reflection or Group Discussion

1. When Forgiveness Feels Out of Reach

Some wounds are too deep. Some betrayals too severe. Some pain too fresh.

You want to forgive. You know you should. But you can't. Corrie ten Boom once found herself face to face with someone she could not forgive. She had no forgiveness in her heart. So, she prayed, "Jesus, I cannot forgive. But You can forgive through me." And he did.

Where does forgiveness feel impossible right now? And what would it mean to pray, "Jesus, I cannot forgive on my own but You can forgive through me"?

2. God's Nearness in Deep Pain

When someone has wounded you deeply, you may feel abandoned not just by them, but by God. "Where were you when this happened?" "Why didn't you stop it?" "How could you let this hurt me so much?"

Psalm 34:18 doesn't answer those questions. It says: "The LORD is near to the brokenhearted." Not "The LORD will explain everything." Not "The LORD will fix it immediately." Just: he is near.

When have you felt God's nearness in the midst of pain, even when you didn't get the answers or the healing you wanted? And what would it look like to trust his presence more than you need his explanations?

3. Forgiveness and Timing

Ten years ago, you couldn't even say their name without anger rising. Five years ago, you could talk about it without crying. Today? You're still not "over it." But something has shifted.

Forgiveness isn't always instant. Sometimes it's layers. Waves. A slow thaw. What does "partial forgiveness" look like for you right now? And what would it mean to trust God with the timeline, even when it feels too slow?

4. Boundaries and Forgiveness

You've forgiven them. You really have. The bitterness is gone. But you're keeping your distance. Maybe for good reason they're not safe yet. The pattern hasn't changed. Some people think forgiveness means opening the gate immediately. But sometimes wisdom says: "I forgive you, but the gate stays closed until trust can be rebuilt."

Is there someone you've genuinely forgiven but are wisely keeping at a distance? How do you know the difference between a healthy boundary and unforgiveness hiding behind "wisdom"?

CHAPTER 10
The Source of All Forgiveness

The previous chapter explored how living by faith enables us to extend forgiveness to others, even when pain or difficult circumstances weigh heavily upon us. This chapter turns our attention toward our own forgiveness. How do we personally experience forgiveness? Can we find lasting freedom from the spiritual and emotional prisons created by our own sins and past wounds? We'll see that although self-forgiveness often falls short, God's forgiveness brings genuine and lasting freedom; and how we can confront the burdens of guilt, shame, regret, trauma, and unresolved sorrow, including grief for those who have passed away. Our first consideration will be the notion of forgiving ourselves, a familiar but often misunderstood idea.

Finding Our Own Forgiveness

Scripture does not give a direct command to forgive ourselves. This concept emerged largely from modern psychology and self-help culture. Many voices encourage self-forgiveness as a path to emotional healing, linking it to self-esteem, personal strength, or independence. These ideas can seem appealing, but they differ from Scripture, which emphasizes humility and our God-given need to receive forgiveness from him.

In today's digital world, this struggle can feel even more intense. Social media often shows idealized images of other people's lives, making our private battles and hidden weaknesses harder to bear. We may find ourselves questioning why we fall short and why past mistakes continue to weigh on us.

Sometimes, the desire for self-forgiveness stems more from wanting to appear good or worthy in the eyes of others than from genuine repentance before God. C. S. Lewis described it this way, "The Christian is in a different position from other people who are trying to be good. He does not think God will love us because we are good, but that God will make us good because he loves us." [73] In other words, the heart of personal forgiveness is not about proving our worth; it is about trusting in God's steadfast love and receiving the grace he freely offers.

Attempts at self-forgiveness can become spiritually unhelpful when they lead us toward either pride or self-pity. Though these responses seem different, both turn our attention inward instead of upward. When our focus is on ourselves rather than on God, we risk becoming disconnected from others and from the one who alone can forgive, restore, and heal.

Accepting God's Forgiveness

God freely offers forgiveness, yet we must choose to receive it. His forgiveness is never forced upon us but patiently extended as from an open, steady hand; yet pride often keeps us from taking hold of it, telling us that we must fix ourselves first or earn the right to feel forgiven. God invites us to rest in the completed work of Jesus on the cross, which is fully sufficient. Nothing we do can add to it or make it more complete.

When we hesitate to accept God's forgiveness, we remain weighed down by fear and guilt. Receiving forgiveness is not an act of self-reliance but an act of surrender to God's love. It means agreeing with him that his mercy is greater than our sin and trusting that his Word is true, even when our emotions have not yet caught up.

When We Struggle to Feel Forgiven

When we struggle to feel forgiven, we can turn to the Holy Spirit for help. He softens our pride, heals our shame, and guides our hearts to trust fully in what Jesus has already accomplished. Even a simple, sincere prayer like this can bring profound change to our lives: *"Holy Spirit, I permit you to change my heart. Where I struggle to believe that I am forgiven, help me to fully receive your mercy. Strengthen my faith and teach me to rest in the forgiveness that Jesus provides. Please deliver me from pride, silence my fear, and let your peace settle deeply within me. In Jesus' name, Amen."*

How Pride Shows Itself

Pride often shows itself in two ways. Sometimes it takes the form of arrogance, leading us to downplay our faults and believe we have little need for God's forgiveness. At other times, it masquerades as self-pity, trapping us in shame and convincing us that God's grace could never reach us. Both forms turn our gaze inward instead of upward, keeping our hearts from the freedom God desires for us. Our worth is not defined by our successes, nor is it diminished by our failures. It is firmly rooted in God's love, freely given through the forgiveness Jesus paid for.

When We Keep Records Against Ourselves

Previously we addressed the truth that love "keeps no record of wrongs" toward others. That same principle applies to how we view ourselves. The ledger principle discussed earlier also extends to our own failures. When we choose not to keep a record of our mistakes, we free ourselves from replaying both real and imagined sins.

Many of us quietly carry an internal list of regrets, as though maintaining secret spiritual ledgers. Yet God invites us to release those ledgers into his hands. He alone is the true soul accountant; and as we trust in Jesus' finished work on the cross, he has already declared our debts, both real and imagined, paid in full. Paul wrote, "And you, who were dead in your trespasses and the uncircumcision of your flesh, God made alive together with him, having forgiven us all our trespasses by canceling the record of debt that stood against us with its legal demands. This he set aside, nailing it to the cross" (Colossians 2:13-14). Rather than striving to absolve ourselves, we are invited to trust in a forgiving Lord: "For you, O Lord, are good and forgiving, abounding in steadfast love to all who call upon you" (Psalm 86:5).

The Joyful Heart

The forgiveness we receive from God creates a ripple effect, filling our hearts with a joy that blesses our families and relationships. To understand this more deeply, we first need to consider what a joyful heart truly is. Looking on each word individually (joyful and heart) helps us grasp the full meaning.

Joy is a God-given delight, happiness, or gladness that runs deeper than our circumstances. This joy is a gift from God, experienced even in life's most difficult moments. It is not a fleeting emotion or a temporary feeling of happiness. As one trusted commentator explains, "Joy is not an isolated or occasional consequence of faith, but an integral part of one's whole relation to God." [74] True joy is strengthened by the grace, love, and mercy that God alone provides. Because it comes from him, we can confidently say "Joy is a delight in life that runs deeper than pain or pleasure." [75]

The word heart carries deep significance. It is "the center or focus of a person's inner life." [76] Our heart reveals our authentic self and can be the source of either evil or righteousness. At times, it may harbor sinful traits such as bitterness, envy, lust, pride, or rage. Yet it can also reflect the fruit of the Spirit: cheerfulness, diligence, joy, love, and wisdom.

When joy and the heart come together, a joyful heart emerges as a God-given, internal part of life that is integral to our relationship with him. It provides a contentment and delight rooted in righteousness, regardless of our circumstances.

It is important to notice the practical fruit of a joyful heart, which offers many lasting benefits. Proverbs 17:22 states, "A joyful heart is good medicine." It inspires hope, encourages peace, and brings perspective. Charles Spurgeon once said, "There is a marvelous medicinal power in joy. Most medicines are distasteful, but this, which is the best of all medicines, is sweet to the taste and comforting to the heart." [77] A joyful heart also naturally encourages reconciliation. Why? Because the condition of our heart shapes our words, tone, and expressions.

Joy is not merely personal it has relational power. A joyful spirit eases conflict, nurtures peace, and strengthens our efforts to restore broken relationships. It uplifts not only the one who carries it but also everyone in the household.

That Your Joy May Be Full

Yet joy goes beyond an inward feeling. Scripture links joy directly to our faith and obedience—a joyful heart flows from walking by faith, trusting Jesus, following his commandments, and relying on him completely. Jesus taught that obedient trust brings fullness of joy, as described in John 15:9–11: "Abide in my love. If you keep my commandments, you will abide in my love, just as I have kept my Father's commandments and abide in his love. These things I have spoken to you, that my joy may be in you, and that your joy may be full."

To maintain joy, we must remain anchored in God's love. This means cultivating a deep, personal relationship with Jesus; not merely acknowledging who he is, but truly living in a close and healthy connection with him. From a mental and emotional perspective, the *Evangelical Dictionary of Theology* notes: "One cannot experience joy while being preoccupied with one's own security, pleasure, or self-interest." [78] It also observes that "Joy is a gift of God, and like all his other gifts, it can be experienced even in the midst of extremely difficult circumstances." [79] However, joy is only complete when we have not just belief in but a true relationship with him. As James 2:19 says, "You believe that God is one; you do well. Even the demons believe, and shudder!"

And knowing about Jesus is not the same as having a

relationship with him. A true, abiding relationship grows from a living connection and ongoing trust in him. This kind of relationship naturally leads to obedience to his commandments, a devotion that is neither burdensome nor joyless. As 1 John 5:3 explains: "For this is the love of God, that we keep his commandments. His commandments are not burdensome." Joy flourishes in the soil of obedience, not because obedience earns God's love, but because it roots us in a steadfast and trustworthy love. Jesus desires that our joy be complete. As noted above, he promises in John 15:11: "That my joy may be in you, and that your joy may be full."

True, abiding joy sustains us through life's most difficult moments and naturally overflows to bless the lives of those around us. The story of Paul and Silas in Acts 16 powerfully illustrates this principle. After being beaten with rods and thrown into prison with their feet secured in stocks, they remained steadfast. Harsh treatment and grim environment notwithstanding, "they were praying and singing hymns to God" (Acts 16:25). Even before the prison walls trembled and the earthquake set them free, they experienced a joy that did not rely on comfort or circumstance. Their story reminds us that true joy comes from the heart, not from external conditions.

This joy sustains and strengthens us as we face life's challenges. James 1:2 exhorts us to "Count it all joy, my brothers, when you meet trials of various kinds." Maintaining joy in difficult times does not mean denying our pain. Instead, it means trusting that God is with us and working for our good, even when the outcome is not yet clear. James continues, "For you know that the testing of your faith produces steadfastness.

And let steadfastness have its full effect, that you may be perfect and complete, lacking in nothing" (James 1:3 4).

Many things can steal our joy and trap us in emotional prisons, with sin, guilt, regret, shame, and painful memories among the most common. Left unaddressed, these forces can drain our joy, isolate us from others, and distort our understanding of God. Breaking free from these strongholds can be challenging, but it is possible. Scripture offers clear guidance and genuine hope for liberation. The journey begins with the primary culprit, sin—the root from which guilt and shame often arise.

Our Sin

Sin brings spiritual death, separating us from intimacy with God and the experience of his goodness. [80] Personal sin can be understood as the voluntary turning away from obedience to God, whether in thought or action. It takes two main forms: sins of commission, which involve actively doing what God forbids, and sins of omission when we fail to do the good we know to do. James 4:17 puts it this way: "So, whoever knows the right thing to do and fails to do it, for him it is sin."

The *Evangelical Dictionary of Theology* describes the essence of sin as "unbelief or hardness of heart, the opposite of a joyful heart." It identifies unbelief, pride, sensuality, and fear as chief manifestations of sin, along with attitudes of self-pity, selfishness, jealousy, and greed. They observe that "the essence of sin is unbelief or hardness of heart [the opposite of a joyful heart]. The chief manifestations of sin are pride, sensuality, and fear. Sin also includes self-pity, selfishness, jealousy, and greed." [81]

If sin separates us from God, guilt acts as a gentle warning, prompting us toward confession and repentance.

Guilt is the Alarm System of the Soul

Living as imperfect human beings in a flawed world constantly reminds us of our shortcomings. We all sin, and when we do, we naturally feel the weight of guilt. It is helpful to define guilt as "the state of a moral agent after intentionally or unintentionally violating a law or principle established by God." [82] Guilt acts as our soul's alarm, alerting us whenever we have strayed from God's standards.

Some may suggest that guilt does not arise merely from breaking external rules but from failing to love God and our neighbors. R. C. Sproul addresses this misunderstanding when he writes: "People have said to me on many occasions that Christianity is not about rules and regulations; it is about love. That is simply not true. Christianity is about love, but that is because love is one of the rules. God commands us to love him and to love one another. Christianity is not just about rules and laws, but rules and laws decreed by God have been a fact of life since the day of creation." [83]

Jesus also clarified that guilt extends beyond external actions. It encompasses the inner attitude of the heart. He says, "You have heard that it was said, 'You shall not commit adultery.' But I say to you that everyone who looks at a woman with lustful intent has already committed adultery with her in his heart" (Matthew 5:27-28).

Guilt can serve a beneficial purpose when we respond to it

wisely. Just as physical pain signals a problem in the body, guilt warns us of a spiritual imbalance. This discomfort gently guides us toward repentance. When we sin, whether through our actions or our omissions, it is natural and right to feel remorse for disobeying God. Yet too often, we try to silence the alarm of guilt by denying it. Denial does not make guilt vanish. As the apostle John writes, "If we say we have no sin, we deceive ourselves, and the truth is not in us" (1 John 1:8).

Healing begins with sincere confession of our sin. Many of us spend years avoiding responsibility for our actions. We may deceive others and even ourselves, but guilt lingers until we bring it honestly before God. Guilt is not meant to be permanent. Imagine a fire alarm in your home blaring nonstop a long time. Eventually, you would address the problem or exhaust yourself by trying to ignore it. In the same way, guilt is meant to guide us toward confession and restoration, not to torment us. The good news is that there is a way to release guilt: "If we confess our sins, he is faithful and just to forgive us our sins and to cleanse us from all unrighteousness" (1 John 1:9). What a beautiful and dependable promise.

Escaping the Cycle of Guilt

Many of us try to ease our guilt through self-punishment, believing mistakenly that our suffering can somehow repay the debt of our sin. The *Evangelical Dictionary of Theology* explains that when we are guilty of sin, "It carries the concept of deserving punishment or payment due, even payment by punishment." [84]

As Steve Brown, a broadcaster, former pastor, and professor, captures this struggle clearly when he writes, "Our natural inclination is to get punished and thereby attempt to be free." He goes on to say, "You will only punish yourself more and, as a result, feel even more guilty. This is a vicious cycle." [85]

Punishment cannot remove guilt; and when we try to carry it alone, we often end up living in fear. Scripture reminds us: "There is no fear in love, but perfect love casts out fear. For fear has to do with punishment, and whoever fears has not been perfected in love" (1 John 4:18). Still, we must be careful, because forgiveness can be either genuine or counterfeit, as the following allegory illustrates.

Lemonade Allegory

Imagine sitting outside on a scorching summer day. The sun blazes overhead, the air hangs heavy, and the heat feels like a weight. Beads of sweat roll down your face, and your parched throat aches for relief. You long for something—anything—cold to drink.

A friend arrives, offering relief; but instead of offering a real drink, they hold up a glowing, eye-catching video screen. On it, a glass of sparkling lemonade shimmers in the light. Ice cubes clink, bubbles rise, and condensation forms of the glass. It looks perfect; but when you reach for it, it is nothing but an image. No matter how convincing, it cannot quench your thirst.

Then another friend steps forward and places a real glass of sparkling lemonade into your hands—chilled and tartly sweet. You lift it eagerly, feeling the cold touch your lips; and as you sip the refreshing liquid, savoring every drop, your thirst is finally quenched.

This contrast illustrates forgiveness. Pride, sometimes disguised as self-forgiveness, is like the video image. While seeming appealing, it is only an illusion. Pride can stir emotion, yet it cannot cleanse the heart. Only God's forgiveness, poured out through Jesus, is the genuine drink that restores the soul.

We might imagine freedom. We might stir feelings of relief. We might even convince ourselves, for a time, that guilt and shame have vanished. Yet until we turn to God, the thirst of the soul remains. The prophet Isaiah describes this longing well: "Let the wicked forsake his way, and the unrighteous man his thoughts; let him return to the Lord, that he may have compassion on him, and to our God, for he will abundantly pardon" (Isaiah 55:7).

But even the most satisfying drink is only effective when received. A glass of lemonade sitting on the table does not quench our thirst until we lift it and drink deeply. Likewise, God's forgiveness becomes real in our lives only when we receive it by faith and turn from sin, trusting that he has fully forgiven us.

But there is the deeper reality: Jesus does not simply offer a refreshing drink for the soul; he offers living water. He said, "Whoever drinks of the water that I will give him will never be thirsty again. The water that I will give him will become in him a spring of water welling up to eternal life" (John 4:14). Lemonade may give us a glimpse of satisfaction, but what we truly need is the living water of God's forgiveness. Only it can fully satisfy; everything else falls short.

Does God Remember Our Sins?

God forgives us. Our sins are not erased from history; but he removes our guilt, pardons us, and sets us free. Though God is omniscient and knows all things, he promises not to remember our forgiven sins. Perhaps this is like a computer drive filled with old files we never open. The information remains, but we no longer access it or even think about it. How God chooses not to remember forgiven sin is a mystery; yet Scripture assures us that he will not hold a Christian's past sins against them. While the mechanics are beyond our understanding, his promise is certain: "I, even I, am he who blots out your transgressions for my own sake, and I will not remember your sins" (Isaiah 43:25).

This promise is echoed in the New Testament. All who believe in Jesus enter into a new covenant, and God promises that he will remember their forgiven sins and lawless deeds no more. As it is written: "I will remember their sins and their lawless deeds no more" (Hebrews 10:17). What a marvelous promise to cherish!

Shame

Guilt and shame often appear together, but they are not the same. It's easy to confuse them, because shame frequently accompanies guilt. Yet, a person can feel shame without having done anything wrong, or experience guilt without feeling ashamed.

So, what is shame? It encompasses a wide range of emotions, yet its deepest pain comes from rejection and separation. While guilt focuses on our wrongdoing or failure, shame reflects how we feel devalued or disgraced in the eyes of others. One dictionary definition puts it plainly: "Shame brings reproach and degrades a person in the estimation of others." [86]

With that in mind, we can see how Jesus bore shame for us. Matthew records that before his crucifixion, a battalion of more than 120 soldiers mocked and humiliated him. They stripped him, dressed him in a scarlet robe to ridicule his royalty, and placed a crown of thorns on his head—all while jeering, "Hail, King of the Jews." They beat him, spat on him, struck him on the head, and scourged him with a multi-lashed whip. Then the Romans publicly crucified him, a method of execution intentionally designed to maximize humiliation. But Scripture says Jesus "despised the shame" and endured it—not because it had power over him, but because he looked forward to the joy and victory it would bring to us (see Hebrews 12:2).

How should we respond when we experience shame? The key is having a clear sense of identity. When we understand who we are in Jesus, we can face shame with confidence. As the Bible reminds us, "Therefore, if anyone is in Christ, he is a new creation. The old has passed away; behold, the new has come" (2 Corinthians 5:17). As new creations in God's image, we no longer need the approval of others; rather, we are called to focus our minds on heavenly things. "If then you have been raised with Christ, seek the things that are above, where Christ is, seated at the right hand of God...For you have died, and your life is hidden with Christ in God. When Christ, who is your life, appears, then you also will appear with him in glory" (Colossians 3:1-4).

This forward-looking mindset helps us stay focused on the future rather than being held back by the past. Jesus emphasized this truth when he said, "No one who puts his hand to the plow and looks back is fit for the kingdom of God" (Luke 9:62). Just as a farmer cannot plow straight rows while looking backward, we cannot experience true victory if we dwell on humiliation and shame. Therefore, we must rise above shame, especially when it comes from others. Condemnation often comes from those who wish to shame us, yet we are not obliged to accept their judgment, especially when our reverence for God outweighs our trust in people. As Proverbs 29:25 tells us, "The fear of man lays a snare, but whoever trusts in the Lord is safe."

When we rest securely in God's love, we find the strength to face shame and rise above it. In doing so, we are called to follow Jesus' example by forgiving those who seek to harm or humiliate us. Even while being mocked, scourged, and crucified, he prayed, "Father, forgive them, for they know not what they do" (Luke 23:34). Many who shame us are themselves guilty of gossip, slander, or false judgment. Their actions are not rooted in love, yet we are still called to forgive.

Shame is not the only burden we carry; we also face the deep pain of regret.

Regret and Wrestling with "What If"

Regret can arise from sin, poor choices, or the pressures of life. It often comes in the form of "could have, should have" memories: missed opportunities, painful decisions, or words left unspoken. Perhaps we failed to visit a loved one in the hospital before their death, sold a stock just before it skyrocketed in value, or missed a life-changing opportunity. We may have lost a relationship, not because of wrongdoing, but because we did not fully express how deeply we cared. Regrets can weigh heavily on us. Even when they do not stem from sin, they still affect us emotionally and may lead us to wonder whether we missed God's will. At times, our regrets arise from moments when we truly did miss his guidance, leaving us to wrestle with "what if" and the pain of what might have been.

How should we respond when regret lingers? Often, the best response is to face the truth honestly. Scripture calls us to cultivate gratitude in every circumstance, even when we feel regret. As Paul writes, "Rejoice always, pray without ceasing, give thanks in all circumstances; for this is the will of God in Christ Jesus for you" (1 Thessalonians 5:16-18). Even in times of loss or disappointment, our hearts can still rejoice. We are called to give thanks in every circumstance, trusting that God is present in both joy and sorrow. Matthew Henry observed, "In him our joy will be full, and it will be our fault if we have not a continual feast. If we are sorrowful upon any worldly account, yet still we may always rejoice. A religious life is a pleasant life; it is a life of constant joy." [87]

As we reflect on our regrets, we must also remember God's sovereignty.

Trusting God's Sovereignty

The Scriptures teach that God is the supreme ruler of all creation, governing the universe with perfect wisdom, justice, and power. Nothing happens outside his authority, and everything he allows aligns with his holy character and divine purpose.

We may never fully comprehend God's sovereignty, for his ways surpass human understanding, yet we can embrace it in faith. His sovereignty is vast and often mysterious, sometimes challenging to grasp. As the prophet Isaiah reflects: "I [the Lord] form light and create darkness; I make well-being and create calamity; I am the Lord, who does all these things" (Isaiah 45:7). Understanding this can be challenging, yet it invites us to trust God even when circumstances feel confusing or painful. We can rely on God's sovereignty, which encompasses not only his authority but also his goodness. He accomplishes all that he intends, fulfills every promise, and acts in ways that reveal both his power and his compassion.

Even when we do not grasp the reasons behind what he allows, we can remain confident that he is holy, just, and purposeful in all of his actions. God can transform our regrets, mistakes, pain, and losses into a part of his perfect plan for our lives. As we reflect on this truth, we find comfort and can proclaim with the psalmist: "Oh give thanks to the Lord, for he is good, for his steadfast love endures forever" (Psalm 107:1).

While trusting in God's sovereignty can bring peace in the midst of regret, certain events leave wounds that run deeper than ordinary remorse, causing emotional pain that lingers. It is important to understand the impact of trauma, and that God's healing can restore hope and bring true restoration.

Healing From Trauma

Trauma can leave lasting scars, like hidden shrapnel embedded in the soul. It can arise from abuse, accidents, betrayal, war, violence, or sudden loss, often leaving deep emotional wounds and sometimes leading to post-traumatic stress disorder — the natural psychological response to overwhelming events. Throughout history, people have endured trauma; and as pastor, counsellor, and author Timothy S. Lane observes: "Read any part of the Bible, and you will see that horrific, traumatic events have been part of the world since the fall of humanity...Life in this world is full of trauma, suffering, and hurt."[88]

Many traumatic experiences are closely intertwined with grief, the deep sorrow that arises from what has been lost or broken. Webster's 1828 *American Dictionary of the English Language* defines grief as "the pain of mind produced by loss, misfortune, injury, or evils of any kind; sorrow; regret."[89] This highlights how grief and trauma often overlap, both striking the soul and leaving wounds that cry out for healing.

It is comforting to know that God is near to the brokenhearted. "The Lord is near to the brokenhearted and saves the crushed in spirit" (Psalm 34:18). We also find strength in the fact that Jesus himself experienced trauma. Scripture says he was "a man of sorrows, and acquainted with grief" (Isaiah 53:3). His sorrows included betrayal, rejection, and the brutal suffering of being whipped and crucified. Because he carried both trauma and grief in his body and soul, he is uniquely able to understand our experience of those things.

Trauma is complex, and healing is often a journey. For some, relief may come quickly; for many, it unfolds slowly over months or even years. Without healing, people can continue to experience persistent symptoms such as anxiety, despair, emotional numbness, or flashbacks. Yet the transformative power of a relationship with Jesus brings hope for recovery. Timothy S. Lane explains where this hope begins: "Acknowledging and believing in your future resurrection and who you are as a child of God will enable you to move forward each day. You will grow in peace and stability as you interact with God in light of this profound relationship you have with him." He also emphasizes that deliverance does not come through "a cognitive exercise where you replace falsehood with truth," but rather through "an actual relationship you have with a personal, redeeming God." [90]

Trauma does not have the final word. In the midst of our darkest moments, Jesus walks with us towards the light, just as he promised. "Come to me, all who labor and are heavy laden, and I will give you rest. Take my yoke upon you, and learn from me, for I am gentle and lowly in heart, and you will find rest for your souls. For my yoke is easy, and my burden is light" (Matthew 11:28–30). Healing may be gradual, but we can still experience rest and victory. Whether our wounds come from trauma or grief, or both, we can bring them to the same Savior who bore sorrow and suffering on our behalf.

The Path to Healing

If your trauma involves immediate danger, such as abuse or thoughts of self-harm, seek help immediately from local authorities, trusted pastors, or counsellors. Scripture reminds us that seeking wisdom and protection is not a sign of unbelief, but an act of obedience. "The prudent sees danger and hides himself, but the simple go on and suffer for it" (Proverbs 27:12).

Even when there is no immediate danger, we may still need help. Scripture does not present spiritual healing and professional care as rivals; they complement one another and often work together. Wise stewardship of our pain can include seeking guidance from trained biblically-grounded counsellors, and pastors who understand trauma and handle Scripture with care. This is not a sign of weak faith but an expression of it. These helpers provide safety, patience, and practical tools to process memories, regulate the body's stress responses, and rebuild trust and joy—all while keeping Jesus at the center. God often weaves together personal faith, and professional care to bring true restoration.

Prayer, worship, and the guidance of the Holy Spirit are also vital for our healing. As Romans 8:26 reminds us, "The Spirit helps us in our weakness. For we do not know what to pray for as we ought, but the Spirit himself intercedes for us with groanings too deep for words. Finally, our church family has an important role in supporting one another, carrying each other's burdens as Galatians 6:2 instructs: "Bear one another's burdens, and so fulfill the law of Christ." In Jesus, trauma does not mark the end of the story. Instead, it becomes the place where God's mercy and healing power shine most clearly.

Another aspect of forgiving ourselves relates to the path of forgiving someone who has passed away.

Forgiving Those Who Have Died

As noted in Chapter 1, we can forgive those who have passed away by choosing to release anger and let go of bitterness; but few burdens cut deeper than unresolved conflict with someone we cherish after their death. When conflicts or deep hurts have gone unaddressed, the death of parents, spouses, siblings, or friends often leaves us mourning not only the loved one but also the broken relationship we can no longer repair. This double grief, losing both the person and the possibility of reconciliation, explains why forgiveness in these moments is particularly weighty. A variety of emotions may surface: guilt over words spoken or left unsaid, anger that reconciliation is no longer possible, regret for missed opportunities, confusion about how to forgive without dialogue, and loneliness from carrying pain without closure.

Many people also fear that forgiveness might excuse the offense. Some worry that forgiving someone who has died implies the person "gets away with" their harmful actions. God is the ultimate judge, fully aware of all things and perfectly just in his judgments. Our forgiveness does not alter his evaluation of a person, nor does it excuse their sin. Instead, forgiveness frees us from bitterness while entrusting justice and mercy to God. When we maintain a loving heart, we can trust that God's mercy will graciously embrace the one we forgive. Judgment belongs to God alone, yet Scripture assures us that he desires to show mercy. As James 2:13 states, "Mercy triumphs over judgment." For all who belong to Jesus, mercy ultimately prevails. By forgiving others, we align our hearts with God's heart, trusting that his mercy endures.

Forgiveness primarily benefits the one who forgives. When we release another's debt, we experience a freedom that does not depend on their response. Jesus forgave those who crucified him, even as they mocked him (Luke 23:34). Their lack of repentance did not diminish the reality of his forgiveness. In the same way, we can forgive the deceased, trusting that God knows the full story of our suffering, their struggles, and the outcome. He will judge or show mercy according to his perfect love.

At the same time, we must acknowledge the full spectrum of our emotions. We should not suppress anger, regret, or sorrow simply because the person has passed away. True forgiveness cannot occur when we hide the truth about what we are forgiving

Expressing What We Cannot Say

Many find comfort in writing a private letter never sent, kept only between themselves and God, to express everything they wish they could resolve with the deceased. In this letter can be shared the impact of their actions, our longing for reconciliation, our choice to forgive, and even the love or appreciation that remains in our hearts despite the pain. While this practice is not required, it can help us pray with greater honesty. Whether or not we write a letter, personal prayer remains vital, because forgiveness is ultimately an act of surrender to God. Here is a sample prayer: *Dear Heavenly Father, I come to you with a burden too heavy to bear alone. You see the hurt that remains. Though I cannot speak to them in person, I choose to forgive and release them from all debts of abuse, lack of love, or neglect.*

You teach us to forgive in the same way that you have forgiven us. I am thankful that you forgave me. Please heal the wounds in my heart, remove any root of bitterness, and fill me with your peace. I entrust all matters of justice and judgment to you, while hoping that your mercy will triumph over judgment. Help me walk in freedom, renewed by your love, even when reconciliation on earth is not possible. In Jesus' name, Amen.

When grief feels particularly heavy or complicated, pastoral or professional support can be invaluable, guiding us through unresolved emotions and offering tools to move toward wholeness. For believers, death is not the end of the story. Even if reconciliation does not happen in this life, we can hold fast to God's promise: "He will wipe away every tear from their eyes, and death shall be no more, neither shall there be mourning, nor crying, nor pain anymore" (Revelation 21:4). One day, brokenness and relational pain will be gone forever. In the meantime, choosing forgiveness even toward those who have died honors God, frees our hearts, and strengthens our love for those who remain with us.

In concluding this chapter, it is important to remember that Christian growth is a journey. It does not happen instantly but unfolds gradually—day by day, step by step, as God's grace shapes our hearts and transforms our relationships.

Sanctification is a Progressive Journey

The journey of Christian growth shapes our hearts and transforms our relationships. As the *Evangelical Dictionary of Theology* states, the Holy Spirit brings about this transformation "not as a sudden miraculous gift; the New Testament knows nothing of any shortcut to that ideal." [91] This transformation is known as sanctification. According to Vine's Expository Dictionary, sanctification involves a "separation to God" and is possible only through our relationship with Jesus. It also emphasizes that sanctification must be pursued earnestly by the believer and is "built up, little by little, as a result of obedience to the Word of God." [92]

Cultivating regular spiritual habits, especially daily Bible reading, nurtures our growth in faith. As we approach Scripture with sincere hearts, we grow in our ability to abide in God's love and reflect his character more fully. Sanctification unfolds in the midst of every circumstance, regardless of the intensity of the trials we face. As Corrie ten Boom famously said, "There is no pit so deep that God's love is not deeper still." [93] Spiritual growth is not measured by speed but by faithful trust in the God who walks with us each day.

Closing Remarks

God's forgiveness frees us from guilt, regret, shame, and trauma. A joyful heart is both a gift from God and a blessing to our families. Sanctification, meanwhile, is a progressive journey, gradually shaping us into the likeness of Jesus. Yet all these truths—everything we know about forgiveness, reconciliation, and joy—rest on a single, unshakable foundation: our relationship with God.

Next is an interlude to consider the peace we can try to secure for our families and friends.

Questions for Personal Reflection or Group Discussion

1. The Difference Between Knowing and Trusting

You believe God forgives sins. You've heard it a hundred times. But do you trust that he's forgiven yours? Believing is intellectual: "Yes, God forgives." Trusting is personal: "God has forgiven me." The demons believe (James 2:19), but they don't trust.

Is there a specific sin you know God forgives in general, but struggle to trust he's totally forgiven you? If so, name it. And what would change if you moved from knowing to trusting?

What's one sin you're still punishing yourself for even though God already forgave it? And what would it take to finally receive what he's already given?

2. When Guilt Becomes a Weapon

Some people use guilt as proof they're serious about repentance. "If I feel bad enough, long enough, maybe God will know I really mean it." But guilt was never meant to be a permanent companion. It's an alarm that should lead us to the cross, then fall silent.

Are you using guilt to prove something to God? If so, what would it look like to confess your sin, receive his forgiveness, then let the guilt go—trusting that his grace is enough?

3. The Memory of God

"Does God remember my sins?" Scripture says he "will remember their sins...no more" (Hebrews 10:17). But how? He's omniscient. He knows everything. Maybe it's like this: The file still exists, but God has chosen never to open it again. Not because he can't but because the case is closed. The debt is canceled. There's nothing left to discuss.

You're forgiven. Completely. But are you living like someone whose file has been permanently closed?

Is there a sin from your past that you keep bringing back up—even though God has chosen never to open that file again? What would it look like to trust his choice and stop reopening what he's closed?

4. The Weight That Won't Lift

Guilt says: "I did something wrong." Shame says: "I am something wrong." Guilt can be healthy it points you to the cross. But shame is a liar. It tells you that what you did has defined who you are. Jesus bore your shame on the cross (Hebrews 12:2). He took it so you don't have to carry it anymore. But are you still carrying it?

Is there shame you're carrying either from something you've done or from how others have treated you or labeled you? What would it look like to let Jesus carry that shame instead of you?

INTERLUDE
Peace for Our Families

A story exists of an art contest with the theme of "peace." Many artists painted serene scenes: still lakes reflecting the sky, quiet meadows blanketed with wildflowers, and soft sunsets casting pastels across the horizon. The first-place painting, however, was strikingly different. It showed a violent storm—black clouds split by jagged lightning, sheets of rain pouring down, and a mighty oak bending under the wind. Yet on a limb of that oak, a small bird sat calmly in her nest, singing through the tempest. The judges declared, "This is peace: not the absence of storm, but calm in the midst of it." [94]

This illustration raises an important question: What kind of peace does the Bible offer our homes and families? Is it the gentle tranquility of a calm meadow, or the steadfast strength to remain grounded through life's storms? Scripture answers with two complementary words: *shalom* in the Old Testament and *eirēnē* in the New, together revealing the fullness of biblical peace that strengthens and sustains families.

To grasp what Scripture teaches, we have to acknowledge a key truth: the English word "peace" cannot fully convey the richness and depth of its biblical meaning. In English, peace is often described as "a state of quiet and tranquility" or "freedom from disturbance." [95] While these definitions are not wrong, they do not capture the meaning of the Hebrew and Greek words used in the Bible for peace. In the Old Testament, *shalom* conveys far more than tranquility or the absence of conflict. It signifies completeness, wholeness, and harmony in every aspect of life—emotional, material, relational, and spiritual. Like *shalom*, *eirēnē* in the New Testament carries a deeper meaning emphasizing spiritual reconciliation and inner peace that comes from God.

For clarity, we will refer to both *shalom* and *eirēnē* as biblical peace—a concept that carries far more significance than the conventional English term. Understanding these biblical words can breathe new life into familiar Scriptures and show how peace can transform a fractured family into a harmonious one. In the pages that follow, we will examine each term in turn to gain deeper understanding of how biblical peace nurtures reconciliation within our families.

Shalom

Shalom appears throughout the Old Testament, occurring over 250 times and rooted in the earliest stories of creation. When Adam and Eve were created, they lived in perfect *shalom*. Although the term itself appears later in Scripture, the concept is evident in Eden's paradise-like state. Their world was beautiful and abundant, nourished by natural streams and irrigation. They experienced no shame and, most importantly, enjoyed intimate fellowship with God until sin disrupted their relationship.

Shalom refers to "completeness, soundness, and wholeness," encompassing harmonious relationships and genuine friendship. [96] It conveys fullness, harmony, and well-being. It is not merely the absence of hostility; rather, it includes everything necessary for a complete and flourishing life. As one author observes, *"Shalom*, in other words, is the way things ought to be."* [97]

Shalom includes the absence of conflict, but is much more than that—it is God's restoration of what is broken. It includes emotional, physical, and spiritual well-being, rest, safety, prosperity, freedom from strife, and a calm heart. Unlike the English word peace, *shalom* emphasizes that God actively imparts his peace. The prophet Isaiah expresses this beautifully: "You [God] will keep him in perfect peace [*shalom*] whose mind is stayed on you" (Isaiah 26:3).

Shalom describes the right relationships between individuals, within communities, and ultimately between humanity and God. It signifies a restored order where justice, righteousness, and God's favor prevail. Its absence is evident in war, disunity, injustice, or the subtle unraveling of relationships and purpose.

Isaiah foretold the coming Messiah with a title that lies at the very heart of *shalom*: the "Prince of Peace." This prophecy points to Jesus as the one who not only brings peace but embodies it, rules over it, and restores it to a broken world. In Hebrew, the word for "Prince" is *sar*, meaning "master," "ruler," or "keeper," emphasizing that Jesus is not merely a messenger of peace but its sovereign source. In a well-known prophecy concerning his birth, Isaiah wrote: "For to us a child is born, to us a son is given...and his name shall be called Wonderful Counselor, Mighty God, Everlasting Father, Prince of Peace" (Isaiah 9:6).

The Bible calls us to actively pursue *shalom*: "Turn away from evil and do good; seek peace [*shalom*] and pursue it" (Psalm 34:14). The value of *shalom* is still evident in Israel today, where people often greet one another or bid farewell by saying *shalom*. But it is more than a simple "hello" or "goodbye." It is a spoken blessing, a heartfelt wish that the other person may experience complete inner peace, harmony, and wholeness.

Eirēnē

In the New Testament, the Greek word *eirēnē* conveys the biblical concept of peace. It appears over ninety times and represents a deeply valued, comprehensive gift from God. Like *shalom*, *eirēnē* emphasizes both spiritual reconciliation and inner rest. This peace reflects the harmony between God and humanity. Biblical scholar Marvin Vincent describes *eirēnē* as "a concept uniquely Christian: the tranquil state of a soul assured of its salvation through Christ, fearing nothing from God and content with its earthly circumstances, whatever they may be."

Unlike the peace offered by the world, which often depends on favorable circumstances, *eirēnē* is not dependent on external situations. This peace is rooted in a relationship with God, rather than in freedom from pain. The apostle Paul describes *eirēnē* as a defining mark of a believer's connection with God: "Therefore, since we have been justified by faith, we have peace [*eirēnē*] with God through our Lord Jesus Christ" (Romans 5:1). Unlike the peace offered by the world, which often depends on favorable circumstances, *eirēnē* is not dependent on external situations. This peace is rooted in a relationship with God, rather than in freedom from pain. The apostle Paul describes eirēnē as a defining mark of a believer's connection with God: This is the peace that "surpasses all understanding" (Philippians 4:7). Guarding our hearts and minds in Jesus is not something we earn or create on our own; it is a gracious gift from God, given through Jesus and inspired by the Holy Spirit.

Eirēnē does not replace shalom; rather, it deepens it. While shalom brings inner wholeness, *eirēnē* emphasizes that this peace is available regardless of our external circumstances.

Shalom and Eirēnē Comparison

As mentioned earlier, the Hebrew word *shalom* paints a picture of complete well-being: physical health, harmonious relationships, safety within the community, prosperity, and favor with God. Sickness or hardship is often seen as a disruption of this wholeness. In the New Testament, the Greek word *eirēnē* deepens this concept by highlighting that true wholeness comes through our relationship with God—in passages such as John 14:27: "Peace [*eirēnē*] I [Jesus] leave with you; my peace I give to you. Not as the world gives do I give to you. Let not your hearts be troubled..."

Unlike *shalom*, *eirēnē* does not depend on external circumstances. You can experience *eirēnē* even amid sickness, sorrow, or persecution. This is the essence of biblical peace—steadfast in every situation and unshaken by life's storms. It is this kind of peace and love that fosters reconciliation within our families.

Both forms of peace are vital for our families. *Shalom* reminds us to pursue wholeness, health, and harmony in our relationships. *Eirēne* assures us that even when life falls short of that ideal—when sickness comes, conflicts arise, or hardships press in—we can still experience deep peace through our relationship with God. Together, they reveal the fullness of biblical peace that we need for our families.

Pursuing Biblical Peace

Promoting biblical peace within our families is one of the most important ways to live out the gospel. It calls for humility, forgiveness, and a willingness to be transformed by God's love. True peace is not merely the absence of conflict; it softens hardened hearts and actively restores broken relationships. This truth is beautifully expressed in the priestly blessing, a declaration worth speaking over our families every day: "The Lord bless you and keep you; the Lord make his face to shine upon you and be gracious to you; the Lord lift up his countenance upon you and give you peace" (Numbers 6:24-26).

We grow in peace as we walk closely with God, turn from sin, and pursue righteousness. True, lasting biblical peace is found only through trusting in Jesus, the Prince of Peace. "Therefore, since we have been justified by faith, we have peace [*eirēne*] with God through our Lord Jesus Christ" (Romans 5:1). The Holy Spirit plays a central role in nurturing and sustaining biblical peace in our hearts and homes. As the Comforter promised by Jesus, the Holy Spirit not only convicts us of sin but also fills us with peace in times of turmoil. This peace, a fruit of the Spirit, shapes our hearts and guides our actions according to God's will. Galatians 5:22 makes this clear: "But the fruit of the Spirit is love, joy, peace, patience, kindness, goodness, faithfulness."

Empowered by his presence, we can forgive, seek reconciliation, and stay calm even in the midst of life's chaos. As A. W. Tozer wrote, "Peace for a believer is not the absence of danger but the presence of God." [98]

Closing Remarks

May true biblical peace overflow in every family. May we forgive as God has forgiven us, love as God has loved us, and seek reconciliation where wounds have lingered too long. May the Lord himself guard our homes, may the Prince of Peace reign in our hearts, restore what is broken, and make our families whole in his love.

Moving forward, may this peace prepare us for the deeper work of reconciliation that God desires to accomplish in and through us.

Questions for Personal Reflection
or Group Discussion

1. Singing in the Storm

In a famous painting, a bird sings calmly in her nest while a storm rages. Lightning splits the sky. Rain pounds down. The oak bends. But the bird is at peace. When have you seen someone be that bird for your family by staying calm in the midst of chaos? How did their peace change everything? And when have you needed to be that bird for someone else?

2. Quiet vs. Real Peace

Your house is quiet. No one's yelling. No one's fighting. But no one's really talking either. No one's connecting. The silence is cold. That's not peace. That's just avoiding active war.

What would warm, real, connected *shalom* look like in your home? What would need to change?

3. The Emotional Climate of a Home

Walk into a home and you can feel it immediately. Tension. Warmth. Safety. Fear. Distance. Connection. What's the emotional temperature of your home right now? And what specific things create that climate? Consistent bedtimes? Family meals? Gentle words? Harsh criticism? Predictable rhythms? Chaos?

Pick one thing. What will you change?

4. Peace in the Midst of Conflict

Scripture uses two words for peace:

Shalom = wholeness, restored harmony, everything made right

Eirēnē = settled trust in God, even when conflict remains

Your family might not have *shalom* yet. The conflict isn't resolved. The relationship isn't restored. But you can have *eirēnē*. Peace with God. Rest in his presence. Trust in his work.

Which kind of peace do you need today? And what would it look like to rest in God's peace?

CHAPTER 11

The Transforming Power of Divine Forgiveness

Throughout this book, we have taken a distinctly Christian view of forgiveness and reconciliation, because only Christianity confronts human pain and wrongdoing with both grace and truth. Nowhere is the transforming power of divine forgiveness more vividly revealed than in the story of a man whose heart was changed completely in a single encounter with God.

The Road to Damascus

Few stories capture the power of transformation more vividly than that of a zealous Pharisee from Tarsus named Saul. A "Jew of Jews," he embodied the highest ideals of Jewish identity: faithfulness to the covenant, devotion to God's law, and a life set apart for holiness. Circumcised on the eighth day, he was born into a devout family that honored the Law of Moses from the very beginning of his life. He belonged to the tribe of Benjamin known for its loyalty to King David's line and its honored place among the tribes of Israel. [99] Proud of his heritage, he held firmly to the traditions of his ancestors and sought to preserve their purity. From childhood, his path was marked by rigorous study and spiritual discipline. In Jerusalem, he studied under Gamaliel, one of the most respected rabbis of the first century. [100] This elite training demanded mastery of Scripture and oral tradition; and he excelled beyond many of his peers in pursuing righteousness with great passion. [101]

Yet that passion soon hardened into hostility toward the followers of Jesus. Convinced they were a threat to God's covenant people, he became a relentless persecutor searching homes, seizing believers, and delivering them to prison. Armed with letters of authority, he set out for Damascus, determined to capture even more and drag them back to Jerusalem in chains. But on that road, everything changed. Suddenly, a light brighter than the noonday sun blazed around him. The very air seemed to pulse with divine presence, and he fell to the ground trembling. Then he heard a clear and commanding voice, calling his name twice: "Saul, Saul, why are you persecuting me?"

Stunned and disoriented, he whispered, "Who are you, Lord?"

The answer came with unmistakable authority: "I am Jesus, whom you are persecuting."

Blinded, he was led by the hand into Damascus, where he spent three days fasting, praying, and wrestling in darkness with the staggering truth that everything he once believed had been overturned. Then a disciple named Ananias, came to him, placed his hands upon him, and spoke words of healing. Instantly, something like scales fell from Saul's eyes, and his sight was restored. He rose, was baptized, and immediately began proclaiming that Jesus is the Son of God. [102]

What is remarkable is not only the suddenness of his conversion but also its profound steadfastness. Saul did not abandon his Jewish heritage or cease to worship the God of Abraham, Isaac, and Jacob. Rather, he came to see that the promises of the Law and the Prophets found their fulfillment in Yeshua Hamashiach, Jesus Christ. As he would later testify, "I worship the God of our fathers, believing everything laid down by the Law and written in the Prophets, having a hope in God … that there will be a resurrection of both the just and the unjust" (Acts 24:14–15) [103]

His Jewish identity was not abandoned but fulfilled. The persecutor became a witness; and his zeal was not extinguished but redirected toward proclaiming forgiveness of sins and reconciliation with God through faith in the Messiah. From that day forward, Saul of Tarsus became known as Paul, a living testimony that no one is beyond the reach of God's forgiveness.

Paul's story reminds us that conversion is not merely an intellectual event but a life-transforming encounter that brings peace with God and fulfills the promises made to Israel, now extend to all who place their faith in Jesus.[104] His conversion marked the moment he became a Jewish believer in Jesus as Messiah. This reality becomes even more alluring when we consider how the message of forgiveness in Jesus Christ stands apart from every other worldview.

The Uniqueness of Christian Forgiveness

Christianity stands apart from every other world religion. It is rooted not in human effort but in the sacrificial love of God, who freely opens the way for reconciliation with him. Unlike belief systems that depend on human striving to earn divine favor or forgiveness, Christianity begins with God graciously reaching toward humanity.

In Eastern religions such as Buddhism and Hinduism, wrongdoing is often explained through the law of karma, the belief that one's future experiences are determined by past actions. In this view, suffering becomes the payment for previous wrongs. While this framework upholds moral responsibility, it offers no true forgiveness, only an endless cycle of cause and effect. [105]

Islam emphasizes Allah's justice and judgment, teaching that each person is rewarded or punished according to their deeds; and that salvation comes through submission to his will. Within this framework, there is no full assurance that sins are truly forgiven or that divine justice has been fully satisfied. [106] If sin carries a penalty, who has paid it?

Secular and humanist worldviews take a different approach, grounding morality in human reasoning rather than divine authority. People become their own standard for what is good or evil. But without a higher moral foundation, it becomes difficult to explain why compassion, dignity, or forgiveness should matter, especially in a worldview shaped by "survival of the fittest." Without a transcendent moral standard guilt loses its meaning and hope for forgiveness fades.

In contrast, Judaism upholds both moral law and the reality of sin. [107] The sacred writings of the Tanakh form the foundation of the Christian faith. The Tanakh shares its core content with the Christian Old Testament, differing mainly in order and emphasis, not in message. After the destruction of the Second Temple, Judaism developed into Rabbinic Judaism, which continues to guide Jewish life and worship today.

Christians believe that the New Testament fulfills the promises of the Old Testament. Prophetic passages such as Psalm 22:7-8, 16-18 and Isaiah 52:13-53:12 foretell a suffering Messiah who will bring lasting forgiveness and reconciliation with God. Christians understand Jesus Christ to be the promised Messiah, the fulfillment of God's redemptive plan.

Some Jews, known as Messianic Jews, have embraced Yeshua as their Savior. They believe that faith in him strengthens rather than diminishes their Jewish identity, fulfilling the promises of the Hebrew Scriptures. Only Christianity, including the faith of Messianic Jews, offers a clear moral foundation that fulfills divine justice through love, teaching that true morality flows from God's righteous and unchanging character. [108] If we belong to Jesus, he has fully paid the debt of our sins (Colossians 2:13-14), offering forgiveness without compromising justice (Romans 3:26). Christianity makes reconciliation with God not only possible but certain for all who believe (2 Corinthians 5:18-19)—which naturally leads to an essential question: why is Jesus the only way to be reconciled with God?

Reconciliation with God is essential to end the estrangement brought about by original sin and to restore our relationship with him. We must recognize Jesus' unique role in making us whole with God. The Bible makes it clear that salvation comes exclusively through him. Numerous Scriptures affirm that there is no reconciliation with God apart from Jesus. Acts 4:12 declares: "And there is salvation in no one else, for there is no other name under heaven given among men by which we must be saved." Jesus himself said, "I am the way, and the truth, and the life. No one comes to the Father except through me" (John 14:6). Christianity is the only faith founded on God's love as revealed through his Son, Jesus (1 John 4:9-10), and the only path that truly satisfies our deepest needs.

What Is Our Greatest Need?

In Mark chapter 2, we encounter a remarkable scene where Jesus healed a paralyzed man. Four devoted friends carried him to see Jesus, but the house was so crowded they couldn't reach the door. Refusing to give up, they climbed onto the roof, made an opening, and lowered their friend before the Lord. Moved by their faith, Jesus looked at the man and said, "Son, your sins are forgiven" (Mark 2:5).

The religious leaders stood in stunned silence. They had expected a simple act of physical healing, not such a daring declaration of forgiveness. Within their hearts, they accused Jesus of blasphemy (disrespecting, dishonoring, or insulting God with our words or actions), believing he had claimed the very authority of God himself. "Who can forgive sins but God alone?" (Mark 2:7).

But Jesus, perceiving their thoughts, said, "'Which is easier: to say to the paralytic, "Your sins are forgiven," or to say, "Rise, take up your bed and walk"? But that you may know that the Son of Man has authority on earth to forgive sins' - he said to the paralytic, 'I tell you, rise, pick up your bed, and go home.'" (Mark 2:9-11).

The man stood, picked up his mat, and walked away before

the astonished crowd.

Why did Jesus first declare the man's sins forgiven? Because he knew that our greatest need is not physical healing, financial provision, emotional stability, or even restored relationships, but forgiveness from God and reconciliation with him. This truth was powerfully revealed to the zealous Pharisee from Tarsus, who learned on the road to Damascus that no amount of law-keeping or religious passion could satisfy his soul's deepest need. Only the risen Messiah could forgive him and restore his relationship with God.

The Greek word for sin, hamartia, means "to miss the mark". It describes falling short of God's perfect and holy standard. Scripture teaches that "All have sinned and fall short of the glory of God" (Romans 3:23) and warns that "The wages of sin is death" (Romans 6:23). This death is not merely physical; it also signifies eternal separation from God.

But the good news of the gospel is that forgiveness is freely offered through Jesus Christ. In his mercy, God did not abandon us in our sin. Instead, he sent his Son to take our punishment and restore us to fellowship with him. "In him we have redemption through his blood, the forgiveness of our trespasses, according to the riches of his grace" (Ephesians 1:7). This forgiveness is not something we can earn; it is a gift received through faith.

When Jesus healed the paralyzed man, he was demonstrating his authority to forgive sins. The physical healing served as a sign pointing to the greater spiritual restoration available to all who believe. As Jesus proclaims:

"Truly, truly, I say to you, whoever hears my word and believes him who sent me has eternal life. He does not come into judgment but has passed from death to life" (John 5:24).

As discussed throughout this book, forgiveness and reconciliation are essential for healthy relationships; yet they ultimately flow from the forgiveness we receive from God. That is why the journey of healing must begin at the cross. All human forgiveness originates in divine forgiveness. When we confess our sins and place our trust in Jesus, we receive much more than cleansing. God adopts us into his family, seals us with the Holy Spirit, and makes us children of God—future citizens of heaven and participants in the divine nature.

The Cost of Our Forgiveness

God sent his Son, Jesus, to be born of a woman, a truth that fills us with wonder. It is both astonishing and mysterious. Pause for a moment and consider this: Jesus, as God incarnate, had a real family. He did not descend from heaven on a cloud; he was born into the ordinary joys and challenges of family life. He had a mother, a step father, and step siblings; and experienced the mess, complexity, and drama of sharing a home with others.

Even his own family initially struggled to understand his identity and purpose. Despite facing rejection and misunderstanding, Jesus not only proclaimed divine forgiveness and reconciliation but also accomplished it through his sacrificial death on the cross and his resurrection. Through the cross, he reconciled humanity to our Heavenly Father.

The greatest act of forgiveness is also the deepest

expression of love. Jesus' birth, suffering, and death were all necessary for our forgiveness, culminating in his victorious resurrection. More than seven hundred years before he came, the prophet Isaiah foretold the anguish of his suffering, describing how his appearance would be disfigured and unsettling to those who saw him: "Marred, beyond human semblance, and his form beyond that of the children of mankind" (Isaiah 52:14). Jesus was so disfigured that his appearance no longer seemed human... Isaiah continues: "But he was pierced for our transgressions; he was crushed for our iniquities; upon him was the chastisement that brought us peace, and with his wounds we are healed" (Isaiah 53:5).

The Son of God entered the world fully aware of the horror that awaited him and, even more astonishingly, he embraced it willingly. He endured humiliation, abuse, torture, and execution, though he was completely innocent and without sin. This is a love that surpasses all human understanding. As Isaiah proclaimed, it fulfills a divine purpose: "All we like sheep have gone astray; we have turned everyone to his own way; and the Lord has laid on him (Jesus) the iniquity of us all" (Isaiah 53:6).

Suffering and Victory

The suffering and death of Jesus are deeply moving. His execution was not only brutal but also marked by abandonment, dishonor, and humiliation. During his arrest and trial, even his closest followers fled; and Peter, their leader, denied knowing him three times. Roman guards spat on him, struck him, and flogged him with leather cords embedded with bone or metal. Bound to a post, he endured lashes that tore his skin and exposed muscle, sometimes even bone. Many victims of such flogging did not survive.

A crown of thorns was pressed onto his head, and he was forced to carry his cross partway to Golgotha, where he was crucified in the most excruciating and humiliating form of execution ever devised. Remarkably, King David had foretold this suffering a thousand years earlier in Psalm 22, long before crucifixion practices existed. "They have pierced my hands and feet...they divide my garments among them, and for my clothing they cast lots" (Psalm 22:16, 18).

Victory followed the cross. God raised Jesus to life and glory, securing our adoption into his family as a blessing beyond comprehension. Through him, we receive eternal life and the strength to live victoriously, even amid life's challenges.

Adoption into God's Family

The New Testament paints a vivid and inspiring picture of our adoption into God's family. It emphasizes key verses that reveal the blessings and privileges of being part of God's household. [109] One foundational verse declares, "But when the fullness of time had come, God sent forth his Son, born of woman, born under the law, to redeem those who were under the law, so that we might receive adoption as sons" (Galatians 4:4-5). Another beautiful verse says, "...in love he predestined us for adoption as sons through Jesus Christ, according to the purpose of his will, to the praise of his glorious grace" (Ephesians 1:4 6).

Being adopted into God's family is an extraordinary act of grace and privilege. It means that all who believe are fully loved by their perfect Heavenly Father and are made his royal sons and daughters. To better understand what this means, we can look at the Roman legal system that shaped the world of the New Testament.

In Roman society, adoption was governed by the Latin *patria potestas*, the full legal authority a Roman father held over his children, whether biological or adopted. [110] Under this system, a son could neither own property nor gain legal independence; and he might even be sold into slavery, regardless of his age. Likewise, apart from Jesus, we live under the bondage of sin, powerless to free ourselves. But just as Roman adoption could elevate someone without authority or status, God's adoption brings us into a new relationship of freedom as children of our Heavenly Father. [111]

Roman adoption created a profoundly different legal relationship. An adopted person gained rights and privileges often surpassing those of a natural-born child. Unlike a natural-born son, an adopted child inherited his father's estate, and the father could neither sell him into slavery nor disown him. Adoption was permanent and legally binding. In some cases, Roman fathers even adopted their own biological sons to ensure greater legal protection. [112]

In Jesus Christ, we experience a reality similar to Roman adoption: we are made heirs of God's kingdom, co-heirs with Christ, and nothing can separate us from God's love. Paul affirms this when he wrote: "The Spirit himself bears witness with our spirit that we are children of God, and if children, then heirs of God and fellow heirs with Christ" (Romans 8:16-17).

Roman adoption had remarkable features. A key aspect was that the law erased the adoptee's past and canceled all debts, giving them a fresh start. In the same way, God cancels the record of debt that stood against us, making every believer a new creation in Christ Jesus. "Therefore, if anyone is in Christ, he is a new creation. The old has passed away; behold, the new has come" (2 Corinthians 5:17). Additionally, to ensure no one could challenge the adoption, seven witnesses formally affirmed it. Similarly, in a Christian's adoption, the Holy Spirit himself bears witness that we are children of God (Romans 8:16).

Having explored how ancient Roman adoption foreshadows our Christian adoption, there is another important topic to address before the next chapter: repentance. Understanding how repentance has been preached from the 19th century to today will help us appreciate why the gospel presentation in the next chapter is more thorough than many modern versions.

The Legacy of Preaching Repentance

John the Baptist, the disciples, and Jesus all began their ministries with a call to repentance. John the Baptist boldly preached, "Repent, for the kingdom of heaven is at hand" (Matthew 3:2). When Jesus first sent out his disciples, they proclaimed that "people should repent" (Mark 6:12). Jesus began his public ministry with a clear call: "Repent, for the kingdom of heaven is at hand" (Matthew 4:17). This focus on repentance has echoed throughout Christian history, particularly among evangelists committed to guiding individuals toward genuine spiritual transformation. Jumping from John, Jesus, and his disciples to modern stories of how various well-known pastors handled the topic of repentance, it is quite interesting to see how preaching has changed.

In the early 20th century, evangelist Billy Sunday (1862–1935) gave powerful sermons across America, urging people to repent and embrace salvation through Jesus. A former professional baseball player turned preacher, Sunday became famous for his passionate delivery and energetic style. His revival meetings often drew tens of thousands of people, and by the end of his career, over one million individuals were estimated to have responded to his invitations to follow Christ. Yet Sunday understood that an emotional response alone was not enough. At his meetings, trained counsellors welcomed those who stepped forward into a quiet space called the "inquiry room." There, they answered questions, explained the significance of repentance, faith, and new life in Jesus, and prayed with each person, encouraging careful reflection rather than rushed decisions.

Later evangelists, such as Billy Graham, followed a similar approach. From the beginning of his crusades, Graham trained thousands of counsellors to meet personally with respondents, offering booklets, prayer, and connections to local churches. While Graham's public preaching emphasized coming to Jesus by faith, his counsellors provided deeper instruction on repentance and the cost of discipleship, ensuring that each new believer understood the commitment required. "Salvation is free, but discipleship costs everything we have." [113]

The great preacher Charles Spurgeon (1834-1892) laid a

strong theological foundation for this approach to evangelism. He emphasized that repentance and faith are inseparable aspects of genuine conversion. Spurgeon often taught that "repentance and faith are the two spokes of the wheel of salvation; you cannot have one without the other." [114]

He cautioned against mere outward sorrow, emphasizing that true repentance requires a change of heart, not just fleeting emotion or guilt. Like Billy Sunday, Spurgeon placed repentance at the center of his preaching, giving it both prominence and doctrinal significance; but Charles Spurgeon, in particular, preached repentance not merely as an initial step but as a central doctrine. He devoted entire sermons to it, exploring its theological depth with remarkable clarity. For him, repentance was indispensable to genuine conversion and formed an integral part of every evangelistic message.

Over time the emphasis has shifted. Although Spurgeon and Sunday preached repentance as a profound, explicit, and urgent message, by the mid-to-late 20th century, while evangelists still affirmed repentance, they often softened its urgency to appeal to a broader audience. Today, many gospel presentations omit repentance entirely, replacing it with well-meaning but diluted phrases like "invite Jesus into your heart," without genuinely calling people to turn from sin.

The next chapter continues in the spirit of those earlier evangelists. The message there is longer than most modern gospel presentations because, in today's fast-paced world, people often reduce profound truths to sound bites, neglecting to address repentance and salvation together. Like those early "inquiry rooms," these pages invite us to slow down, reflect, and respond, not with empty emotion, but with understanding and faith.

Closing Remarks

Chapter 11 explored the uniqueness of the Christian faith, how we can be adopted by God, and an introduction to repentance; and in the closing chapter we will see that God's forgiveness is not merely the cancellation of a debt, but the radical transformation of our identity and destiny. This is why being forgiven by God and reconciled with him is essential for building a truly loving home. Whether you are just looking into Christianity or have been following Jesus for years, the next chapter offers timeless truths about how we can be forgiven by God and reconciled with him—which is the most important topic of all.

Questions for Personal Reflection or Group Discussion

1. A Heart Transformed

Paul was hunting Christians. Ravaging churches. Dragging believers to prison. Three days later, he was preaching the gospel he had tried to destroy. Only God can do that.

Where have you seen a transformation that could only be God's work, either in yourself or someone you know? What made it unmistakably divine, not just human effort?

2. Forgiveness That Changes Identity

You're not on probation. You're not a servant trying to earn your place. You're adopted. You're family. You're a son. You're a daughter.

In Roman adoption, the adopted child received full rights above those of a biological child. Permanent. Irrevocable. Secure.

Do you live like you're on probation, or like you're adopted into God's family? What would change if you truly believed your status is permanent, not performance-based?

3. More Than a Moment

You became a Christian in a moment. But becoming *like Christ*? That's taking a lifetime. "We are being transformed" (2 Corinthians 3:18). Present tense. Ongoing. Where are you being impatient with yourself or someone else, expecting instant transformation instead of gradual growth?

What grace do you need to extend today, knowing God isn't finished yet?

4. When Transformation Meets Resistance

You've been forgiven. You've been set free. You know the gospel. So why do the same old patterns keep showing up? The same defensiveness. The same fear. The same pride. You thought you were done with these. But transformation isn't instant.

What old pattern is God still working on in you? And what would it mean to trust that he's not finished, that resistance doesn't mean failure?

CHAPTER 12
Faith and Repentance

Moving from what God has done to how we respond, Chapter 12 examines faith and repentance, twin gifts that enable us to receive God's grace and live as reconciled people. It explores what true faith looks like, what genuine repentance involves, and how this transformation fosters forgiveness and reconciliation.

The Gift of Faith

What does becoming a believer have to do with forgiving or reconciling with others? Simply put, it initiates an inner transformation that makes genuine forgiveness and reconciliation possible.

Before exploring this transformation, we must first understand what it means to be a believer—which is both an event and a process. It begins with the action of the Holy Spirit, prompting us to respond to Jesus in faith; and continues as the Spirit works within us, purifying us from discord and willful disobedience, gradually remolding us into the image of Christ. This purification unfolds as we continually repent and cling to Christ anew. [115]

New believers receive an infusion of divine grace. This is not something we can achieve by our own effort; it begins when we repent of unbelief and receive God's gift, a gift that opens our spiritual eyes and transforms our minds. We can never do enough good to outweigh our sins, yet God has provided a way for them to be forgiven and completely removed. When we trust that Jesus died on the cross for our sins and place our faith in his death and resurrection, God grants us full and lasting forgiveness.

In the New Testament, the Greek word for faith is *pistis*. Its full meaning is difficult to capture in English. Pistis is not merely intellectual belief; it also involves trust, loyalty, and commitment. It reflects a vow of faithful relationship, rooted in the early church's understanding of covenant loyalty. In fact, it could be translated as "vow" or "pledge," emphasizing enduring commitment and covenantal faithfulness, much like a wedding vow. [116]

This raises a deeper question: how does genuine belief actually begin in a person's life?

Repentance and Faith Together

Receiving and trusting in Jesus' substitutionary death reconciles us to the one true God and serves as the climax of the biblical story—one into which God graciously invites each of us. At the heart of Paul's conversion was this union of repentance and faith: he turned from persecuting the Church to proclaiming the very name he once despised. This transformation involves "an inner re-creating of fallen human nature by the gracious, sovereign action of the Holy Spirit."[117]

All of this occurs when repentance and faith come together. Repentance may begin in an immature form, but it starts the moment we honor and place our trust in Jesus. As Paul wrote,

"If you confess with your mouth that Jesus is Lord and believe in your heart that God raised him from the dead [repent of unbelief], you will be saved" (Romans 10:9). Faith is more than an intellectual belief; it is a wholehearted loyalty of the heart. With this foundation, we can now look at what distinguishes true repentance from false.

True and False Repentance

When we turn from unbelief to faith and place our trust in Jesus, we embrace the gift of salvation and begin a new journey defined not by perfection but by transformation. This journey leads us toward growing righteousness and away from persistent sin. At the heart of this path is repentance.

Repentance is more than regret. It is a change of heart, a renewal of the mind, and a redirection of life. Becoming a Christian does not bring instant victory over all sin. Believers continue to stumble and struggle as they grow in the ongoing process of sanctification. Yet repentance marks a pivotal moment: the heart begins to turn in a new direction, away from self and toward Jesus, motivated by a desire to reflect his character more faithfully.

Many people regret their actions, especially when they are exposed or they damage their reputation; but Biblical repentance goes beyond mere remorse. One can feel sorry without experiencing true transformation. An adulterer may grieve being caught but feel no sorrow for the betrayal itself. A liar may promise to do better, yet only become more careful to conceal deception. Fear of consequences can modify behavior, but it cannot transform the heart. True repentance goes much deeper.

The key question is whether sorrow over wrongdoing leads to genuine change. For many, it does not. The liar may simply become more cautious and the adulterer more discreet. Countless people regret the outcomes of sin yet remain unchanged; but when we turn from unbelief to faith and receive Jesus, we embrace the gift of salvation and begin a new journey defined not by perfection but by transformation—motivated by a desire to reflect his character more faithfully.

True and False Conversions

Paul's story reminds us that true conversion is more than a fleeting emotional experience; it is a lifelong, living relationship with the risen Messiah. When Saul encountered Jesus on the road to Damascus, his life was completely changed: the persecutor became a preacher, the enemy became a friend, and the self-reliant Pharisee became a humble servant of Christ. This is the unmistakable fruit of genuine conversion

Jesus also gave a sobering warning: "Not everyone who says to me, 'Lord, Lord,' will enter the kingdom of heaven, but the one who does the will of my Father who is in heaven" (Matthew 7:21). Some may claim mighty works in his name, yet he will declare, "I never knew you" (Matthew 7:23). The issue is not how much they did or how loudly they professed their faith, but that they never had a genuine relationship with him. They knew about Jesus, but he did not know them as his own.

True conversion is not about perfection; it is about a transformation that springs from a relationship. Repentance and faith open the door, but walking with Jesus each day demonstrates the reality of new life. Like Paul, every genuine believer can say, "I once was blind, but now I see; and now I belong to him."

New Life in Jesus

True repentance begins with a changed heart, one that depends on God's power to leave darkness behind and walk in the light. Biblical repentance involves heartfelt sorrow for sinning against God and a genuine desire to turn from sin, no matter the cost.

When Jesus called us to follow him and put our sinful nature to death daily, he made it clear that genuine faith produces a transformed life. This does not mean Christians never sin; rather, it means we confess our sins and strive to turn away from them. We do not live in willful, unrepentant sin. The book of 1 John assures us that when Christians stumble, they have an advocate with God. John writes, "I am writing these things to you so that you may not sin. But if anyone does sin, we have an advocate with the Father, Jesus Christ the righteous" (1 John 2:1); and adds, "If we confess our sins, he is faithful and just to forgive us our sins and to cleanse us from all unrighteousness" (1 John 1:9). This kind of repentance gives us confidence that we are never separated from our Heavenly Father.

Believing in Jesus transforms our inner nature, making us spiritually alive and guiding us into a new way of living marked by a growing desire to obey God. As our renewed nature develops, our character and temperament begin to change, making forgiveness and reconciliation increasingly natural. While anyone can forgive, the grace and mercy believers receive uniquely empower them to forgive from the heart. Rather than holding grudges, we grow eager to forgive and love.

Faith in Jesus delivers us from spiritual death and grants us eternal life. This transformation should be evident in a changed life and in a growing desire to follow God.

Trusting and Obeying

Obedience to God is included here, because it is closely connected to the command to forgive others. Trusting and obeying him is essential for a healthy and vibrant Christian life. Jesus says, "If anyone would come after me, let him deny himself and take up his cross daily and follow me" (Luke 9:23). He also says, "If you love me, you will keep my commandments" (John 14:15). What does it mean to trust and obey Jesus? It means seeking God's guidance in every decision like Israel's King David did, and choosing to live by faith. It means placing our confidence in him above all other sources of security.

Charles Spurgeon shared a story that perfectly illustrates the importance of clinging to Jesus alone: Years ago, above Niagara Falls, a boat carrying two men overturned. The men were caught in the strong current and swept toward the falls. Someone onshore floated a rope to them, and both men grabbed hold. One man held tightly and was safely pulled to the bank. The other saw a large log drifting nearby. Believing it to be stronger, he loosened his grip on the rope and clung to the log instead. Although the log looked solid, it had no connection to the shore. The man and the log were swept over the falls, since the size of the log was not anchored to anything that could save him and provided no safety. [118]

Charles Spurgeon used this illustration to explain a vital spiritual truth. When a person trusts in works, prayer, generosity, church attendance, or anything apart from Jesus Christ, there is no salvation; as there is no true connection with God through Christ alone. Faith may appear fragile—like a slender rope—but it is held firmly in the hands of the Almighty. God himself secures the connection and draws the soul away from destruction and into safety.

True safety comes only from holding fast to Jesus, the one who is firmly anchored and able to save. Faith in the one God appointed is the lifeline that unites us to him. Our part is to hold fast to the cord God has provided—faith in Jesus Christ.

Turning to him awakens a new desire to obey God. As John writes, "This is the love of God, that we keep his commandments" (1 John 5:3). Genuine faith is never passive; it draws us toward his ways and shapes our obedience. A. W. Tozer described it this way: "Faith, as Paul saw it, was a living, flaming thing leading to surrender and obedience to the commandments of Christ." [119]

The following sections explore the divine work that reconciles us to God and transforms us into new creations—a transformation that empowers us to forgive others and gives us the desire to pursue reconciliation in our relationships.

The Divine Exchange

Through a divine exchange, God makes reconciliation possible.

Jesus takes upon himself, and we are credited with his righteousness. This exchange removes the alienation caused by sin and restores our relationship with God. As Paul writes, "For our sake he made him to be sin who knew no sin, so that in him we might become the righteousness of God" (2 Corinthians 5:21).

What an astonishing truth that sinless Jesus bore our moral debt so that we could receive his perfect righteousness! We can picture him taking our sins and giving us his flawless record, like exchanging an over-spent ledger for one that is perfectly balanced. This extraordinary transfer is not just awe-inspiring but is deeply personal, transforming our standing before God forever.

God's Work in Reconciliation

Reconciliation is more than a legal transaction. It is a transformation of the heart—and it is entirely God's work, not ours. Only God can restore our relationship with himself. Perfect and trustworthy, he adopts us freely, requiring nothing from us. Reconciliation is a gift of his mercy, delivered through his power, not ours, "He has delivered us from the domain of darkness and transferred us to the kingdom of his beloved Son, in whom we have redemption, the forgiveness of sins" (Colossians 1:13-14).

Our redemption comes solely through his grace: "In him we have redemption through his blood, the forgiveness of our trespasses, according to the riches of his grace" (Ephesians 1:7). His mercy is our only hope, rescuing us from the darkness of sin.

The Bible records countless miracles and wonders, yet

perhaps the most profound is that the Son of God became fully human in Jesus while remaining eternally God. This truth is deeply significant. Because he is fully God, he is sinless. Because he is fully human, his perfect obedience opens the way for his righteousness to be credited to all who are born again. Paul summarizes this miracle well: "Therefore, as one trespass led to condemnation for all men, so one act of righteousness leads to justification and life for all men. For as by the one man's disobedience the many were made sinners, so by the one man's obedience the many will be made righteous" (Romans 5:18-19).

A New Heart

When we are reconciled to God, he not only restores our relationship with him, but he also renews our inner life. Paul offers a living example of this transformation. Once an enemy of Christ, he was remade as an ambassador of reconciliation, calling others to "be reconciled to God" (2 Corinthians 5:20). This reconciliation is an act of divine grace and mercy, with God himself bearing judgment, removing guilt, and turning hostility into fellowship. As Paul wrote: "In Christ God was reconciling the world to himself, not counting their trespasses against them" (2 Corinthians 5:19). Reconciliation, then, is more than a legal pardon; it is an inward transformation. As the *International Standard Bible Encyclopedia* explains, God "simultaneously effects a change in sinners so that they no longer desire alienation from God, but rather, reconciliation with God." [120]

Both the prophets and apostles testify to this truth. God's reconciliation begins within. Ezekiel promises: "I will give you a new heart, and a new spirit I will put within you. I will remove the heart of stone from your flesh and give you a heart of flesh" (Ezekiel 36:26). Paul echoes this prophetic vision when he exhorts believers, "Do not be conformed to this world, but be transformed by the renewal of your mind" (Romans 12:2).

Reconciliation with God is not only about being declared righteous; it also involves inward transformation. God's pardon restores our fellowship with him, and his Holy Spirit renews our hearts, enabling us to live no longer in alienation but in close communion with him.

New Creations

Through this redemption, we receive not only forgiveness but also the joy of becoming new creations in Jesus. Because of Jesus' love for us, we no longer live for ourselves. We become a new creation, held and shaped by his love. As new creations, we receive wisdom and strength from him to pursue reconciliation with others and to experience the blessings that come from restored relationships. Because of his death and resurrection, we are forgiven, renewed, and reconciled to God:

For if, while we were enemies, we were reconciled to God through the death of his Son, how much more, now that we are reconciled, shall we be saved through his life! And not only that, but we also rejoice in God through our Lord Jesus Christ, through whom we have now received reconciliation (Romans 5:10-11).

Perhaps you are not reconciled with God, or you have doubts. Redemption is more comprehensive than knowing who Jesus is—

the Bible says that even evil spirits who are not redeemed know who Jesus is: "You believe that God is one; you do well. Even the demons believe and shudder!" (James 2:19) Being redeemed means you have a personal relationship with Jesus.

When making a decision to become a new creation and to follow Jesus, a sincere prayer is proper. Such a prayer should acknowledge your sins, request forgiveness for your sins, express your belief in Jesus' death and resurrection, and make a commitment to follow him. You can say a prayer with your own words that covers these things.

Closing Remarks

In this final chapter we affirm that being reconciled to God through faith in Jesus brings both forgiveness and a new identity, a renewed purpose, and the power to forgive others. Like Paul, our story is transformed from resisting Jesus to bearing witness to his grace and mercy. In this way, we become agents of forgiveness and reconciliation within our families, ambassadors of the very grace and mercy we have received

Forgiveness is more than a single event; it becomes a way of life. It forms a steady rhythm in a heart shaped by grace and mercy, sometimes easy to embrace, sometimes a hard-won battle fought through prayer. Forgiveness does not always mean forgetting, but it does mean releasing the desire for revenge. When we remember that Jesus has forgiven all our sins, every unkind thought, careless word, moment of anger, and selfish deed, how can we withhold forgiveness from others? The answer lies in understanding the work God has been doing in us.

This book looked at forgiveness through the image of a portrait being painted. Stepping back now, we see what has taken shape. At the beginning of Part One, a canvas was prepared, and colors were mixed and brushes selected. In Part Two, the artist began applying bold strokes of truth, gentle layers of grace, and patient touches of mercy. Now, at the end, the portrait is becoming clearer.

Perhaps we can see our own portrait emerging: conversations beginning, forgiveness being extended, and reconciliation pursued. Faithful steps, hard-won choices, and prayers whispered in the night when forgiveness felt out of reach.

Looking closer, we see light finding its way into places that once felt dark; and colors have been blended with a wisdom beyond our own. The composition holds together in ways we could not have planned. The truth being revealed from the first page of *Family Forgiveness and Reconciliation* is that God is the artist. He is the one who has been painting this portrait all along. Every moment of grace, every act of forgiveness, and every step toward reconciliation have been his brushstrokes guided by his hand.

The portrait is not finished. There are still layers to add, and light is still finding its way into hidden corners. But beauty is already emerging. The Bible is a portrait of love painted on a canvas of forgiveness, and so are we.

Questions for Personal Reflection
or Group Discussion

These questions are especially suited for personal reflection. If used in a group, leaders may wish to allow additional quiet time for consideration.

1. Our Greatest Need

The paralytic came for healing. His friends lowered him through the roof, expecting Jesus to fix his legs. Instead, Jesus said, "Your sins are forgiven" (Mark 2:5). Everyone wanted the miracle, but Jesus gave him something deeper. What do you want most from God right now? And what if he's offering you something you didn't even know you needed?

2. True Repentance

Judas felt terrible about betraying Jesus. He even gave the money back (Matthew 27:3-5). But he didn't repent. He gave up hope. Peter denied Jesus three times. He wept bitterly (Luke 22:62). And he repented. What's the difference? Judas ran from Jesus. Peter ran to him.

When you sin, where do you run? Away from God in shame or toward him in repentance?

3. Grace as a Gift

"For by grace you have been saved through faith... not a result of works" (Ephesians 2:8-9). No payment. No earning. No working it off. Just receive.

So why is that so hard? What makes you think you need to bring something to the table when Jesus says, "It is finished"?

4. Faith and Assurance

"Did I really believe? Am I doing enough? What if I lose my salvation?" Stop looking at yourself. Look at Jesus. Your assurance should not be based on your grip on him. It should be based on *his* grip on you. "I give them eternal life, and they will never perish, and no one will snatch them out of my hand" (John 10:28).

When doubt comes, where are you looking—at your performance or at the cross? Have you asked Jesus to immerse you in the Holy Spirit? (Matthew 3:11, Mark 1:8, Luke 3:16, John 1:33, and Acts 1:5)

Appendices

APPENDIX ONE
Voices We Cite

Throughout this book, we draw from voices across the centuries who spoke with wisdom about forgiveness and reconciliation. The brief profiles below introduce a select group of authors quoted in this book. This list is representative, not comprehensive; additional voices and all reference works appear in the endnotes.

Matthew Henry (1662–1714)— English (Welsh-born) Presbyterian pastor who ministered in Chester and London. His devotional *Exposition of the Old and New Testaments* (often called the *Commentary on the Whole Bible*) has nourished personal and pastoral study for over three centuries.

Charles H. Spurgeon (1834–1892)— English Baptist pastor in London, long-time preacher at the Metropolitan Tabernacle. Nicknamed the "Prince of Preachers," he left thousands of sermons and launched ministries including a pastors' college and orphan care.

Dwight L. Moody (1837–1899)— American evangelist from Northfield, Massachusetts, who led major urban revivals in the U.S. and U.K. Founder of Moody Church in Chicago and Moody Bible Institute, his preaching emphasized conversion, Scripture, and practical mercy.

Corrie ten Boom (1892–1983)— Dutch watchmaker from Haarlem, Netherlands, who, with her family, sheltered Jews during World War II. Authorities imprisoned her and sent her to Ravensbrück, and later she wrote *The Hiding Place* and traveled globally with a message of forgiveness and hope.

C. S. Lewis (1898–1963)— Irish-born British scholar who taught at Oxford and Cambridge. Known for clear, imaginative apologetics and literary gifts, he authored *Mere Christianity, The Screwtape Letters,* and *The Chronicles of Narnia.*

A. W. Tozer (1897–1963)— American pastor in the Christian and Missionary Alliance, serving congregations in Chicago and Toronto. His devotional classics *The Pursuit of God* and *The Knowledge of the Holy* call believers to reverent worship and a deeper knowledge of God.

Elisabeth Elliot (1926–2015)— American missionary and author who worked as a missionary in Ecuador. Widely read for books like *Through Gates of Splendor* and *Passion and Purity,* she wrote on obedience, suffering, forgiveness, and costly love shaped by her husband Jim Elliot's death and her subsequent service among the people he sought to reach.

R. C. Sproul (1939–2017)— American Reformed theologian and pastor—founded Ligonier Ministries in Pennsylvania (later in Florida). A clear, accessible teacher of doctrine and worldview, he wrote *The Holiness of God* and taught widely through radio, books, and teaching series.

APPENDIX TWO

Forgiveness Involving Financial Debt and Disputes

Forgiveness is most difficult when money is involved. Whether involving a large institution or another person, financial wrongs create unique challenges calling for both mercy and wisdom. Many Christians wrestle with a troubling question: *If I forgive a company, government, or person who owes me money, does that mean I must cancel the debt?*

The answer involves a complex interaction of biblical principles, personal circumstances, and spiritual discernment, on which much more could be written than what appears in this brief appendix. The subject of debt, forgiveness, and financial disputes is not the primary focus of this book. What is offered here are general principles drawn from Scripture, while the specific application in any situation must be guided by the Holy Spirit. In one case, he may lead you to cancel a debt. In another, he may release you to pursue the legitimate recovery of what is owed.

While personal discernment and sensitivity to the Holy Spirit are essential, Scripture never presents spiritual guidance as subjective or detached from God's revealed Word. The Holy Spirit works in harmony with the Scriptures he inspired, the wisdom God provides through lived experience, and the counsel of mature believers. As Psalm 119:130 says, "The unfolding of your words gives light; it imparts understanding to the simple." Decisions involving forgiveness, debt, and justice should therefore be grounded in Scripture, tested by godly wisdom, and examined honestly before God in prayer, rather than resting solely on our own impressions.

R. C. Sproul cautioned against separating spiritual guidance from Scripture when he wrote, "The Spirit of God works with the Word of God. The Holy Spirit does not whisper messages into our hearts that contradict or bypass Scripture." [121] Discernment, then, is not a choice between the Spirit and Scripture, but faithful submission to both.

The answer to the opening question is clear. Forgiveness and debt repayment are separate issues that operate on different principles and serve different purposes. Forgiveness is a posture of the heart that releases bitterness, resentment, and the desire for revenge. It frees us from the emotional bondage that comes from holding a grudge.

Debt repayment, by contrast, is a legal and moral obligation. It involves honoring commitments, restoring what was taken or borrowed, and maintaining financial integrity. A person can fully forgive another while still requesting repayment of a legitimate debt.

These two positions are not contradictory. We are not required to choose between extending grace and pursuing justice, as both can exist together. We can hold others accountable with reasonable expectations while fully releasing bitterness from our hearts. At the same time, we must remain open to the Holy Spirit's leading in each situation, recognizing that there are times when mercy may call us to release the financial obligation as well.

Personal Debts and Financial Obligations

Scripture speaks directly to the matter of debt, particularly among those who follow Jesus. Paul writes, "Owe no one anything, except to love each other" (Romans 13:8). Some misunderstand this verse to mean that Christians should avoid all borrowing or that they are exempt from repaying what they owe. This, however, misreads Paul's intent.

In the verses immediately preceding this instruction, Paul commands believers to pay what is due, including taxes, revenue, respect, and honor (Romans 13:7). Verse 8 continues this emphasis by urging believers to leave no debt unpaid. The only obligation that remains ongoing is love, which can never be fully discharged because we are always called to love one another. Financial debts, by contrast, are meant to be paid and completed. Matthew Henry affirms this understanding by saying, "Financial debts should be paid and finished, while love can never be fully discharged." [122] Christians are not instructed to avoid borrowing altogether, but to fulfill their obligations faithfully and avoid leaving debts unresolved.

Therefore, when someone borrows money, repaying it is not optional. It is a biblical responsibility. Proverbs 22:7 warns that "the borrower is slave to the lender," which shows that debt creates obligation. While borrowing itself is not sinful, wisdom calls for caution. The real moral issue is not borrowing, but failing to repay. As Psalm 37:21 states, "The wicked borrows but does not pay back, but the righteous is generous and gives." The contrast is not between borrowing and avoiding borrowing, but between honoring commitments and neglecting them. Christians are called to honor their financial obligations as a matter of integrity and obedience.

When we are the ones owed money, forgiveness does not require pretending the debt does not exist. We may, and often should, remind the borrower of their obligation with clarity and restraint. This reminder should be offered in a spirit of love rather than anger. A gentle approach may include proposing a realistic payment plan that allows the debtor to fulfill the commitment without undue pressure or shame. In this way, mercy and accountability work together.

One guiding principle should shape such arrangements: Christians should not charge interest when lending to fellow believers. The Old Testament prohibits charging interest to "your brother", [123] reflecting God's concern for fairness, compassion, and community well-being." [124] Scripture presents this prohibition as a covenantal principle rather than a situational guideline. God's people are not to profit from one another's obligations within the household of faith. Lending among believers is meant to be relational rather than commercial, governed by love rather than financial advantage, regardless of the borrower's circumstances. John Piper reflects this when he writes, "When Christians lend to one another, love, not leverage, must govern the transaction. We are not called to turn the needs or obligations of our brothers into opportunities for gain."[125]

We must also guard our hearts carefully. The parable of the unforgiving servant warns against demanding what is owed while forgetting how much we have been forgiven (Matthew 18:23–35). As shown early in the parable, the master canceled an unpayable debt, yet the servant immediately demanded full repayment from someone whose debt was insignificant by comparison. Notably, the unforgiving servant rejected his fellow servant's plea for patience and time to repay: "Have patience with me, and I will pay you" (Matthew 18:29). Instead of granting even a brief extension, he had the man thrown into prison. This response revealed a heart hardened by bitterness.

The warning Jesus gives is not against acknowledging legitimate obligation, but against pursuing repayment with a hard and merciless spirit that contradicts the grace we ourselves have received. Forgiveness reshapes how justice is pursued, even when accountability remains appropriate. This balance between mercy and accountability is central to the Christian understanding of grace. Grace does not eliminate moral responsibility; it restores it. As R. C. Sproul observed, grace does not eliminate moral responsibility but restores it by transforming the heart.[126] The gospel does not excuse wrongdoing or erase legitimate obligations, but it transforms the heart from which responsibility is exercised. Forgiven people are not freed from integrity; they are freed to walk in it.

At the same time, there may be circumstances where additional mercy becomes the most loving response. Exodus 22:25 addresses lending to the poor: "If you lend money to any of my people with you who is poor, you shall not be like a moneylender to him, and you shall not exact interest from him." When someone genuinely cannot repay because of poverty, job loss, medical crisis, or other hardship beyond their control, Scripture calls us to show compassion. This may include eliminating interest, delaying payments until hardship passes, extending the loan term to reduce payments, reducing the amount owed, or canceling the debt entirely. Jesus reinforced this teaching: "If you lend to those from whom you expect to receive, what credit is that to you? Even sinners lend to sinners, to get back the same amount. But love your enemies, and do good, and lend, expecting nothing in return" (Luke 6:34-35). While this does not require us to cancel every debt, it does call us to hold our financial claims loosely and to extend extraordinary mercy when dealing with genuine poverty or hardship.

We should also distinguish between genuine inability to repay and deliberate fraud. If someone borrowed money with no intention of repaying, or if they misrepresented their circumstances to obtain the loan, that constitutes theft rather than simple financial hardship. Even in cases of fraud, we are called to forgive—releasing bitterness and the desire for revenge from our hearts. However, forgiveness does not require us to enable ongoing deception or protect others from similar harm. When fraud is involved, especially if it puts others at risk, reporting it to appropriate authorities may be both a legal obligation and an act of responsible stewardship. We can pursue justice through proper channels while maintaining a forgiving heart toward the person who wronged us.

Forgiving Institutions and Organizations

The principles of forgiveness discussed in relation to personal debts also apply when wrongdoing comes from larger entities. Throughout this book, we have focused on our responsibility to forgive family members, friends, or even enemies, regardless of their repentance or the severity of the offense. It is appropriate, however, to briefly address a question many readers face: how do these principles forgiveness apply to our interactions with institutions and organizations?

Organizations can certainly wrong us. For example, if we hold a valid insurance policy and a company refuses to honor a legitimate claim, how should we respond? Should we overlook the offense, appeal to a regulatory authority, or pursue legal action? All three responses may align with biblical teaching, depending on the motive of the heart and the manner in which they are pursued.

While modern corporate organizations did not exist in biblical times, organized covenantal leaders and governmental authorities certainly did. The apostle Paul, for example, appealed to a higher authority in Rome when officials in Caesarea improperly detained him after Jewish leaders falsely accused him (Acts 25:1–12). As a Roman citizen, he exercised his legal right to have his case heard before Caesar. In the same way, we may appeal to lawful authority when an organization or government agency falsely accuses us, takes advantage of us, or acts abusively. Seeking fairness through governmental involvement, including legal processes, can be consistent with Christian values. At the same time, we are called to avoid bitterness and vindictiveness, to show respect for officials, and to pray for them. Our goal should be to resolve disputes fairly, standing firm for what is right with humility and a preference for negotiation and peaceful resolution whenever possible.

Closing Remarks

In all these situations, whether dealing with institutions, fellow believers, or nonbelievers, the path of forgiveness remains central. We are called to release bitterness, seek reconciliation where possible, and honor God by pursuing justice with humility and integrity. No two situations are identical, and the steps we take will vary depending on the circumstances, the relationships involved, and the condition of our own hearts. For this reason, seeking guidance through prayer, wise counsel, and the leading of the Holy Spirit is essential. He knows the full story, including motivations, hardships, and history, and he directs us toward wisdom, mercy, and right action. As we navigate these difficult decisions, we can trust that the same God who has forgiven us an immeasurable debt will provide what we need to handle our own disputes with justice and compassion.

Scripture Index

299 Different Scripture References from Genesis to Revelation

GENESIS

Genesis 2:24 - Man and woman become one ....p. 162

Genesis 39:2 - Lord was with Joseph ....p. 67

Genesis 39:2, 21 - God was with Joseph ....p. 53

Genesis 39:21 - Lord showed Joseph mercy ....p. 67

Genesis 42:13 - We are twelve brothers ....p. 55

Genesis 42:21 - Brothers recall their guilt ....p. 57

Genesis 42:28 - What has God done ....p. 58

Genesis 43:11 - Take gifts to the man ....p. 58

Genesis 43:23 - Your God gave you treasure ....p. 58

Genesis 43:34 - Benjamin's portion was largest ....p. 59

Genesis 44:1 - Fill the men's sacks ....p. 59

Genesis 44:9 - Let him die ....p. 60

Genesis 44:14-34 - Judah pleads for Benjamin ....p. 60

Genesis 44:33 - Let me remain as slave ....p. 61

Genesis 45:3 - I am Joseph ....p. 62

Genesis 45:4-15 - Joseph reveals his identity ....p. 62, 63, 71

Genesis 45:5 - God sent me to preserve ....p. 68

Genesis 45:14-15 - Joseph kisses his brothers ....p. 64

Genesis 45:24 - Do not quarrel on way ....p. 70

Genesis 50:19-21 - You meant evil God meant good ....p. 68

EXODUS

Exodus 21:24 - Eye for eye tooth for tooth.....................................p. 24

Exodus 22:25 - Lending to the poor..p. 297

LEVITICUS

Leviticus 25:35 - Support the poor brother....................................p. 313

NUMBERS

Numbers 6:24 - The Lord bless you and keep you.......................p. 250

DEUTERONOMY

Deuteronomy 23:19 - No interest from brother ....p. 313

Deuteronomy 32:35 - Vengeance is mine......................................p. 148

1 SAMUEL

1 Samuel 15:22 - To obey is better ....p. 101

1 KINGS

1 Kings 12:21 - Rehoboam assembles army..................................p. 311

2 CHRONICLES

2 Chronicles 1:7 - God appears to Solomon.................................p. 132

2 Chronicles 1:10 - Give me wisdom and knowledge.................p. 132

2 Chronicles 1:11 - Solomon receives wisdom and wealth ....p. 132

PSALM

Psalm 18:2 - The Lord is my rock and fortress............................p. 206

Psalm 19:9 - Fear of Lord is clean..p. 135

Psalm 22:7 - 8, 16-18 - Prophecy of crucifixion............................p. 259

Psalm 22:16, 18 - They pierced my hands.....................................p. 264

Psalm 34:14 - Seek peace and pursue it..p. 248

Psalm 34:18 - Lord is near brokenhearted ....p. 205, 214, 234

Psalm 37:7-9 - Be still before the Lord ....p. 149

Psalm 51:4 - Against you only have I sinned.................................p. 42

Psalm 62:1 - God alone is my rock...p. 204

Psalm 85:10 - Steadfast love and faithfulness meet......................p. 37

Psalm 86:5 - You Lord are forgiving ....p. 220

Psalm 103:10-11 - His steadfast love is great........................p. 27, 147

Psalm 107:1 - Give thanks for his steadfast love ....p. 233

Psalm 115:1 - Not to us but to your name......................................p. 191

Psalm 118:8 - Better to trust Lord than man ....p. 140

Psalm 139:4 - You know it altogether ....p. 150

Psalm 139:23 - Search me O God know my heart.........................p. 150

Psalm 141:3 - Set a guard over my mouth ....p. 151

PROVERBS

Proverbs 2:10-14 - Wisdom will come into heart..........................p. 136

Proverbs 3:5-6 - Trust in Lord with all heart........................p. 145, 211

Proverbs 3:12 - Lord disciplines those he loves ....p. 25

Proverbs 3:13-18 - Blessed is one who finds wisdom...................p. 131

Proverbs 3:19 - Lord by wisdom founded earth ....p. 131

Proverbs 4:7 - Beginning of wisdom get wisdom.........................p. 130

Proverbs 4:18 - Path of righteous like dawn........................p. 104, 140

Proverbs 4:23 - Guard your heart above all...................................p. 150

Proverbs 9:7-8 - Do not reprove a scoffer.....................................p. 153

Proverbs 9:10 - Fear of Lord is beginning ....p. 132

Proverbs 11:2 - With pride comes disgrace ....p. 130

Proverbs 11:14 - In abundance of counselors safety....................p. 153

Proverbs 12:18 - Rash words pierce like sword ....p. 87

Proverbs 14:27 - Fear of Lord is fountain.....................................p. 135

Proverbs 15:1 - Soft answer turns away wrath..............................p. 152

Proverbs 17:9 - Whoever covers offense seeks love.....................p. 147

Proverbs 17:22 - Cheerful heart is good medicine........................p. 221

Proverbs 19:11 - Good sense makes one slow to anger ....p. 146, 157

Proverbs 19:20 - Listen to advice accept instruction ....p. 154

Proverbs 20:22 - Do not say I will repay ....p. 148

Proverbs 21:3 - To do righteousness and justice.........................p. 101

Proverbs 22:7 - Borrower is slave to lender ....p. 295

Proverbs 27:12 - Prudent sees danger and hides ....p. 236

Proverbs 31:11 - Heart of husband trusts in her ....p. 140

ISAIAH

Isaiah 1:18 - Though sins are like scarlet.....................................p. 16

Isaiah 9:6 - His name shall be called ....p. 247

Isaiah 26:3 - You keep him in perfect peace................................p. 247

Isaiah 43:25 - I will not remember your sins ....p. 229

Isaiah 45:7 - I make well-being create calamity...........................p. 233

Isaiah 52:13-53 - Suffering Servant prophecy ....p. 259

Isaiah 52:14 - His appearance was marred ....p. 263

Isaiah 53:3 - He was despised and rejected ....p. 234

Isaiah 53:5 - By his wounds we are healed ....p. 263

Isaiah 53:6 - All like sheep have gone astray...............................p. 263

Isaiah 55:7 - Let wicked forsake his way.....................................p. 228

Isaiah 59:1-2 - Your iniquities have made separation.................p. 88

Isaiah 59:2 - Sins have hidden his face ....p. 309

JEREMIAH

Jeremiah 17:9 - The heart is deceitful ....p. 206

LAMENTATIONS

Lamentations 3:22 - Steadfast love never ceases............................p. 27

EZEKIEL

Ezekiel 36:26 - New heart and new spirit ....p. 282

DANIEL

Daniel 3:17-18 - Our God is able to deliver..................................p. 210

MATTHEW

Matthew 3:2 - Repent for kingdom is at hand.............................p. 266

Matthew 3:11 - He will baptize with Spirit..................................p. 287

Matthew 4:17 - Repent for kingdom is at hand...........................p. 266

Matthew 5:9 - Blessed are the peacemakers ....p. 102, 109

Matthew 5:23-24 - Reconcile before offering gift ....p. 101

Matthew 5:27-28 - Do not commit adultery or lust ....p. 225

Matthew 5:38-39 - Do not resist the one who is evil....................p. 117

Matthew 5:43 - Love your enemies pray for persecutors ....p. 38

Matthew 6:9-13 – The Lord's Prayer...p. 144

Matthew 6:12 - Forgive us our debts ....p. 86

Matthew 6:14-15 - If you forgive others ....p. 94

Matthew 7:1-5 – Judge not, lest you be judged ....p. 208

Matthew 7:6 - Do not give dogs what is holy ....p. 201

Matthew 7:21 - Not everyone who says Lord Lord.....................p. 276

Matthew 7:23 - I never knew you depart from me.......................p. 276

Matthew 10:16 - Wise as serpents innocent as doves.................p. 309

Matthew 10:28 - Do not fear those who kill body.......................p. 135

Matthew 11:28 - Come to me all who are weary ....p. 235

Matthew 18:15 - If brother sins go tell him...............p. 138, 152, 157

Matthew 18:16 - Take one or two others ....p. 152

Matthew 18:17 - Tell it to the church ....p. 152

Matthew 18:21 - How many times shall I forgive..................p. 82, 304

Matt 18:23 - Kingdom like a king settling accounts...................p. 305

Matthew 18:23 - Kingdom like a king settling accounts...................p. 83, 297

Matt 18:24 - One was brought owing talents............................p. 305

Matt 18:24, 28 -Servant owed talents…..............................p. 305

Matthew 18:24 - One was brought owing talents.......................p. 304

Matthew 18:27 - Master released him forgave debt ....p. 304

Matthew 18:29 - Have patience I will pay you............................p. 297

Matthew 18:33-35 - Should you not have had mercy...................p. 86

Matthew 18:35 - Forgive from your heart...............................p. 86

Matthew 19:6 - What God has joined let not separate ....p. 162

Matthew 19:19 - Love your neighbor as yourself ....p. 306

Matthew 22:37-39 - Love God and love neighbor.......................p. 113

Matthew 22:39 - Love your neighbor as yourself ....p. 306

Matthew 27:3 - Judas regretted and returned silver...................p. 286

MARK

Mark 1:8 - He will baptize with Holy Spirit.............................p. 287

Mark 2:5 - Son your sins are forgiven ....p. 260, 286

Mark 2:7 - Who can forgive sins but God ....p. 260

Mark 2:9-11 - Which is easier to say forgiven ....p. 260

Mark 6:12 - They went out and proclaimed repentance................p. 266

Mark 12:31 - Love your neighbor as yourself...........................p. 306

LUKE

Luke 2:52 - Jesus increased in wisdom and stature...................p. 136

Luke 3:11 - Whoever has two tunics share ....p. 117

Luke 3:16 - He will baptize with Spirit ....p. 287

Luke 4:28 - All in synagogue were filled wrath .... p. 309

Luke 6:27 - Love enemies do good to haters .... p. 144, 313

Luke 6:34 - Lend expecting nothing in return.......................... p. 298

Luke 6:37 - Judge not and not be judged .... p. 39, 304

Luke 7:41-43 - Two debtors parable.. p. 181

Luke 9:23 - Take up cross daily follow me........................... p. 40, 278

Luke 9:62 - No one who puts hand to plow .... p. 231

Luke 10:27 - Love Lord with all your heart................................ p. 306

Luke 10:37 - Go and do likewise good Samaritan .... p. 114

Luke 15:7 - Joy over one sinner repents .... p. 34

Luke 15:18-19 - I have sinned against heaven............................. p. 32

Luke 15:22-24 - Bring robe and ring celebrate........................... p. 33

Luke 15:29 - I never disobeyed your command.......................... p. 35

Luke 15:31 - All that is mine is yours .... p. 35

Luke 17:3-4 - If he repents forgive him .... p. 39

Luke 17:5 - Increase our faith .... p. 212

Luke 19:8 - Zacchaeus gives half to poor.................................. p. 43

Luke 22:62 - Peter went out and wept bitterly .... p. 286

Luke 23:34 - Father forgive them .... p. 169, 231, 238

JOHN

John 1:33 - He will baptize with Holy Spirit .... p. 287

John 4:14 - Water I give becomes spring .... p. 228

John 5:24 - Whoever hears and believes has life .... p. 262

John 7:24 - Do not judge by appearances.................................. p. 208

John 10:28 - I give them eternal life .... p. 287

John 13:14-15 - Wash one another's feet................................... p. 117

John 14:6 - I am way truth and life.. p. 260

John 14:15 - If you love me keep commandments...................... p. 278

John 14:27 - Peace I leave with you... p. 249

John 15:5 - I am vine you are branches.................................p. 212

John 15:7 - Ask whatever you wish bear fruit.....................p. 89

John 15:9 - Abide in my love...p. 222

John 15:11 - That your joy may be full ....p. 223

John 19:30 - It is finished ....p. 185

ACTS

Acts 1:5 - Baptized with Holy Spirit.................................p. 287

Acts 4:12 - No other name under heaven...........................p. 259

Acts 5:34 - Gamaliel a Pharisee stood up.........................p. 311

Acts 8:3 - Saul ravaging the church ....p. 311

Acts 16:25 - Paul and Silas praying singing hymns...................p. 223

Acts 22:3 - Paul educated under Gamaliel.........................p. 311

Acts 24:14 - I worship God of our fathers.....................p. 257, 311

Acts 25:1 - Festus went up to Jerusalem...........................p. 299

ROMANS

Romans 1:17 - Righteous shall live by faith.....................p. 209

Romans 3:23 - All have sinned fall short...........................p. 261

Romans 3:25 - God put forward as propitiation.................p. 311

Romans 3:26 - He justifies one who has faith....................p. 259

Romans 4:8 - Blessed one against whom sin not counted ....p. 182

Romans 5:1 - Justified by faith we have peace ....p. 248, 250, 311

Romans 5:8 - God shows his love for us ....p. 27

Romans 5:10-11 - Reconciled through death of Son..................p. 283

Romans 5:18-19 - One act of righteousness leads to life...........................p. 281

Romans 6:23 - Wages of sin is death.................................p. 261

Romans 8:15 - Spirit of adoption as sons ....p. 311

Romans 8:16 - Spirit bears witness with our spirit..................p. 266

Romans 8:23 - Wait for adoption as sons ....p. 311

Romans 9:4 - To them belong adoption sonship ....p. 311

Romans 10:9 - If you confess and believe saved ....p. 275

Romans 10:17 - Faith comes from hearing the word...................p. 211

Romans 12:1 - Present bodies as living sacrifice............................p. 36

Romans 12:2 - Be transformed by renewal of mind ....p. 282

Romans 12:3 - Do not think more highly than ought.................p. 116

Romans 12:17 - Do not repay evil vengeance is mine.................p. 148

Romans 12:18 - Live peaceably with all ....p. 108, 138

Romans 12:19 - Vengeance is mine says Lord ....p. 189, 208

Romans 13:1-2 - Be subject to governing authorities ....p. 149, 307

Romans 13:4 - He is God's servant for good................................p. 208

Romans 13:7 - Pay to all what is owed ....p. 295

Romans 13:8 - Owe no one anything except love ....p. 295, 312

Romans 13:9 - Love your neighbor as yourself............................p. 306

1 CORINTHIANS

1 Corinthians 3:19 - Wisdom of world is folly ....p. 133

1 Corinthians 5:11 - Do not associate with immoral ....p. 309

1 Corinthians 10:31 - Do all to glory of God...............................p. 191

1 Corinthians 13:2 - If I have not love nothing...........................p. 133

1 Corinthians 13:3 - 7 - Love is patient and kind ....p. 115

1 Corinthians 13:4 - Love is patient and kind.............................p. 122

1 Corinthians 13:5 - Love keeps no record of wrongs.................p. 188

2 CORINTHIANS

2 Corinthians 3:18 - Being transformed into same image...................p. 271

2 Corinthians 5:17 - If in Christ new creation...............................p. 230

2 Corinthians 5:18 - 19 - Ministry of reconciliation......................p. 138, 259

2 Corinthians 5:19 - God was reconciling world to himself ....p. 281

2 Corinthians 5:20 - We are ambassadors for Christ ....p. 281

2 Corinthians 5:21 - Made him to be sin..p. 280

2 Corinthians 9:6 - Sow bountifully reap bountifully ....p. 166

2 Corinthians 10:5 - Take every thought captive to Christ .p. 151, 185

2 Corinthians 12:9 - My grace is sufficient for you ....p. 204

GALATIANS

Galatians 2:20 - I have been crucified with Christ ....p. 209

Galatians 4:4-5 – God sent his Son to redeem us ....p. 264

Galatians 4:5 - To redeem those under law ....p. 311

Galatians 5:14 - Love your neighbor as yourself ....p. 306

Galatians 5:16-24 - Walk by Spirit not gratify flesh ....p. 210

Galatians 5:22 - Fruit of Spirit is love joy ....p. 250

Galatians 6:1 - Restore him in spirit of gentleness........................p. 141

Galatians 6:2 - Bear one another's burdens...................................p. 236

Galatians 6:7-8 - Sow to flesh reap corruption ....p. 166

Galatians 6:9 - Do not grow weary doing good ....p. 167

EPHESIANS

Ephesians 1:4 - He chose us in him before foundation...............p. 264

Ephesians 1:5 - He predestined us for adoption ....p. 311

Ephesians 1:7 - Redemption through his blood ....p. 27, 261, 281

Ephesians 2:8-9 - By grace through faith not works....................p. 287

Ephesians 2:10 - Created in Christ for good works...............p. 86, 212

Ephesians 4:2 - With all humility and gentleness........................p. 146

Ephesians 4:15 - Speaking truth in love ....p. 26

Ephesians 4:26 - Be angry and do not sin ....p. 165

Ephesians 4:32 - Be kind forgiving one another ....p. 25, 39

Ephesians 5:25 - Husbands love your wives ....p. 140, 165

PHILIPPIANS

Philippians 2:3 - Do nothing from selfish ambition .... p. 115

Philippians 2:5-8 – Christ humbled himself unto death .... p. 119

Philippians 3:5 - Hebrew of Hebrews Pharisee .... p. 311

Philippians 4:6 - Do not be anxious pray with thanksgiving p. 143, 212

Philippians 4:7 - Peace of God will guard hearts .... p. 249

Philippians 4:8 - Whatever is true think on these .... p. 150

COLOSSIANS

Colossians 1:13 - Delivered from darkness into kingdom .. p. 280, 312

Colossians 2:3 - In whom are hidden treasures wisdom .... p. 136

Colossians 2:13-14 - Having forgiven all our trespasses ..... p. 38, 180, 220, 259

Colossians 2:14 - Having canceled record of debt .... p. 29

Colossians 3:1 - Set your minds on things above .... p. 230

Colossians 3:12 - Put on compassion kindness humility .... p. 164

Colossians 3:13 - Forgive as Lord forgave you .... p. 146, 304

Colossians 3:14 - Put on love binds all together .... p. 112

Colossians 3:16 - Let word of Christ dwell richly .... p. 153

1 THESSALONIANS

1 Thessalonians 5:16 - 18 - Rejoice always pray without ceasing ...... p. 232

1 TIMOTHY

1 Timothy 1:13 - I received mercy because ignorant .... p. 183

2 TIMOTHY

2 Timothy 2:13 - He remains faithful cannot deny .... p. 161

TITUS

Titus 3:4-5 - God's loving kindness appeared ....p. 26

PHILEMON

Philemon 1:16 - No longer as slave but brother...........................p. 72

Philemon 1:18 - Charge that to my account.................................p. 73

HEBREWS

Hebrews 4:12 - Word of God is living and active.......................p. 150

Hebrews 8:12 - I will forgive their iniquity ....p. 41

Hebrews 9:27 - Appointed for man to die once ....p. 311

Hebrews 10:17 - I will remember sins no more ....p. 229, 243

Hebrews 11:33-38 - Through faith conquered kingdoms...........p. 197

Hebrews 12:1-2 - Run race looking to Jesus ....p. 197

Hebrews 12:2 - Looking to Jesus author finisher faith........p. 230, 243

Hebrews 12:5-6 - Lord disciplines those he loves.....................p. 135

Hebrews 12:15 - See that no root of bitterness ....p. 42, 91

Hebrews 13:5 - I will never leave you forsake ....p. 174

JAMES

James 1:2 - Count it joy when you meet trials...........................p. 223

James 1:3 - Testing of faith produces steadfastness...................p. 224

James 1:5 - If any lacks wisdom ask God...........................p. 137, 143

James 1:6 - Ask in faith with no doubting.................................p. 212

James 1:17 - Every good gift from above ....p. 311

James 1:19 - Quick to hear slow to speak.................................p. 145

James 2:8 - Love your neighbor as yourself..............................p. 306

James 2:13 - Mercy triumphs over judgment ....p. 39

James 2:17 - Faith apart from works is dead ....p. 85

James 2:19 - Even demons believe and shudder..................p. 242, 283

James 3:8 - No human can tame the tongue................................p. 151

James 3:15 - This is not wisdom from above................................p. 133

James 3:17 - Wisdom from above is pure gentle........................p. 132

James 4:17 - Whoever knows right and fails to do......................p. 224

James 5:16 - Confess sins to one another pray.......................p. 88, 154

1 PETER

1 Peter 2:23 - He did not revile in return..p. 149

1 Peter 3:9 - Do not repay evil bless instead...............................p. 103

1 Peter 4:8 - Love covers multitude of sins..................................p. 146

1 Peter 5:5 - God opposes proud gives grace humble................p. 115

1 JOHN

1 John 1:8 - If we say we have no sin.....................................p. 36, 226

1 John 1:9 - If we confess our sins faithful......................p. 43, 226, 277

1 John 2:1 - We have advocate with Father Jesus........................p. 277

1 John 3:21 - 22 - If heart does not condemn us..............................p. 88

1 John 4:9 - 10 - God sent his Son as propitiation.........................p. 260

1 John 4:18 - Perfect love casts out fear..p. 227

1 John 5:3 - This is love keep his commandments..............p. 223, 279

REVELATION

Revelation 5:5 - Lion of Judah has conquered................................p. 66

Revelation 21:4 - He will wipe away every tear...................p. 172, 239

APPENDIX FOUR

References and Supplementary Notes

[1] C. S. Lewis, *The Weight of Glory and Other Addresses* (New York: HarperOne, 2001), 182.

[2] A. W. Tozer, *Tozer on the Holy Spirit: A 365-Day Devotional*, ed. Marilynne E. Foster (Ventura, CA: Regal Books, 2007), 85.

[3] A. W. Tozer, *Tozer on the Holy Spirit: A 365-Day Devotional*, ed. Marilynne E. Foster (Ventura, CA: Regal Books, 2007), 85.

[4] Kenneth E. Bailey, *The Cross and the Prodigal: Luke 15 Through the Eyes of Middle Eastern Peasants*, 2nd ed. (Downers Grove, IL: InterVarsity Press, 2005), 69; Craig S. Keener, The IVP Bible Background Commentary: New Testament (Downers Grove, IL: InterVarsity Press, 1993), 210.

[5] Bailey, *The Cross and the Prodigal*, 68; Keener, *Bible Background Commentary*, 210. "The ring indicated restored sonship and authority, often used to seal agreements or represent delegated power in the household."

[6] Bailey, *The Cross and the Prodigal*, 68–69; Keener, *Bible Background Commentary*, 210. "Sandals were not worn by servants; they marked freedom and sonship. Providing sandals signaled that the son was not returning as a hired hand, but as a beloved child."

[7] Kenneth E. Bailey, The Cross and the Prodigal: Luke 15 Through the Eyes of Middle Eastern Peasants, 2nd ed. (Downers Grove, IL: InterVarsity Press, 2005), 69; Craig S. Keener, The IVP Bible Background Commentary: New Testament (Downers Grove, IL: InterVarsity Press, 1993), 210.

[8] Margaret MacMillan, *Paris 1919: Six Months That Changed the World* (New York: Random House, 2001), 167–71; Richard J. Evans, *The Coming of the Third Reich* (New York: Penguin Press, 2003), 31–36.

[9] John W. Dower, *Embracing Defeat: Japan in the Wake of World War II* (New

York: W.W. Norton, 1999), 281–84.

[10] Douglas MacArthur, *Reminiscences* (New York: McGraw-Hill, 1964), 302–6.

[11] Richard B. Frank, *Downfall: The End of the Imperial Japanese Empire* (New York: Random House, 1999), 348–51.

[12] Lawrence S. Wittner, "MacArthur and the Missionaries: God and Man in Occupied Japan," *Pacific Historical Review* 40, no. 1 (Feb. 1971): 77-102; John Gunther, *The Riddle of MacArthur* (New York: Harper & Brothers, 1951), 281-83.

[13] D.L. Moody, Notes from My Bible (Chicago: Fleming H. Revell Company, 1895), 147.

[14] International Standard Bible Encyclopedia, vol. 4: 55-56.

[15] "About the ten Booms: Meet the Family," Ten Boom House Foundation,https://www.tenboom.org/about-the-ten-booms/. Used with permission.

[16] Corrie ten Boom and Jamie Buckingham, *Tramp for the Lord*, (Fort Washington, PA: CLC Publications, 1974), 55–57. Used with permission.

[17] Corrie ten Boom and Jamie Buckingham, *Tramp for the Lord*, (Fort Washington, PA: CLC Publications, 1974), 55–57. Used with permission.

[18] C.S. Lewis, *The Weight of Glory and Other Addresses* (New York: HarperOne, 2001), 182.

[19] God commanded us to forgive others in a number of verses that are quoted in this book, including verses from Luke 6:37, Colossians 3:13, and Matthew 18:21–22.

[20] *Talmud, Yoma* 87a (The William Davidson Talmud, Sefaria.org). See also Maimonides, *Mishneh Torah, Hilchot Teshuvah* 2:9–10, in *Mishneh Torah: The Book of Knowledge*, trans. Eliyahu Touger (Moznaim Publishing, 1987).

[21] *ESV Study Bible*, Larger Print ed. (Wheaton, IL: Crossway, 2008), 1859, note on Matthew 18:27 ("about six billion dollars"); and *New International Version*, footnote to Matthew 18:24 ("A talent was worth about twenty years of a day laborer's wages"). Establishes: (a) the modern about US$6 billion estimate for 10,000 talents; (b) the years-of-wages magnitude — 10,000 talents × ~20 years ≈ 200,000 years. (For alternative reckoning by workdays: 10,000 talents = 60,000,000 denarii, ≈ ~160,000–200,000 years depending on workdays/year; see note 2.)

[22] Methods note (units and smaller-debt estimate). A talent ≈ 6,000 denarii; thus 10,000 talents = 60,000,000 denarii. One denarius ≈ a day's wage; 100 denarii ≈ ~100 days' wages (≈ three to four months). Using a conservative modern proxy of US$100–US$120/day yields ≈ US$10,000–US$12,000 for the smaller debt. For base units, see *NET Bible*, notes on Matt 18:24–28; and *NIV*, footnotes on Matt 18:24, 28. Establishes: **The US$10k–US$12k figure for 100 denarii and the standard conversions used.

[23] Combined scholarly corroboration. Leon Morris, *The Gospel According to Matthew*, Pillar New Testament Commentary (Grand Rapids: Eerdmans; Leicester: IVP, 1992), 473 (on Matt 18:23–35); Donald A. Hagner, *Matthew 14–28*, Word Biblical Commentary 33B (Dallas: Word, 1995), on Matt 18:23–35. Establishes: The hyperbolic scale of the 10,000-talent debt and the talent/denarius ratio (≈6,000:1) as standard background.

[24] Craig L. Blomberg, *Matthew*, New American Commentary 22 (Nashville: B&H, 1992), on Matt 18:23–35. Establishes: The moral contrast at the heart of the parable — receiving immeasurable mercy vs. refusing modest mercy to others.

[25] Julie J. Exline and Roy F. Baumeister, "Expressing Forgiveness and Repentance: Benefits and Barriers," *Psychological Science* 11, no. 4 (2000): 314-318.

[26] Yoichi Chida and Andrew Steptoe, "The Association of Anger and Hostility With Future Coronary Heart Disease: A Meta-Analytic Review of Prospective Evidence," *Journal of the American College of Cardiology* 53, no. 11 (2009): 936-946.

[27] Everett L. Worthington Jr., ed., *Handbook of Forgiveness* (New York: Routledge, 2005), 127-145.

[28] Gayle L. Reed and Robert D. Enright, "The Effects of Forgiveness Therapy on Depression, Anxiety, and Posttraumatic Stress for Women After Spousal Emotional Abuse," *Journal of Consulting and Clinical Psychology* 74, no. 5 (2006): 920-929.

[29] Mike Lunsford, "The Straight Story: A True Journey of Reconciliation," *Terre Haute Tribune-Star*, July 9, 2006. *The Straight Story* film and supporting details confirmed by *The New York Times*, June 1996 obituary and "The True Story Behind The Straight Story," *History vs. Hollywood*, https://www.historyvshollywood.com/reelfaces/straightstory/. Accessed July 2025.

[30] Kylie Agllias, "Missing Family: The Adult Child's Experience of Parental Estrangement," *Journal of Social Work Practice, 32,* (2017): 1–15. 10.1080/02650533.2017.1326471.

[31] Kylie Agllias, "Missing Family: The Adult Child's Experience of Parental Estrangement," *Journal of Social Work Practice, 32,* (2017): 1–15. 10.1080/02650533.2017.1326471.

[32] The University of Virginia, "The National Marriage Project." https://nationalmarriageproject.org/wp-content/uploads/2012/06/WMM_summary.pdf

[33] Solangel Maldonado, "Facilitating Forgiveness and Reconciliation in 'Good Enough' Marriages," *Pepperdine Dispute Resolution Law Journal, 13,* no.1 (2013). https://digitalcommons.pepperdine.edu/cgi/viewcontent.cgi?article=1239&context=drlj

[34] Wayne Grudem, *Christian Ethics: An Introduction to Biblical Moral Reasoning* (Wheaton, IL: Crossway, 2018), 857–859.

[35] Richard Wurmbrand, *Tortured for Christ. The 50th Anniversary Edition* (Colorado Springs: David C. Cook, 2017), 52.

[36] Richard Wurmbrand, *Tortured for Christ. The 50th Anniversary Edition* (Colorado Springs: David C. Cook, 2017), 51.

[37] Richard Wurmbrand, *Tortured for Christ. The 50th Anniversary Edition* (Colorado Springs: David C. Cook, 2017), 51.

[38] Richard Wurmbrand, *Tortured for Christ. The 50th Anniversary Edition* (Colorado Springs: David C. Cook, 2017), 61.

[39] Richard Wurmbrand, *Tortured for Christ. The 50th Anniversary Edition* (Colorado Springs: David C. Cook, 2017), 56.

[40] The seven verses in the New Testament that instruct us to love our neighbor as we love ourselves are Matthew 19:19, Matthew 22:39, Mark 12:31, Luke 10:27, Romans 13:9, Galatians 5:14, and James 2:8.

[41] Webster's Dictionary, s.v. "Humble."

[42] International Standard Bible Encyclopedia, vol. 2, 776.

[43] *White Star Line* brochure for *Olympic* and *Titanic*, 1910–11: "As far as it is possible to do so, these two wonderful vessels are designed to be unsinkable." Quoted in Castleford Academy, *Was Titanic Unsinkable?* (accessed September 2025).

[44] Eloise Hughes Smith, affidavit before U.S. Senate Inquiry, May 20, 1912, describing her husband's final words and her placement into a lifeboat.

[45] British Board of Trade, *Report on the Loss of the "Titanic"*, 1912, p. 41: lists total lives lost as approximately 1,503.

[46] Webster, Noah. *American Dictionary of the English Language*. New York: S. Converse, 1828.

[47] Spurgeon, Charles Haddon. *A Fear to Be Desired*. Sermon #2458, delivered in 1897. In *The Metropolitan Tabernacle Pulpit Sermons*, Vol. 41. London: Passmore & Alabaster, 1895–1917.

[48] Tozer, Aiden Wilson. *The Knowledge of the Holy*. New York: Harper & Brothers, 1961. *The Root of the Righteous*. Harrisburg, PA: Christian Publications, 1955.

[49] Elisabeth Elliot, *Keep a Quiet Heart* (Grand Rapids, MI: Revell, 1995), 18.

[50] A.W. Tozer, *God's Pursuit of Man* (Chicago: Moody Publishers; originally *The Divine Conquest*), chap. 1, "The Eternal Continuum"

[51] A. W. Tozer, *The Knowledge of the Holy* (Chicago: Moody Publishers, 2015), chap. 17.

[52] Romans 13:1-2: Let every person be subject to the governing authorities. For there is no authority except from God, and those that exist have been instituted by God. Therefore, whoever resists the authorities resists what God has appointed, and those who resist will incur judgment.

[53] Charles H. Spurgeon, *Divine Forgiveness Admired and Imitated* (sermon, Metropolitan Tabernacle, London, May 17, 1885), in *The Complete Works of C. H. Spurgeon*, vol. 31: *Sermons 1816–1876* (Delmarva Publications, 2014), 374.

[54] Elisabeth Elliot, *The Mark of a Man* (Old Tappan, NJ: Fleming H. Revell, 1981), 172.

[55] —Elisabeth Elliot, *Loneliness: It Can Be a Wilderness. It Can Be a Pathway to God* (Old Tappan, NJ: Fleming H. Revell, 1988), 118.

[56] See *A Greek-English Lexicon of the New Testament and Other Early Christian Literature*, 3rd ed., s.v. "χαρίζομαι."

[57] The Holy Bible: New King James Version (Nashville: Thomas Nelson, 1982); The Holy Bible: New American Standard Bible (La Habra, CA: Lockman Foundation, 2020).

[58] Franco Montanari, ed. Madeleine Goh, and Chad Schroeder, *The Brill Dictionary of Ancient Greek* (Leiden; Boston: Brill, 2015).

[59] Scripture from 1 Corinthians 13 taken from the (NASB®) New American Standard Bible®, Copyright © 1960, 1971, 1977, 1995, 2020 by The Lockman Foundation. Used with permission. All rights reserved,Lockman.org.rg"

[60] Spurgeon, Charles H. *The Treasury of the New Testament*. Vol. 9. London: Passmore and Alabaster, 1886.

[61] A. W. Tozer, *The Root of the Righteous* (Harrisburg, PA: Christian Publications, 1955).

---

[62] Hiram Erb Steinmetz, "Peter Miller and Michael Witman: A Revolutionary Episode," Lancaster County Historical Society 6, no. 3–4 (1901–1902): 73.

[63] Henry Stuber and Benjamin Rush, *The Life and Character of Peter Miller of Ephrata* (Philadelphia, 1815), 17–20.

[64] Steinmetz, "Peter Miller and Michael Witman," 76. Some later retellings mistakenly describe the men as *British agents*, but only American authorities could have prosecuted Wittman for treason.

[65] Steinmetz, "Peter Miller and Michael Witman," 76.

[66] Steinmetz, "Peter Miller and Michael Witman," 77. Stuber and Rush (1815) confirm Washington's decision but do not preserve his exact words; later accounts record the dialogue in this traditional form.

[67] Steinmetz, "Peter Miller and Michael Witman," 77.

[68] Renée Napier, interview by Robert Kraus, September 21, 2022.

[69] C.S. Lewis, *The Weight of Glory* (New York: HarperOne, 2001), 182.

[70] Luke 4:28–30

[71] Matthew 10:16

[72] 1 Corinthians 5:11

[73] C. S. Lewis, *Mere Christianity* (New York: HarperCollins, 1952), Book IV, chap. 12, "Faith."

[74] *Evangelical Dictionary of Theology*, Daniel J. Treier and Walter A. Elwell, 2nd ed.

[75] *Evangelical Dictionary of Theology*, Daniel J. Treier and Walter A. Elwell, 2nd ed.

[76] *Evangelical Dictionary of Theology*, Daniel J. Treier and Walter A. Elwell, 2nd ed

[77] Charles H. Spurgeon, *The Treasury of David: An Exposition of the Book of Psalms,* vol. 7 (Peabody, MA: Hendrickson Publishers, 1988), 175.

[78] *Evangelical Dictionary of Theology,* Daniel J. Treier and Walter A. Elwell, 2nd ed., 637

[79] *Evangelical Dictionary of Theology,* Daniel J. Treier and Walter A. Elwell, 2nd ed., pg.636

[80] "But your iniquities have made a separation between you and your God," (Isaiah 59:2).

[81] Walter A. Elwell, ed., *Evangelical Dictionary of Theology,* 2nd ed. (Grand Rapids: Baker Academic, 2001), 1104.

[82] Ibid., 530.

[83] R.C. Sproul, *What Can I Do with My Guilt?* (Sanford, FL: Reformation Trust Publishing, 2011), 4.

[84] *Evangelical Dictionary of Theology,* Daniel J. Treier and Walter A. Elwell, 2nd ed., Pg. 530 - paraphrased

[85] Steve Brown, *Feeling Guilty?* (Greensboro, NC: New Growth Press, 2016), 8. Used with permission.

[86] Webster's Dictionary, s.v. "Shame."

[87] Matthew Henry, Matthew Henry's Commentary on the Whole Bible: Complete and Unabridged (Iowa Falls, IA: World Bible Publishers, 2008), vol. 6, 790. This reference was subsequently published by Hendrickson Publishers (2014) and does not require permission as the original material was published before 1923.

[88] Timothy S. Lane, Timothy Lane, *PTSD Healing for Bad Memories* (Greensboro, NC: New Growth Press, 2012), a 23-page booklet. Used with permission.

---

[89] Webster's Dictionary, s.v. "Guilt"

[90] Timothy S. Lane, Timothy Lane, *PTSD Healing for Bad Memories* (Greensboro, NC: New Growth Press, 2012), a 23-page booklet. Used with permission.

[91] *Evangelical Dictionary of Theology,* Daniel J. Treier and Walter A. Elwell, 2nd ed.

[92] Vine's Expository Dictionary, William Edwy Vine.

[93] Corrie ten Boom, *The Hiding Place* (Grand Rapids: Chosen Books, 1971), 217.

[94] This illustration of the "peace painting contest" has circulated widely in sermons and devotional literature, in various forms. Because it is a traditional story, no single source is definitive.

[95] Webster's Dictionary, s.v. "Peace."

[96] Evangelical Dictionary of Theology, Daniel J. Treier and Walter A. Elwell, 2nd ed.

[97] Cornelius Plantinga, *Not the Way It's Supposed to Be: A Breviary of Sin* (Grand Rapids: Eerdmans, 1996), 10. Italics original.

[98] A. W. Tozer, as quoted in Precept Austin, s.v. "Peace (eirene)," https://www.preceptaustin.org/peace_eirene.

[99] *Tribe of Benjamin* – Benjamin was one of the twelve tribes of Israel, descended from Jacob's youngest son. The tribe held a place of honor, giving Israel its first king (Saul) and remaining loyal to the house of David when the kingdom divided (1 Kings 12:21).

[100] *Gamaliel* – A highly respected Pharisee and member of the Sanhedrin, known for his wisdom and moderation (Acts 5:34). Paul mentions being educated under him in Acts 22:3.

[101] Philippians 3:5–6 – Paul describes himself as "circumcised on the eighth day, of the people of Israel, of the tribe of Benjamin, a Hebrew of Hebrews; as to the law, a Pharisee; as to zeal, a persecutor of the church; as to righteousness under the law, blameless."

[102] Acts 8:3; 9:1–20; 26:13 – These passages narrate Saul's persecution of Christians, his encounter with Jesus on the road to Damascus, and his immediate transformation.

[103] Acts 24:14–15 – Paul's testimony before Felix, affirming his continued faith in the God of Israel and the hope of the resurrection.

[104] Romans 5:1–2 – "Therefore, since we have been justified by faith, we have peace with God through our Lord Jesus Christ. Through him we have also obtained access by faith into this grace in which we stand, and we rejoice in hope of the glory of God."

[105] Hebrews 9:27 – "And just as it is appointed for man to die once, and after that comes judgment."

[106] Romans 3:25–26 – "...whom God put forward as a propitiation by his blood, to be received by faith. This was to show God's righteousness... so that he might be just and the justifier of the one who has faith in Jesus."

[107] Exodus 20; Psalm 51 – The Ten Commandments (Exodus 20) reveal God's moral law, and Psalm 51 expresses the reality of sin and the need for cleansing and mercy.

[108] James 1:17 – "Every good gift and every perfect gift is from above, coming down from the father of lights, with whom there is no variation or shadow due to change."

[109] The five New Testament verses that include the word adoption are: Romans 8:15; Romans 8:23; Romans 9:4; Galatians 4:5; and Ephesians 1:5.

[110] David A. deSilva, *Honor, Patronage, Kinship & Purity: Unlocking New Testament Culture* (Downers Grove, IL: InterVarsity Press, 2000), 178–181.

[111] *Colossians 1:13* — "He has delivered us from the domain of darkness and transferred us to the kingdom of his beloved Son."

112 The understanding of Roman adoption is supported by scholars such as William Barclay and resources like the Zondervan Bible Background Commentary. William Barclay, The Letter to the Romans (Westminster Press, 1957); Zondervan Illustrated Bible Backgrounds Commentary: Romans, vol. 3, ed. Clinton E. Arnold (Zondervan, 2002).

113 *The Holy Spirit: Activating God's Power in Your Life* by Billy Graham (W Publishing Group, 2000), paraphrased from page 176.

114 *Faith and Repentance Inseparable"* (Sermon No. 44, New Park Street Pulpit, 1856): "Repentance and faith must go together; they are the two spokes of the wheel of salvation. You cannot have the one without the other." Charles H. Spurgeon, *The Metropolitan Tabernacle Pulpit Sermons*, vol. 37 (London: Passmore & Alabaster, 1891), Sermon No. 2217, "Forgiveness Made Easy," 585.

115 *Evangelical Dictionary of Theology*, Daniel J. Treier and Walter A. Elwell, 2nd ed.

116https://thelogosofagape.wordpress.com/2018/07/25/pistis-pisteos-and-pisteuo-a-greek-word-study/

117 *Evangelical Dictionary of Theology*, Daniel J. Treier and Walter A. Elwell, 2nd ed.

118 C. H. Spurgeon, revised by Robert Kraus, *Around the Wicket Gate.*

119 A.W. Tozer, *The Root of the Righteous* (Camp Hill, PA: Christian Publications, 1955), 27.

120 International Standard Bible Encyclopedia, vol. 4: 55-56.

121 R. C. Sproul, Knowing Scripture (Downers Grove, IL: InterVarsity Press, 1977), 45–46.

122 Matthew Henry, Commentary on the Whole Bible, vol. 6 (Peabody, MA: Hendrickson Publishers, 1991), comment on Romans 13:8.

123 The prohibition against charging interest to fellow believers appears in multiple Old Testament passages:

Exodus 22:25 – "If you lend money to any of my people with you who is poor, you shall not be like a moneylender to him, and you shall not exact interest from him."

Leviticus 25:35–37 – "If your brother becomes poor and cannot maintain himself with you, you shall support him as though he were a stranger and a sojourner, and he shall live with you. Take no interest from him or profit, but fear your God, that your brother may live beside you. You shall not lend him your money at interest, nor give him your food for profit."

Deuteronomy 23:19–20 – "You shall not charge interest on loans to your brother, interest on money, interest on food, interest on anything that is lent for interest. You may charge a foreigner interest, but you may not charge your brother interest, that the Lord your God may bless you in all that you undertake in the land that you are entering to take possession of it."

[124] Christians differ on how to apply Old Testament civil laws to the New Testament church. Some see this as a binding command for all believers. Others view it as expressing the underlying principle that we should not profit from the needs of our brothers and sisters in Christ. This book emphasizes the latter approach—that the spirit of the law calls us to lend with generosity and compassion rather than viewing loans as opportunities for financial gain.

[125] John Piper, Desiring God: Meditations of a Christian Hedonist, rev. ed. (Sisters, OR: Multnomah, 2011), 191–194; see also John Piper, sermon, "Love Your Enemies," on Luke 6:27–36, Desiring God Ministries.

[126] R. C. Sproul, What Is Reformed Theology? Understanding the Basics (Grand Rapids: Baker Books, 1997), esp. chapters 6–7.

www.ingramcontent.com/pod-product-compliance
Lightning Source LLC
Chambersburg PA
CBHW071014280326
41935CB00011B/1353